Overcoming Post-Deployment Syndrome

A Six-Step Mission to Health

Overcoming Post-Deployment Syndrome

A Six-Step Mission to Health

David X. Cifu, MD
Herman J. Flax Professor and Chairman
Department of Physical Medicine and Rehabilitation
Executive Director
Center for Rehabilitation Sciences and Engineering
Virginia Commonwealth University

National Director
Physical Medicine Rehabilitation Program Office
Veterans Administration Central Office (VACO)
Veterans Health Administration
Richmond, Virginia

Cory Blake
Authorized Continuum Movement Teacher
Music and Movement Therapist
Hunter Holmes McGuire Polytrauma Rehabilitation Center
Richmond, Virginia

 **demos**HEALTH

New York

ISBN: 978-1-936303-0-45
eISBN: 978-1617050398

Acquisitions Editor: Noreen Henson
Cover Design: Carlos Maldonado
Compositor: Absolute Services, Inc.
Printer: Bang Printing

Visit our website at www.demosmedpub.com

Medicine is an ever-changing science. Research and clinical experience are continually expanding our knowledge, in particular our understanding of proper treatment and drug therapy. The authors, editors, and publisher have made every effort to ensure that all information in this book is in accordance with the state of knowledge at the time of production of the book. Nevertheless, the authors, editors, and publisher are not responsible for errors or omissions or for any consequences from application of the information in this book and make no warranty, express or implied, with respect to the contents of the publication. Every reader should examine carefully the package inserts accompanying each drug and should carefully check whether the dosage schedules mentioned therein or the contraindications stated by the manufacturer differ from the statements made in this book. Such examination is particularly important with drugs that are either rarely used or have been newly released on the market.

Library of Congress Cataloging-in-Publication Data

CIP data is available from the Library of Congress.

Made in the United States of America

11 12 13 14 15 / 5 4 3 2 1

This book is dedicated to the men and woman of the Armed Services who have served in Iraq and Afghanistan. The world needs the wisdom that your strength and experience are growing in you.

Contents

Preface

History has taught us repeatedly that it is possible to overcome adversity. Cities and nations have been rebuilt after war and calamity. Entire companies and even industries have come back from economic failure and ruin. There are scores of books and movies filled with individuals who have beaten the odds and returned to their personal greatness. The goal of this book is to teach you the techniques needed to help you to rebuild, to aid you in your comeback, and to allow you to return to your own greatness. It won't necessarily be easy. It won't be given to you on a silver platter. You'll need to work for it. You'll need to strap on your boots to make it happen. You will have to fully engage to meet this new mission. But it can happen. Your road to wellness is in front of you. It's as real as the road outside your door. It's as possible as any success story. It's your own personal miracle waiting to happen.

So when you turn this page, be prepared to begin on a journey that will show you a new way to begin to heal. Be prepared to take the steps we've laid out for you. Six simple steps that will guide you from the point you are now toward the place where you want to go:

- First Step: Understanding your body's symptoms
- Second Step: Discovering your strengths
- Third Step: Applying healing principles
- Fourth Step: Re-establishing normalcy
- Fifth Step: Integrating health into your life
- Sixth Step: Resuming the productive mission

These steps are designed to complement and supplement, not replace, all that you have already been doing to get well and everything else that is available to help you get well. Just as any well-designed staircase is built with handrails, so too are the elements of this book improved by using the care and services available from the military, veterans, and private health care systems. Similarly, less traditional healing techniques can also be used with the principles in these pages. Actually, using this program will allow you to benefit *more* from all of these types of programs. You'll even notice that some of the things that didn't work well in the past will now start to have a positive effect. You just didn't have a body and mind that were prepared to fully benefit from them. You will now. Read this book. Use it as both a how-to guide and as a resource. Your time to heal is now. Begin the journey to wellness.

David X. Cifu
Cory Blake

Acknowledgments

After 35 years as a musician, educator, and more recently as a Continuum movement teacher, it has been my great honor to come to know and work with both the men and woman of the military and the health care providers that work with them.

I would like to acknowledge a few people who have influenced my thinking over the years. First off the Mexican guitarist, teacher, and poet Jesus Silva: the teacher that opened me to the idea that music itself is the best teacher and that nature always finds a way to bring forth her intelligence if one listens. I want to acknowledge the visionary teacher, Emilie Conrad, the founder of Continuum. Her brilliance and tenacity created a work that altered the course of my life. To my teacher, Susan Harper, whose always open and compassionate heart has never failed to amaze and inspire me. She has been my primary guide in finding an authentic way to live. To the co-author of this book Dr. David Cifu—what a profound and inspiring journey this has been. Thanks Dave. I've learned a lot from your words and even more from your being. And then there is my lovely and gifted wife Amy and whip smart, funny, and creative daughter Grace. I love you both with all the 70 trillion cells that I am.

Cory Blake

This book has come about as a result of a natural blending of my traditional left brain training and approach to life with Cory Blake's phenomenal right brain training and approach to life, in an effort to restore the minds and bodies of America's Heroes by bridging the chasm that exists in America's approach to health care. While our neurosurgical skills at brain-splicing may be somewhat flawed and this is still only the first step in a long journey of wellness, this process of melding these seemingly opposite approaches is the only clear hope to meet the challenges of post-deployment syndrome. For accepting me into his world of creativity, spirituality and exploration, thanks Cory. Your limitless patience and ethereal fluidity inspire me.

I would like to acknowledge the scores of teachers I have had throughout my career who have all influenced and shaped me in innumerable ways. All have contributed to enrich my skills as a clinician, researcher, and educator, some have also helped me become a better person. In particular, I'd like to recognize William Donovan, MD, Marty Grabois, MD, Susan Garrison, MD, Paul Wehman, PhD, and Jeffery Kreutzer, PhD. I'd also like to acknowledge the work, support, and tireless efforts of my faculty, fellows, residents and staff at the Virginia Commonwealth University School of Medicine and my PM&R Program Office team and leadership at the Veterans Administration Central Office. Most importantly, the support and love of my family is what motivates me to be all that I can be. Thanks and love to my parents, John and Rose, my brothers, John and Douglas, my daughters, Brie and Belle, and to the one person who makes me whole, my wife, Ingrid.

David X. Cifu

Overcoming Post-Deployment Syndrome

A Six-Step Mission to Health

Putting It All Together: A Holistic System for Health

A military force has no constant formation, water has no shape. The ability to gain victory by changing and adapting according to the opponent is called genius.

—Sun Tzu, from *The Art of War*

A WARRIOR'S MISSION

True warriors are called to honorable missions. All warriors take pride in their personal achievements of athleticism, toughness, inner discipline, and becoming *all that they can be*. But, there is a deeper calling to that mission and that's their calling to *genuine service*. It infuses the warrior's life with meaning. It is the ultimate goal of any warrior. No mission is more honorable, or urgent, than *taking care of your own*.

> *The best feeling I ever had in my life was draggin' Fernandez back inside the wire . . . after I knew he was gonna be alright. The second best feeling was shooting the bastard who had tried to kill him.*
> —Cpl Leon T. Church, Afghanistan War Veteran

This focus on taking care of a fellow warrior has been a guiding principle of the U.S. military for more than 200 years. No marine or soldier is ever left behind. It's something that separates the American fighting force from almost all others. With this in mind, remember, you *are one of your own*. If you have made it home from a tour in theater but do not feel you are the person you were before leaving, that is completely normal. Whether you were wounded severely and have obvious changes in your appearance or functioning, or if you suffered one of the war's *invisible wounds* and nothing really feels right, then you have been given a new mission. Your new

1

mission is to drag yourself back inside the wire. It is your new mission to figure out what's wrong and to understand how to fix it. This book can help to serve as your guide to help you do this. Your personal heal-ing—physical, mental, emotional, and spiritual—and how you bring that healing into the world around you is your new mission. It is a mission of profound importance. It is a mission that is without end, an ongoing one into which you can invest your whole life. It is a mission that begins anew at this very moment and in every moment. It requires, first and foremost, a certain state of mind, a warrior's mind, and a certain state of heart, a warrior's heart. This book is dedicated to helping you with that mission. By the end of this book, you'll better understand why you feel so differ-ent and so bad. You'll also better understand what it will take to begin the process of feeling better, the process of recovering.

Your new mission is to drag yourself inside the wire. This book will give you the tools and techniques to meet that mission.

Just because this mission has been thrust upon you, it doesn't mean that you have to accept it. The choice is yours. Maybe you've already figured out what's wrong and how to fix it. Or you may decide to just ease the pain the best way you can, to ride it out and to see if time changes things. You'll actually find out that time alone itself will help you heal. This healing power is at work whether you are engaged with it or not. You may have already found that deep cuts heal over time, broken and fragmented bones will eventually knit themselves back together, and even intense memories will gradually fade over time. Whether you fully engage in treating these injuries or not, the healing process will begin and will proceed with time. The process even works while we are asleep. Sometimes healing works *best* when we are asleep, so just finding a way to sleep may be one answer to many of your problems. You can use the techniques in this book to just help you figure out how to get the sleep you need.

On the other hand, the full circle of healing, the type that allows you to truly recover, can't occur with time or rest alone. Or sometimes, by the time recovery occurs, you've been suffering for so long that it has severely damaged your life. So you may be searching for ways to *jump start* re-covery so you can get back on the path and move along the process more quickly. This book can be part of that jump start, part of the push (or pull) you need to get that engine humming along again. Maybe you don't even feel ready to get back out there and resume your life. You need more than just a little push; you need some new fuel to get the process going again. Let this book be the fuel needed to make it all happen. Even if your recov-ery has gone astray and you are headed down a path that won't lead to wellness, a road that is bringing you into greater difficulties and a deeper hole, this book can be part of the system of healing that you need to right yourself. It will take something more that a simple push or refueling to get your recovery back on course and to allow you to return to your full potential. This book offers you a blueprint to get on that recovery curve and help move you along it. But, this book is only the beginning of the answer. The strategies, the solutions, even the system that make up the chapters of this manual are there to help get you moving along the road to recovery, but it is you who must decide if you'll initiate these activities, how much you'll commit to the system outlined and if you'll fully engage in that recovery. You can have many supporters and have all of the assistance you need along the way, but it must begin with you.

So, the decision to actively lead the way in your personal mission is up to you. The good news is that it's likely that you'll make improvements in your recovery regardless of which path you choose or don't choose. But, we hope you'll choose to fully participate in the process. To give your all to this mission. If you do commit to the program, something extraordinary will happen; you'll notice almost immediately that there's more juice to your recovery. Purposely committing yourself to involvement in something (almost anything) fires up your body's healing ability. The cells of our body draw strength from the linkage between our consciousness and our commitment. So what this means to you is that diving headlong into the recovery process will allow you to jumpstart it. It's a pretty cool thought, that you can play an active role in getting yourself well. But don't be fooled into thinking it's that easy. You can't just pledge to give it your all and then you'll be well. The commitment is the first step on the journey. But, it's the most important step.

A WARRIOR'S IDENTITY

> *I can't say I really liked the army that much, all the freaking rules and everybody on you all the time. And I hated Iraq. Never been that hot or that wasted in my life. I was just walking around dead . . . a year of that hell. And then they sent me back again. That stuff gets real old. It just wouldn't let up . . . but for all the nightmare of being there, at least I was something, I was somebody in Iraq.*
> —PFC Lori Stefano, Iraq War Veteran

Purpose and meaning are the stuff of an authentic life. The military provides one system of meaning in life. It may be a complex system to folks on the outside, but it is absolutely a system that you get to understand and eventually live by. A person's responsibilities are distinctly outlined. Your loyalties are clearly defined and duties are completely understood. An entire galaxy of belief is laid out and, if accepted, makes for a profoundly organized way of being. Codes are honored, command is respected, and mission is paramount. There's also the whole military community that you are made a part of. For some of you from military families, this has already been a way of life and a clear identity for a generation or more. For others, it may have been the first sense of true belonging, a family. For some of you, it might just be a community of people that you tolerated. A really big community that you were part of, but didn't always want to belong to. However, for all, the agreement to live within this military community and the system of ideas and conduct that come with it, is deeply affecting. Being a soldier, marine, airman, or sailor is a distinct and upright identity.

> *When I was a kid I wanted to be a marine just like my uncle. He was the only one who seemed to have a clear idea about life. It looked like everybody else I knew was just screwing around. He'd run ten miles just for the fun of it. He'd been all over the world and he had the coolest car, a Shelby Cobra, I've ever seen. Even when he drank he was in control. He was definitely my hero.*
>
> —Lt Gen James Mathews

Being faced with a significant physical or emotional trauma can profoundly affect the identity you have established for yourself. The injuries or stressors that are caused by the trauma of war can change who we are. Most of us have had multiple shifts in our identity imposed on us during our lives, but usually over lengthy spans of time. We go from 10-year-old grade school students to 18-year-olds graduating from high school. We are single, next we're in a relationship, then married, and sometimes with children. We are students or unemployed after graduation and then we are employed in the workforce or in the military. We are young, middle aged, and then old. Although each of these shifts is profound in scope, for the most part, there has been time to acclimate and the change has been expected. It's part of nearly everyone's lives and what we expect. However, sometimes changes in our identities occur rapidly, with little time to adjust, and in ways that we never would have expected. This makes it very difficult to integrate these changes into our identities. For example, we may be employed one day and unemployed the next, or suddenly faced with a life changing illness. Although change is inevitable, it is almost always stressful. This is especially true when it occurs rapidly, unpredictably, or without the input of the person it effects. Changes in how we see ourselves can be the most stressful, particularly when we see a negative or distorted view of ourselves. In someone returning from war with the loss of physical skills, mental abilities, limbs, or loved ones; this radical change in identity; and the sense of helplessness in the face of fate, can be devastating. It also can prove to be an additional crushing burden on top of the consequences of the trauma. This change in identity alone can be the biggest challenge of returning from deployment. You don't feel like the same person or part of the same group you were before, maybe you even feel like you are nobody.

It's important to recognize that our identity is fluid in nature. In reality, who and what we are is constantly changing. Although this fluidity of identity may be quite obvious in someone who has suffered an acute trauma, it is also present in the warrior who returns with a more minor issues or significant negative memories of the experiences or of a single, traumatic event. We are all forever changing who we are in life, it's just not always as obvious. Looking deeply into this truth leads to an expanded sense of self. It's a way of better understanding that the ability to change and to adjust to change is what may in fact give us our identity. It can give you a better appreciation of possibilities in the way we meet life as it unfolds before us. Perhaps, being a warrior is not a static or fixed identity, but actually a much bigger and more fluid identity than we thought or could imagine. Perhaps, being a warrior is way of approaching life, a way of adapting to what life challenges us with, and a way of meeting death. Maybe it doesn't require being in a war zone or even being in the service at all. Maybe realizing that the ability to react and to change to the challenges of your mission and of your life is what being a warrior is really about. Maybe being a truly fluid warrior is a way of staking your claim on this earth as a human being. This book is here to help you better see the value of accepting this ability to change to meet the need and to help you to do so in order to get well and to return to your full potential.

DEDICATING TO THE MISSION

To get the most out of this book, we ask you to consider fully dedicating yourself to the mission of recovery. We propose that by dedicating yourself to the art of healing, your mission, your identity, and your sense of meaning grows. The sense of aliveness and power that comes with this dedication cannot be overemphasized and is the force that will allow you to succeed.

Until one is committed, there is hesitancy, the chance to draw back, always ineffectiveness. Concerning all acts of initiative and creation, there is one elementary truth the ignorance of which kills countless ideas and splendid plans: that the moment one definitely commits oneself, then providence moves too . . . Whatever you can do, begin it. Boldness has genius, power and magic in it. Begin it now.

— Johann Wolfgang von Goethe

A good solution applied now with vigor is better than a perfect solution applied ten minutes from now.
—Gen George S. Patton

This book is one possible beginning for you, the beginning of a new way to see yourself, your mission, and your place in the world. It is a new basic training and a new opportunity to look into what it means to be a warrior—a warrior dedicated to healing. It means becoming the captain of your own ship and deciding at every tack what course does or doesn't work for you. You are at the helm. What doctors and therapists know and suggest is important; you should listen to and weigh what they have to say. It has been their life's work to study and understand the body and mind and to help us get better when there is illness. But, they are merely consultants in healing, employees if you will. What they know about your body is miniscule compared to what you know. That's because you live in there. And whether you are listening or not, your body is in direct communication with you at all times—it's hot, it's cold, this hurts, I'm freaked, that feels good, this is exciting, I'm pumped, I'm pissed, I'm sad, I'm scared. No one knows you better than you. This same thing may be said about your family and friends. It may even be said about your squad or platoon buddies. All of these people understand some special piece of you. All of them want to do whatever it takes to help and support you. They are there for you. However, no one has got the full picture of just who you are, except for you. This book will show you how you can use your knowledge and wisdom about yourself and turn that into healing. Even more, this book will serve as a guide to help you, your family, your friends, your buddies, and your health care providers to all work together toward the common goals of a return to activity and wellness. But, you've got to lead the way.

We suggest you take everything in this book with a grain of salt. Examine everything and take nothing for granted. We want to caution you, however, to keep an open mind. Do not rush to judgment before you have really given the information, the ideas, and the exercises in this book a chance to sink in. Sometimes things can sound or feel strange just because they are new to us. Try things out. Give everything your full effort. Walk around in these ideas for a while. We've made sure that none of the recommendations in this book can be of any harm to you. Although not everything in this book pertains to everyone, the information in it can only help you and make you feel better. We have worked directly with many warriors just like you and use these strategies in our own lives. But, it's important that you feel that these practices are for you. If there is any power in them, it will be because they have become your practices. If they are to help you generate new growth in your life, they have to become part of the rhythm *of your life*.

The ultimate warrior leaves no openings—except in his mind.

—Sei Shin Kan

Throughout this book you will see this symbol: ☯. When you see this symbol, it signals an opportunity to stop; notice your breathing; muse over some section of reading, a quote, or an exercise; and consider whether what is being offered has any relevance for you. More than that, it is a space for resting and thinking. This book and this program are not necessarily easy to take in all at once. It can't be rushed through. There are no extra points or benefits to finishing it quickly. This symbol: ☯ is a reminder to come completely back to this present moment *just as it is*. Reread the section or quote. Try out the exercise again. Take inventory of where you are and how you feel right now. Not tomorrow, not yesterday, but today, right now. There's nothing that is more important than what's happening now.

We will talk more about this *just being* later, but let us just say that at the very least, we hope that you will find reading this book a relaxing and pleasurable part of your journey.

When you see the symbol ☯, take a moment and reflect on how things are going right now without thinking about the past or the future. Let's give it a try;

See it? Stop what you're doing, what you're thinking. Stop and just breathe. Please enjoy three . . . . long . . . . easy . . . . breaths through the nose. Take your time and really feel each one, in and out. Stop reading for the moment and do nothing but enjoy those breaths. Stop and take three long, slow breaths through your nose with your eyes closed.

How does that feel? Take three more if you wish. This is the beginning of healing. This is how you begin to figure out how you're feeling. This is how to begin taking steps to bringing your life, your body and your mind back in synch. How does what you've read so far sit with you? Really, put down the book—take a moment, take a break—look around at your surroundings, notice your thoughts, enjoy another breath, just be.

A New Basic Training

This new mission requires new basic training. We will be learning about and submitting to a new kind of rigor.

- Do you remember how you felt when you completed basic training?
- Do you have memories of before and after?
- What was it to have come through that challenge?
- What was your inner response?
- Were you ready to engage in that which you had been trained for?

You must summon the strength that got you through that. Training, however, is not a substitute for the learning that takes place in the mission itself. So, in addition to exercises and practice, we will be focusing on the actual mission at hand, returning your life to wellness. We will be acquiring the skills to learn from our life, as we live it. There really is no dividing line between training, and mission, and life. All of it is of utmost importance.

> *I loved most of basic training. Of course, I was already in pretty good shape even before, but really being pushed; it made me realize I could handle a whole lot more than I thought. I got stronger and stronger. It felt really good to run. I miss that.*
>
> —Cpl Leon T. Church

Can you be your own drill sergeant? Can you be your own commanding officer? We are advocating a daily and lifelong commitment to healing and growth. At first, just like basic training, this will require tremendous effort and perseverance, but, eventually, once its effects are felt and a new life rhythm is established, a new sense of flow can emerge. Flow is the secret to your success. It's your own personal Holy Grail. We wish it for you as we strive for it ourselves.

> *You must concentrate upon and consecrate yourself wholly to each day, as though a fire were raging in your hair.*
>
> —Taisen Deshimaru

HOW TO USE THIS BOOK

Who's this book for? First and foremost it's for service members and Veterans. But this book is also for the service members' and Veterans' families and friends; for their buddies from the military or at work; for their pastors, rabbis, and other religious leaders; for their doctors and therapists. This book is for anyone else who is part of the service member's or Veteran's world. Although there's not really a right or wrong way to read or to use this book, there are a number of suggestions that we have to help you get the most out of it. Here a few of these suggestions or rules;

Rules of Engagement

1. Keep an open mind.
2. Read this book straight through if you can. But, if that's too much, it's okay to skip around and go directly to those parts that are most applicable to you, such as quick treatments for your headaches or sleeplessness.
3. Come to understand this book as a *complete system of healing* designed to integrate body, mind, and spirit toward a common mission of healing. Although many parts of it are helpful in themselves, the overall approach is what will bring the full measure of wellness.
4. If reading is difficult for you, as it is for many war-weary veterans, read it *with* someone, or have them read it *to* you. Maybe have them record parts of it and listen to it that way. The more folks you read it with, the more you will gain from the shared experience of it. Take your time with it, there's really no hurry.
5. Share this book with all relevant people. If you are a service member, share it with family and caregivers. If a family member, share it with your Veteran and their doctors. And if you are a doctor or therapist, share it with your patients, your staff, and even your family. This book is designed to put everyone on the same page.
6. Form a study and practice group. There is power in community, especially a healing community.
7. Create a physical place in your home or office devoted to the processes outlined. Although many, if not all, of the exercises and activities outlined in the book can be performed almost anywhere with little or no equipment or preparation, it often works best if you have a specific place or two dedicated to your recovery.
8. Obtain the *Gear for the Mission* listed in Chapter 10.

9. Give each recommended practice at least a 1 week trial period before making any decisions regarding their effectiveness. Although many exercises and practices will make you feel better (and different), some may take some practice and repetition before you can fully benefit.

10. Integrate these practices into your daily life by establishing a regular practice time. This is a key to success in any life system. It must not be something you do only when you have some free time or are feeling up to it. You must see this as the key to everyday activities. To have full effect, these strategies must become ingrained in your day-to-day living.

11. Follow the activities schedules listed in the Chapter 10, they are a menu of what to do and when.

12. None of this will work for you, unless you work for it.

13. If you don't like these rules, bend them. Creativity rules all. Make the rules to fit who you are and to help you recover. If need be, ignore them.

14. Engage in your mission.

It's never easy to start something new, to try something you've never tried before. It's much easier to just continue on with what you're used to. It's always easiest to just push forward with the mission that you've already begun on. For many of you, this perseverance is what has made you a successful warrior all along. It's what has shaped the inner determination that's kept you going this far. The traumas and stresses of the combat that you've experienced, however, have worked against you. This military deployment has caused you to have a range of symptoms that are preventing you from a return to normal. Through this book, we'll explain many of the reasons why you are feeling the way you do. We'll then review what you can do to feel better. As you've probably already discovered, there are a range of options available to assist you in your recovery. Some of these options can be found at your local health care center, Veteran's center, military base, or Veterans Administration hospital. Others may exist in a counselor's office, your health club, or your local health food store. This book will take a look at many of these options and show you how to incorporate them into an overall system to help you to get well. This book isn't a stand-alone answer to all of your problems; instead, it's a way to take charge of your recovery so you can find and take advantage of these answers.

Throughout this book you'll see comments from a number of Iraq and Afghan warriors who have come through combat with many of the same feelings and difficulties that you have. These quotes are compilations of words and thoughts from service members and Veterans who we've had the pleasure of working with directly. Although their names, ranks, and/or exact stories have been altered to protect their identities and to help simplify the message, you'll see that they feel the way you do, that they are struggling to push through the same way you are. We'll follow these folks throughout the book and show you the challenges that they have within the system and within their lives. Like you, these warriors have been through the fire and are searching for a way to return to their missions. Some will be able to get back on with their lives, but others will not. As you'll see, for some of them, this book will give them the guidance and support they need. The help they need to begin this new mission. Read along and see which of these warriors you can relate to, who is most like you. Just as you've been trained to provide support to your fellow warriors, the figures described in this book are there to give you the support that you may need. Pick one of them and follow them on their journey through post-deployment. Engage in their new mission and, if you can, make it your own as well.

TO THE FAMILY

He was gone for a long time. You didn't want him to go at all. Even with the phone calls, the Skypes and the emails, his distance seemed to increase. Over the months and months there was a shift in him and in you. In many cases you shifted together, but in others the changes have made you feel further apart, somehow different. You had put together a life in his absence. It was running smoothly enough. But always there was that sense of dread that that he might be killed, or wounded. Perhaps he was exposed to a blast or other trauma. Or perhaps he just had to face challenges that you can't even imagine. After these events, you resisted thinking about what it might mean and clenched your whole being with a resounding no. And then he came home.

The first few months you were in crisis mode, but, over time, as grinding as this tragedy was, you may have gotten used to it: the trips to see him or her, the time in VA offices talking to doctors or commanding officers, the stacks of paperwork from the military, the bills you never knew could exist. You're tired of talking about it with all of his and your friends and relatives. It's the way life is now. It may suck, but that's the way it is. Hopefully he can talk now at least, maybe even tell you some things about how he's doing. All those months of intensive services, or counseling, or trying come to terms with this different person who came back from the war are becoming past history. A new routine is setting in and it can feel like wading in molasses.

Although his physical wounds seem to be healing slowly, his emotional wounds do not. There is bitterness over the loss of his ability to work or be in the military. Or you can't believe he wants to try and go back to being a warrior. You have kids to raise for Christ's sake. He's short with you and them, and has no interest in any social occasions. He's drinking too much and smoking like a smokestack. Living with him feels like being in a pressure cooker, and you're already well done. Most of the time, it's best to just leave him alone. Now what? What role should you be playing in all of this?

No one cares more about or will eventually provide as much care for your wounded warrior than you do. Your involvement is the most essential ingredient in her or his recovery. If you are family—wife, husband, mother, father, a child, cousin—or friend of a returning service member or Veteran who is wrestling with any of the problems that you'll see described in this book, then this book is for you too. First and foremost, this is because you, like him or her, are in a lot of pain. That pain is calling you to action.

- What do you do?
- How can you help?
- Who do you contact?
- How do you keep yourself well in the midst of it all?

You know that even though the doctors appear to be doing all they can, more can be done. More has to be done. How can you rearrange yourself and your life around a program of healing? What can be done on a day-to-day basis to create a full and satisfying life for all of you? How do you turn on the fountains of life? This book is all about wellness, letting you know what that really means, how you can become in touch with it, how you can value it, and how you can create it. The book contains practical steps and healing exercises that you can do at home to help create a soothing and nurturing life for all of you. This book can serve as an organizing center of wellness to help guide your hopes and actions.

No two people, no two warriors, no two families, and no two situations are ever exactly the same. Some of you have children with your Veteran and some of you are parents of your service member. Some of these warriors have chronic pain and some have lost eyesight. You may be experiencing the intense heartbreak of caring for a warrior with a severe polytrauma injury, a brain injury, a burn, or an amputation, where you know deep down that your life will never be the same again. Or you may be coming to grips with how debilitating and frustrating the invisible wounds that cause mild traumatic brain injury can be. The insidious specter of post-traumatic stress disorder (or PTSD) may be over shadowing your life. You may have doctors, therapists, commanding officers, and caseworkers to whom you are extremely grateful, or you may have ones you'd like to drop kick into the next state. Again, no two scenarios are alike. That's what makes one-to-one personal therapists and doctors addressing your particular needs so important and, at the same time, it's what makes using a single, specific book addressing all these varied illnesses so challenging. We will do our best in this book to show you how you can help the warrior to take back his or her life by making use of the special clinicians and programs that are available across the country, while at the same time becoming empowered to better understand what he or she can do to augment their own recovery. Prescribing these universal wellness practices is the main goal of this book, is the core principle to allowing one's body and mind to get back on course, and is the key strategy to how you can support your warrior's recovery. It will be important that you understand how these general principles can be tailored to the specific needs of your loved one and how embracing these specially formatted core principles as the mission of recovery is crucial for the warrior.

2

Post-Deployment Syndrome:
The Illness of War

Only the dead have seen the end of the war.

—George Santayana

SETTING THE STAGE

Military researchers have reported that nearly *one in five of the more than two million U.S. service members* who have been deployed to either Iraq or Afghanistan have returned with an array of signs and symptoms that we are now calling post-deployment syndrome (or PDS). These official, conservative estimates confirm that at least 400,000 U.S. troops have been impacted with PDS. You may have seen terms like traumatic brain injury, polytrauma, combat stress, blast injury, post-traumatic stress disorder (PTSD), post-concussive syndrome, or other names, but each of these fits into the spectrum of symptoms called PDS. Four hundred thousand previously healthy young men and women now live with a range of signs and symptoms that, at times, causes them to be completely disabled or to suffer so much that they even may take their own lives.

Step # 1: Understanding your body's symptoms. Learning about and understanding the background and causes of post-deployment syndrome is a key to beginning the recovery process.

Although this number may seem staggering, as we'll see, it's actually just the tip of the iceberg. PDS affects not just these service members, reservists, National Guardsmen, and Veterans, but also their friends, family members, employers, communities, and even the very health care workers who are desperately trying to help them. Amazingly, despite how common this syndrome is, it still remains challenging to fully define and understand. Here's how one Iraq War Veteran who is trying to get help for his PDS describes his feelings:

> I wish I was back in Iraq. People don't understand, but it's just what we do. I'm a marine, not a patient. I remember when I first got there. I was so strong. It was intense. In Faluja we were kickin' ass. We were total warriors. I had no idea it would be this hard when I got back. As hard as the 15 months in Iraq were they don't compare with how hard it is to be back here. I spent eight months at Walter Reed. That was a couple of years ago now. The way I feel now . . . everything's a pain. My back is killing me. I wonder if I'm ever gonna really walk right again. These headaches won't let up. Everywhere I go the lights are way too bright; and I can't stand being around people, they're constantly staring at me. These meds just wipe me out. I don't feel right. I just feel like sleeping, but with the meds I can't wake up and without them I can't get to sleep, and when I can my dreams are horrible, mostly about that kid. I can't concentrate, and I can't remember anything. I can barely play video games. And trying to play bass just bums me out, my hearing's all messed up. My parents, and Jill, and those doctors: they don't have clue. I feel better when I'm hanging with Jason and Sean. They were there. But my body feels like shit, my mind feels like shit, and my heart feels like shit. I even look like shit. How can that really be my eye? When will it all go away? I can't get Will's getting blown up out of my head. And now they are telling me that along with this brain injury, I've got PTSD, too. I wish I was back in Iraq. I gotta buck up. Fuck it.

How could such a level of suffering and angst have come out of the very mission that this Marine had exquisitely trained to be in? Where has PDS come from? The two wars that have ensued from the September 11, 2001 attacks on New York's Twin Towers have had a whole range of unplanned effects. Some of these effects were so important as to have changed the world we once knew, some of them so utterly meaningless that it makes us question war's sensibilities, some of them so positive that it reminds us what it means to be an American, and some of them so negative that we fear for the future. PDS is one of the unplanned, negative effects.

These two wars, designated Operations Enduring Freedom (OEF) and Iraqi Freedom (OIF), have been the longest wars in America's more than 240-year history. They have also been the driving force behind tremendous advances in weaponry, innovations in military tactics, an enhanced appreciation of the cultures of Iraq and Afghanistan, the development of a worldwide system of combat health care delivery, and incredible breakthroughs in medical techniques and technology. As with every major American war, OEF/OIF has helped to generate major health care initiatives in this country, including the ramping up of trauma services in the Department of Defense (DoD), the establishment of a comprehensive Polytrauma System of Care (PSC) in the Veterans Administration (VA), and an unprecedented level of cooperation between the DoD and VA, as well as the private and academic health care providers. It has aided in the development of integrated systems of trauma and rehabilitation care and an ever expanding field of research into *blast injury* to combat the relatively new use of improvised explosive devises (IEDs) by Iraqi and Afghani combatants. The American and worldwide public have also demonstrated a startling outpouring of community and corporate support directed toward helping America's newest heroes. All of these activities have been the direct or indirect result of two commercial airplanes being deliberated crashed into a symbol of wealth and power in New York City, as well as the two other planes destined for the Washington, DC centers of power. These are the obvious impacts of the 9-11 terrorist attacks on America. These are the stories we all have read in newspapers and magazines, seen on television and in the movies, listened to on the radio, and perhaps heard through the grapevine. But what is the untold story of OEF/OIF? What has happened to more than 400,000 of America's heroes who have fought our Global War on Terror? What is PDS?

The wife of our devastated Marine whose feelings were expressed previously provides some additional insights into PDS, the so-called *signature injury of the OEF/OIF* conflicts:

> His face doesn't look nearly as bad as he thinks. I've gotten used to it. But he's just not the same guy. We used to have so much fun. The whole time he was gone all I could think of was God, keep him safe, keep him safe. It was so stressful. And when I heard he got wounded I just fell apart. They said he was gonna make it, but it was still my worst nightmare. Before, he wasn't perfect, he could get mad, but now it's like he's always angry and irritable. The least little thing sets him off. Or he just sits there watching TV and won't even talk to me. Sometimes he watches TV all night long. To tell you the truth I'm a little scared of him. It feels like he has to keep himself from doing something violent. He laughs at stuff that doesn't make any sense.
>
> I have to do everything. I have to make sure he's taking all his medications. It seems like all I do is cook and clean up his mess and drive him to appointments. If I don't go with him he won't even remember what the doctor told him to do. He really needs to go back to the VA for a while. His drinking is really starting to be a problem. When he's drunk I'm outta here. Last week, Jason and Sean came and got him and they went out for a while, and I realized what a relief it was to just be in the house alone. I wish I could help him but it seems like all I do is piss him off. I love him but I don't know how much more of this I can take.

Post-deployment syndrome is the signature injury of the OEF/OIF conflicts

BEEN THERE, SEEN THAT

Poorly explained health conditions, like PDS, have been associated with nearly every war in the recorded history of man. That's right, the often devastating symptoms of PDS are extremely similar to symptoms from nearly every major war in recorded times. Although given a vast variety of names depending on the era or belief systems in play, many of the poorly explained conditions seen in hundreds of years of wars sound eerily alike. Psychological and physical difficulties arising from the horrors of warfare have been recorded in Trojan warriors from the times of Homer, during the ancient wars of the armies of King Saul of Israel, from the world-conquering armies of Alexander the Great, and in all of America's wars. Known as *soldier's heart* in the Civil War; *shell shock, shell concussion, traumatic war neurosis,* or *effort syndrome* in the Great War; *shell shock* or war *neurosis* in World War II; *battle fatigue* in the Korean War; *PTSD* in the Vietnam War; and *Gulf War syndrome* in the Persian Gulf War, a similar constellation of symptoms is seen with all recorded wars. Each war may have its unique emphasis on one or more symptom, or additional complications due to multiple injuries or stressors, but the underlying cause of the symptoms remain the same. Fortunately, the underlying treatment of these conditions is also the same.

Although these types of symptoms and disorders are not unique to wars and can also be seen in those exposed to brief periods of extreme physical or emotional stress (e.g., environmental disasters, terrorist attacks, kidnappings) or prolonged periods of moderate physical or emotional stress (genocide, domestic abuse, sexual trauma), they occur most commonly and consistently as a result of wars. These symptoms range from sleep problems (insomnia), to difficulty concentrating, to headaches, to emotional disturbances, and have been attributed to a range of causes, including lack of sleep, poor dietary habits, psychologic stresses, concussion injuries from artillery blasts and shellings, and toxins and chemicals in the environment. In the OEF/OIF wars, the same phenomenon has been described. Although it has been labeled a number of things since 2003, including *combat stress, blast injury, P3 or P4* (polytrauma + post-traumatic stress syndrome + pain + polysubstance abuse), the name that best fits this range of interrelated symptoms resulting from military deployment is PDS. PDS has been blamed on exposure to blast explosions (like IEDs), single or multiple traumatic brain injuries or concussions, psychological stressors of battle and military theater, poor sleep patterns, poor dietary habits, environmental and warfare toxins, effects of impurities in the sand, and a host of other factors. So what really is going on here? What is PDS and what can be done to treat it?

A variant of PDS has been around for centuries and has been seen in almost every war across cultures. PDS is the result of all aspects of the Iraq and Afghan Wars, from injuries to stressors.

SO WHERE DO WE START?

Maybe the ultimate wound is the one that makes you miss the war you got it in.

—Sebastian Junger

Figuring out PDS isn't easy, but it's also not some new and profound mystery. To some extent, a systematic demystification of PDS and its varied manifestations is one of the first key steps toward managing it. If you know what something is, it becomes less scary, less confusing, and easier to begin to deal with. The greatest challenge, and the first step in recovery, is developing a clearer understanding of the many components that make up PDS. These multiple factors *must* be understood and addressed in order to begin to help improve these symptoms. This is the jumpstart needed to diffuse the effects of PDS on the service member, Veteran, the family, and even the very health care workers (doctors, nurses, counselors, therapists, social workers, and more) who are trying to help fix the problem. If the very clinicians who are designated to provide care for our wounded warriors are at a loss as to what PDS is all about and how to institute reasonable care for it, how can we expect to achieve resolution? Here's how a treating physician saw our OIF Marine with PDS symptoms:

> I've seen guys in much worse condition. That's what makes him so frustrating. His face and eye have healed nicely. If he would stick with the program, I know he would keep getting better. I thought his medications were helping him but he's stopped taking them. I wish he would go to the veterans group that meets at the VA, but he thinks the older guys don't understand. I definitely feel for the guy: Traumatic Brain Injury, PTSD, and he lost his eye, but considering how far he has come . . . he was really starting to get better. He's an outpatient now. When he was on the transition unit he was exercising every day and opening up a little in group. But now it seems like he's slipping. I can't run the guys life. He's got a long road ahead of him and I think he can make it, but if he keeps going this way, drinking and not doing anything, he'll be a total mess and won't be any use to himself or anyone else. I do think Jill is the best thing he's got going. If he could go

back to school or if I could just get him interested in something besides his own pain. It's really frustrating. He just shuts down.

All three of these affected people, the Marine, his wife, and the doctor trying to care for him are joined in the same hope: the hope of healing. The traumatic events and the suffering that the service member has experienced directly affect all of these individual's lives in a multitude of ways. Just as war radiates from its center and permeates everything within its circumference, so too do the PDS symptoms of that war. Just as this Marine needs the support and care of his family and the input and skills of his health care workers, his spouse and his doctor also need him in order to fully realize their lives and their roles. His healing is their healing. His growth is their growth and, at the same time, their growth is his growth. The family, parents, spouse, friends, children, and friends of the wounded warrior desperately want their lives to return to some sense of normalcy. To achieve this however, they need their loved one to regain his sense of normalcy. So, too, is the recovering service member a validation of the role and the success of the doctor or therapist. Indeed, caregivers draw some of the very meaning of their lives from the well of the soldier's recovery. This is truly a linked community.

This is the illness of war. Those of you who are affected by this illness do not have to imagine any of this. You are living it. More than anything, there is a sense that the ability to rest has been obliterated—that there is no restful space in the mind. There is no peace. Nowhere has this been more eloquently stated than by the Vietnam War veteran John Wolfe:

> Few things in this world are as unforgiving, pitiless, ungovernable, and irrecoverable as lead and steel loosed from a weapon. The transfigurations they affect on the bodies of friend and foe alike form a permanent backdrop to all a man's future visions. While others experience intervals of silence between thoughts, a combat veteran's intervals will be filled with rubbery Halloween mask heads housing skulls shattered into tiny shards, schemeless mutilations, and shocked, pained expressions that violent and premature death casts on a dead boy's face.
>
> These images are war's graffiti. They are scrawled across the veterans mind defacing the silence and peace that others enjoy. At times the images may seem to fade, but an unguarded glance into the gloom is sufficient to exhume them.

War leaves this imagery in injuries of the flesh and the mind. But, even after the body seems to heal, these images often remain. They are more than just images and more than mere psychological processes. They can create ongoing suffering and are often actual *physiologic* processes and *physical* symptoms. War's stressors and injuries change neurotransmitters in the brain and hormones in the blood, cause these neurotransmitters to be out of sync, and cause sensations, feelings, and real-world difficulties. These feelings can burn so intensely that they inevitably lead to a desire to avoid and withdraw from them. Not surprisingly, depression is the most common mental illness associated with the OEF/OIF conflicts. Another common desire is to find ways to deaden these feelings, which is why poly-substance abuse with alcohol or illicit drugs is so common during and after war. Finally, many will go into some kind of attack mode—either towards one's self or others. It is precisely this tendency to escape that drives the symptoms of PTSD and combat stress deeper into the body and mind.

> *There are two kinds of suffering: the suffering that you run away from, which follows you everywhere, and the suffering that you are willing to turn and face and thereby find liberation.*
>
> —Ajhan Chah

UNDERSTANDING THE ROOTS OF POST-DEPLOYMENT SYNDROME

It is in the light of awareness that the experiences of war can be integrated, learned from, and moved on from. War is not a pleasant state of affairs. It's really not supposed to be. Although it has been glorified in older mov-ies and public relations campaigns, the increasingly realistic descriptions of the everyday horrors and stressors of war seen in modern movies and books are closer to the reality of what war has always really been like. Even in settings where war is so common and prolonged that is appears to be the norm, such as the Hundreds Years Wars of Europe or generations of tribal wars of Africa, it is still not a condition that the human body can adapt to. War is *supposed* to be horrible. Injury, death, deprivation, and stress are underpinnings of all wars and being exposed to combat—where these conditions are a regular part of one's existence for weeks, months, or even years on end—is *never* beneficial or even tolerable. Persisting for a long period of time in a nearly constant state of readiness, brought on by the necessities of war, will always result in some degree of deterioration of functioning over time. Although humans and animals have highly effec-tive stress responses to acute events, we are not wired to be able to main-tain these responses for more than a few minutes to hours. The normal stress response, also called the *fight or flight* response, entails a coordinated effort of the body's hormonal, cardiovascular, pulmonary, digestive, mus-cular, and nervous systems that allows us to rapidly respond to perceived or real threats. In order to do this, high energy sugar reserves are made ready, muscular tissue is filled with blood, the brain and nerves are invigorated with stimulants, the heart and lungs are set into high gear, blood vessels become rapidly able direct blood flow where needed and to clot, and the digestive and urinary systems are turned off. Our bodies become (seemingly) invincible fighting or flighting machines. Although this may be a great way to stay alive in a battlefield, it takes a tremendous toll on the body. This would be like ratcheting up the performance of your family car to meet the rigors of a NASCAR race. It's a great way to go from 0 to 200 miles per hour and to call up your inner Ricky Bobby, but not very good for your vehicle's longevity or your fuel bill. But, this is exactly what we're asking of our modern warriors (and their predecessors) and it's just not realistic to run a car on nitro boosters all the time or a warrior on adrenaline for 12 months at a time.

 No one's body can tolerate being revved up and ready to go all the time.

As if the intense stressors of warfare and the battlefield weren't bad enough, often the impact of a new injury (or two) that isn't urgently and adequately managed is added to this. If a service member gets injured and can't respond at the high level that he or she had been used to, then a cycle of both physical and psychological failure will begin. Imagine what it feels like to live in constant pain—a ruptured spinal disc, a dull or acute headache, and a crushing sense of fatigue. What about not being able to easily comprehend your situation or control your emotions because of a new brain injury? What is like to have lost your sure-footedness, especially when compared to your previous strength and athleticism? What does it feel like to move from situations of totally focused heightened purpose to the sense of an absolute loss of meaning?

Imagine never again being able to engage in the activity in which you have gained the most skill and pride. Imagine the impact of being unable to prevent injury to another. Envision in your body the sensation of deep grief over the loss of a mentor, a brother, or many brothers. Empathize, if you will, with the guilt, sense of failed responsibility, and helplessness over not being able to affect the outcome of an IED attack or a firefight. Consider the penetrating guilt of breaking your own moral code in a misguided response to outrageous injustice, or just because your blood got too hot. And now remove yourself from the love of the family of soldiers who know what you have been through and who know because they have been through it themselves. Imagine frequent moments of utter confusion or horrid nightmares that startle you awake with pounding heartbeat and sweat-soaked sheets. Consider facing life as an amputee or imagine being the family of a soldier with a traumatic brain injury that's reduced your loved one to a remnant of their former self. Now, add a constant feeling of unease, where the sensations of your entire body and mind are filled with dread, anxiety, mistrust, and the molten fire of rage. A rage made up of intrusive memories of violence in the past and intrusive thoughts of the possibility of violence in your future. Finally, add the icy, cold, empty sensation of seeing no future and the fathomless depression of staring into the abyss and the prospect of death could seem downright welcome. This is your personal introduction to the beginnings of PDS.

POST-DEPLOYMENT SYNDROME: SO WHAT IS IT?

Although not all of the 400,000 service members and Veterans who've been identified as having some elements of PDS have all of the features of the syndrome, nor are they necessarily disabled by it, but nearly all have returned from combat changed and affected by it. It can be difficult to make global or cross-cutting statements about PDS because the underlying causes are typically multifactorial and therefore differ from person to person. We'll explore some of these key factors and then try and help you understand how these factors may have impacted you.

So, what are some of these factors that bring about or contribute to PDS? Some factors are difficulties that were present before going into battle, difficulties that many of us have always had, but that we were able to manage with before. Other factors are the nearly constant life stressors that pervade the military theater: waking up each morning thankful for being alive, dreading your tour on guard duty, not sleeping well or consistently, filling your body with inadequate nutrition, and not having the time or space to clear your head. Add to these factors the specific combat exposures that war can bring, such as physical injuries or intense psychological traumas. Finally, take into consideration the variety of things that occur even after you've been injured or traumatized, well-meaning but suboptimal treatments, fellow service members or leaders who don't recognize or understand your "silent injuries," and then the array of issues from the post-deployment period after returning home, from the transition back to being a civilian to some of the hassles of getting benefits from the military or VA. One, several, or all of these many factors contribute to whether PDS will arise and how it will be expressed. With so many variables and potential factors, it's a wonder that only one in five service members actually manifest symptoms of PDS. It's both a testament to the strength of the modern warrior and to the resiliency of human beings. But, when these factors simply overwhelm the defense mechanisms in place, or overcome the newly formed adjustment or treatment strategies, the typical spectrum of symptoms and difficulties arise.

Like most things that cannot be easily seen, touched, x-rayed, or otherwise easily tested, clinical and research experts do not fully agree on what PDS is, when symptoms reach a threshold to be labeled as PDS or when they're something else, and when your symptoms are significant enough to warrant different types of treatments. Similarly, we are still trying to understand why some people can handle or at least overcome these problems, and why others cannot. At the very least, the term PDS implies that the service member or Veteran is dealing with:

- more than just a single symptom or two,
- more than just the results of a single injury,
- more than just a reaction to stress, and
- more than just some minor difficulty readjusting to home after a tour of duty.

At a minimum, in order to be accurately labeled as PDS, these symptoms must

- be fairly consistent in nature and intensity,
- be significant enough to limit some aspect of your day-to-day functioning,
- be there for at least 3 months after all physical injuries have healed, and/or
- be there for at least 3 months after a return to home.

However, even if you are not quite at the 3-month point and can't quite yet be labeled with PDS, but you still are experiencing these symptoms it would make sense for you to begin treating yourself with the program in this book. Similarly, even if you've had your symptoms for years and the number or complexity of the symptoms is increasing, there is no reason to accept the chronic nature of any disorder. It's really never too early or too late time to begin the recovery. The best time to start is right now.

A syndrome is a collection of related symptoms, and in this case, PDS is not just the annoying symptoms of pain, sleeplessness, or forgetfulness, but it is the profound impact on a person's day-to-day functioning that makes PDS such a challenging condition. These impacts on your day-to-day functioning and your overall life may be seen in a variety of ways, from physical limitations, to the secondary medical diagnoses these symptoms generate and seemingly endless number of tests and health care visits that are needed, to the elevated rates of job loss and homelessness seen with PDS. Importantly, these often life-altering problems persist long after

- the initial insult or injury is over,
- spontaneous healing would have been expected, and
- the expected period of readjustment to being back home has been completed.

Although there are certain symptoms of PDS (see the asterisks in the following list) that are extremely common and seem to be the main "drivers" of difficulties, there are nearly two dozen that are accepted as occurring often. These include:

- Irritability*
- Poor frustration tolerance
- Anxiety
- Depression
- Headaches*
- Fatigue or loss of energy
- Difficulty making decisions
- Slowed thinking
- Poor concentration*
- Forgetfulness
- Difficulty falling or staying asleep*
- Nightmares
- Poor coordination or clumsiness
- Feeling dizzy
- Loss of balance
- Nausea
- Vision problems or blurring
- Loss of or increased appetite
- Numbness in parts of the body
- Sensitivity to noise
- Sensitivity to light
- Difficulty hearing
- Change in taste or smell

This list is pretty exhaustive and includes many problems that can come and go in almost anyone. Those symptoms that first occurred at the time of or just after battlefield stressors and have continued to be present even after a return to less stressful military or civilian life are the ones that are most indicative of PDS.

As noted, although no one date or time period applies to all people, a persistence of symptoms that are preventing a return to full and normal functioning for a period of more than 3 months after the exposure/trauma and at least 3 months after the completion of a deployment is clear evidence of PDS. Labeling a service member with PDS earlier than this *can* be helpful, but only if it motivates early education, care, and treatment. It's important to be aware that there must be careful consideration of other conditions that can resemble PDS (depression, post-concussive symptoms, substance abuse), because a simpler diagnoses that requires simpler treatments that are more likely to work quickly is a much easier path to wellness. Unfortunately, because the overlap of all of these conditions is so common and a multitude of symptoms are frequently seen after being in military theater, a more multilevel management is usually needed to treat even early PDS.

Although you could choose to not be labeled with PDS and just be identified by the symptoms that you are having, it is usually in your interest to consolidate the multitude of difficulties you are having into a condition or syndrome that can be relatively easy to convey. Because most folks who have PDS have more than five symptoms, it becomes easier to take into account the full list of possible symptoms that are commonly seen, so that smaller ones that you may not recognize or forget to mention are considered. These lists tend to be helpful to both clinicians and the patients because they allow for a relatively thorough review of possible symptoms without having to focus on the best way to label them. It can often be quite hard to clearly describe many of the difficulties you're having because many of them may seem strange to you. It also helps to allow for clustering of overlapping problems, thus potentially simplifying the diagnosis and the management strategies. Just as importantly, it allows the clinician to get a handle on the range of difficulties a person is having and to compare them to other patients with similar findings, which can allow them to

- gauge the severity of the problem
- understand how often the symptoms are occurring
- realize how the symptoms are affecting the person
- utilize treatments that worked on similar patients
- predict who will make a rapid or a slow recovery
- understand when someone is not making a usual recovery

An estimation of the severity of the problem can be made more accurate if the clinician asks you to quantify or rate how severe the symptoms are. At the same time, it is important to note that one really bad symptom can be far more debilitating than three or four minor ones. Often times, these questions about symptoms for PDS may initially take place in the form of a screening form or interview such as:

- Did you get exposed to a blast injury or other exposure in the field?
- Did you have new symptoms as an immediate or delayed result of that blast or exposure?
- Do you still have any or all of these symptoms?

If the answers to these questions are positive, a more detailed and PDS-specific questioning will occur.

But, not everyone who fights in war develops problems. So why do some warriors develop PDS and others come back home and get on with their lives? There are a number of factors that influence how war affects people. Although no one is sure of all of the interactions involved, we do have some ideas of who is at risk for developing PDS.

THE IMPACT OF MILITARY EXPOSURES AND POST-DEPLOYMENT SYNDROME

First, everyone who is exposed to the rigors and the horrors of war (or any traumatic event) has some short- and long-term effects from it. This is normal. It actually highlights the important notion that war's effects on service members should be broken down into its components. Not all wars or their effects are created equal. The multitude of events or traumas of war must be seen as each individual's unique exposures. Some people have high doses of exposure over a short period of time; for example, they are involved in an intense firefight or battle with a great deal of injury and killing all around them. Whereas others have low doses of exposure for their entire period of deployment, such as soldiers who work in the Green Zone preparing their killed-in-action comrades' bodies for return stateside. Each of these exposures is potentially devastating and may actually cause similar symptoms, but clearly they are different. This is similar to the idea of being exposed to a lot of germs all at once (e.g., if someone sneezes or coughs on you) or a smaller amount over the course of a longer period of time (e.g., if you're tending to your sick children or if you work around people with illnesses). We'll call these *high-intensity exposures* and *low-intensity exposures*, respectively. Other factors may intensify these exposures for you. For example, if you received a physical injury at the same time that a major catastrophe occurs or if your buddy is killed in the same blast that injured your back or leg, you're more likely to have difficulties.

Or, if you get a high-intensity exposure but immediately receive the needed care—debriefing, rest, physical exercise—you are more likely to fully recover, whereas even a low-intensity exposure can develop into PDS if limited, inappropriate, or no care is delivered while still in military theater. Regardless of the specifics of your unique exposure to the horrors of war, everyone has some effects from these exposures. In fact, based on the extensive testing done from the Gulf War service members, we know that on average it takes 3 months after completing a military deployment for the typical service member to return to his or her baseline brain performance, stress level, and overall functioning. Again, this is not a unique phenomenon of the OEF/OIF wars. Interviews of Veterans of WWII, who were exposed to wars horrors, sustained a number of physical injuries that went untreated, and rarely received any type of medical diagnosis, reveal that many of these GIs experienced years to decades of psychological challenges and physical symptoms after returning home. Back in the 1940s and 1950s, awareness of these difficulties was limited in the medical system and little got documented, so we've always assumed that this "Greatest Generation" somehow rose above the countless exposures of America's bloodiest war. Others have attributed the apparent success of WWII Veterans to the "moral correctness" of the conflicts, the warm welcome that these Veterans received, and the unprecedented economic opportunities that existed in the post-war era. The reality of it seems to suggest that thousands of this generation suffered in many of the same ways that our current service members and Veterans are suffering, we just didn't know to ask and they didn't know to tell us.

Today, many factors are in play that have heightened our awareness of the difficulties that OEF/OIF service members are having. Increasing awareness of the public to the lasting effects of war may be attributed to the incredible advances in information and communication technology we have in the world today. We are able to view the battlefields in real time, to learn about the devastation of modern weaponry firsthand, and to keep up communications to actual service members on an almost daily basis. Additionally, television series (*Band of Brothers, Pacific*), movies (*Saving Private Ryan, Coming Home, Black Hawk Down, The Hurt Locker*), and myriad books have given us a service member's view of war, including the effects of physical and emotional stress.

Every war has short- and long-term effects on everyone involved in it, whether they sustain a physical injury, psychological injury, or just spend time involved.

How Pre-exposure Factors Affect PDS

A second key to the mystery of why only some folks get PDS is what we call pre-exposure risks. Just as a healthy, well-fed, and strong animal is more likely to survive a fight with another animal, the physical and emotional quality of the human being behind the service member plays an integral role in their ability to withstand a military deployment. This ability is often called one's *innate resiliency* or their built-in ability to withstand the exposures of warfare. People who have significant physical and emotional strengths and have built up a solid foundation of successes (stable family and friends, productive job, pleasurable hobbies, advancement in the military) during their lifetime are most likely to have enhanced resiliency to exposures. These strengths are often based on a healthy upbringing that included good eating habits (plenty of vegetables and fruits, lean meat, small amounts of fats and carbohydrates, avoiding alcohol and tobacco products), regular exercise and vigorous activity, normal sleep patterns, a sense of spirituality, and a structured family environment. Service members who have come into the military in poor states of physical fitness are more likely to continue the bad behaviors that produced this poor fitness (poor diet, limited exercise, unstructured sleep habits) after their wartime exposures. This poor fitness coming into the exposure will predispose them to poorer resiliency after the exposure. Similarly, service members who come from unstable family structures (poor parental supervision, limited interpersonal skills) or have been exposed to domestic or sexual abuse are less likely to have developed the emotional maturity and strengths, which again can contribute to poor resiliency. Service members with limited innate resiliency are much more likely to develop elements of PDS as a result of almost any negative experience of war time, whereas those with greater resiliency are often able to withstand even high intensity exposures and still do well.

The degree of formal education and inborn intelligence can also play a huge role in providing a service member with the resiliency needed to deal with war's exposures. Individuals who have been able to develop their intellectual abilities through schooling and life experiences are more likely to have optimized the functioning and integration of their brains and thus achieved a significant degree of mental flexibility (they can adapt to changing conditions, they can understand why things are happening around them). This adaptable mind makes them more likely to tolerate some of the unique conditions and hardships associated with warfare, including the alien environments of foreign battlefields, the conflicts of killing others, and the countless other challenges created by war.

Unfortunately, although one can often blame one's past for your present day difficulties, there's typically little to be gained from doing so. Instead of bemoaning the past, appreciating that elements of your past may be influencing or worsening symptoms is often one of the steps toward improving those symptoms. Just because you may have had some limitations in your background is not a sentence to suffering or difficulties. Instead, these realizations may give you the motivation to want to alter those negative ways that you can to provide optimal conditions of strength for recovery.

 One's upbringing plays a key role in the development of resiliency from deployment exposures.

The Role of Secondary Events on the Battlefield

A third key that helps to explain why some service member's wartime exposures lead to long-term difficulties, whereas others are able to prosper, has to do with the events surrounding the exposure or exposures. Sustaining a physical injury during your deployment will put you at higher risk for developing PDS because the feelings of pain, fear, discomfort, burden, embarrassment, and any others associated with that injury will commonly resurface whenever you think about any element of your wartime experience. This resurfacing of negative feelings in turn is more likely to magnify the negative experiences your exposures cause you to have. Any time you experience a new injury or have an experience that gives you similar feelings of pain, fear, or discomfort, you may easily relive the combat-related trauma over and over again. In fact, very often people will assume that the difficulties they're experiencing—such as a headache, poor sleep, anxiety, forgetfulness—are not just similar to what they have felt after the original war-related exposure, but are actually *caused* by these prior injuries. Even if the headache had previously resolved months or years ago, any new headache can also be ascribed to the original military experience.

If your injury is one that directly affects your brain's ability to fully understand or process all that was happening at the time of your injury, such as a mild traumatic brain injury or concussion, then not only is there likely to be difficult negative feelings or emotions associated with your military experience, but, because your brain was not functioning perfectly afterward, you may never have fully processed all that went on. So you may have incorrectly remembered or dealt with the inciting exposure event and are therefore more likely to have challenges dealing with either the effects of this concussion or with new events that produce similar feelings. Although we'll spend a lot more time discussing concussions, it's very important to understand this overall concept of how a whole variety of other injuries (new and old) can magnify all of your difficulties (new and old). Even more importantly, this concept emphasizes the crucial need to address all of these injuries and the symptoms they cause.

Your body and mind's memories of new and old injuries can worsen your PDS.

How Stressors Impact PDS

A fourth key to why combat exposure can affect different people in different ways is how well you were doing physically and mentally at the time of your actual exposure or injury. Overall, service members who are deployed often have significant baseline alterations in their normal life functioning, diets, day-to-day routines, exercise regimens, sleep patterns, and the like. Although some folks may actually get more physical activity on an active military base than their usually sedentary lives, overall these life alterations have a deleterious effect on the impact of battlefield exposures. Although these temporary differences in lifestyles for the 12 to 18 months of deployment are not necessarily bad or harmful in themselves, they do create changes in how your body functions. Even if your body is able to adequately adjust to all of these new changes, once you are redeployed and return to your home, there will be a period of up to 3 months of readjustment before your body is functioning as it did before deployment. This is normal. During this period, you may have a hard time fully healing from injuries or of dealing with day-to-day stresses and activities, which puts you at a high risk to develop PDS. Even if you didn't have any specific injury or high-intensity exposures, but rather were just exposed to the normal low-level stressors of being in a battle zone, you may be at risk for PDS if your body and mind had been negatively affected by your lowered life functioning. If the changes that occurred in your routine (i.e., sleep deprivation, a constant level of anxiety or fear, an excess of fat-related calories) in the military theater are not ones that your body and mind can adequately adjust to, then you will be at greater risk to have a poor response to subsequent exposures or injuries during your deployment and during this period of normal recovery and readjustment after your return home. If the exposure you had from combat is a low intensity one over a sustained period of time, such as the emotional stress of having to decide which troops get chosen for specific tasks or rotations, which may result in the injury or death of some of those troops, and your body and mind is in a constant state of stress because of the difficulties of your new routine, then you will have essentially been damaging yourself for the many months you served before being able to return home and have a chance to heal. Even though the degree of actual damage from this low level of exposure may be small, the background stressors of this routine, plus any injuries you incurred will compound it, so the overall effects may be significant. There are treatments available while in the field—

such as counseling, rotating duties, medications, and improving your daily routines such as improving your diet or sleep—that can begin the process of recovery. But there are rarely quick fixes for these types of things. Very often it may take a longer period of time after returning home to continue this recovery process and sometimes it may even become a lifelong activity. A lifelong activity doesn't necessarily have to be the same thing as a chronic disorder or life sentence, but rather a strategy for ongoing success. If the exposure is a more intensive, short-lived injury (concussion, amputation, musculoskeletal injury, witnessing death), then the acute treatments will similarly likely be more intensive (assuming you have reported the injury or someone is aware of it). However, the same background stressors to your body from an altered routine will still be in place. So again, the recovery from this high intensity exposure may take far longer than would be expected in a civilian setting or than you might expect.

Often, service members have all three of these factors going on:

- altered routines,
- low-intensity exposures over a long time, and
- a high-intensity exposure.

Obviously, this may take a multilevel treatment program applied over a long period of time to facilitate recovery. The recurring theme you'll be seeing in this book is to focus on ways to both improve your short-term symptoms and difficulties, but at the same time develop a set of strategies to help your body and mind heal over a longer period of time, possibly throughout your whole life.

 The stressors of routine living in military theater can heighten your chances of developing PDS.

The Effect of Multiple Exposures and Injuries

Whoever came up with the concept of modern warfare forgot to build in time outs. Although probably not as big a part of older warfare as Hollywood would have us believe, the ability to just stop the roller coaster from going when things got too intense or when the injured needed to be removed from the battlefield isn't built into the wars in Iraq and Afghanistan. There are no time outs, regardless of the extent or type of injuries. In fact, as was learned in the Vietnam War, the best way to wound or kill several U.S. service members at once is to injure a single service member and wait for his multiple buddies to try and help him. Oftentimes, the intensity of battle results in multiple moderate- to high-intensity exposures and injuries. Additionally, the prolonged duration and multiplicity of warfare does not allow for periods of rest or removal from the military theater. Although one significant exposure or a moderate duration period of low intensity exposure is bad enough and may predispose you to develop PDS, a series of high-intensity exposure injuries or 12+ months of low-level exposure is exponentially more likely to bring about PDS. Unfortunately, we are seeing more and more service members who have had multiple high-intensity exposures, everything from several blast exposures with multiple concussions, to multiple bodily injuries causing the condition known as polytrauma. Technically, polytrauma is a brain injury plus another bodily or psychologic injury, but this term is also used to express the concept of two or more injuries or injury locations. Just as those folks with greater risk factors pre-injury (or innate resiliency) or more alterations to their routines (long-duration, low-intensity exposures) are more likely to have the persistent symptoms of PDS, those individuals with multiple injuries (multiple, short-duration, high-intensity exposures) are also more likely to have PDS. So how can you use this information? Be aware, that if you've had multiple separate exposures, even though the combined effects may come across as specific symptoms, usually each of the separate injuries must be addressed individually to understand the extent of injury and potentially unique ways of treating the related symptoms. So, it's best to be able to identify each of the separate injuries as carefully as you can, so that you can be as clear as possible about when things started or when they got worse. This doesn't mean that there aren't overlapping tests or treatments that help to assess and treat symptoms caused by a variety of causes. It also doesn't mean that these separate treatments should be applied at separate times. Actually, the best practice is to treat the multiple causes and symptoms at the same time, when possible. What it really means is that the people helping you with your recovery should be aware of these multiple exposures so that they can fully formulate your care and you should be aware of the challenges and time duration it takes to deal with these multiple issues.

> The more exposures or injuries you've had the more likely it is that you'll need multiple and longer treatments.

How Does Time Between Exposures Affect Post-Deployment Syndrome?

Although just having had more than one high-intensity exposure is important, a more significant issue is whether or not the first exposure has had time to adequately recover or heal before the second (or third) one occurred. Although it's a bit vague when it comes to a new high-level exposure on top of an existing low-intensity one, it's very clear that high-level exposures need both a period of time to heal and often a specific therapeutic treatment (or environment) to recover with. If these injuries are not cared for adequately and another high-intensity exposure occurs, then full recovery will be challenging. Of course, the same may be true with the low-intensity exposures (whether they begin before or after the high-intensity one), but the urgency of treatment may be less of an issue. The cumulative effects of these repeated, high-intensity exposures are also seen outside of the combat arena. In the world of sports, specific guidelines exist for athletes ranging from junior high to professional who have sustained an injury, including a concussion. These guidelines recommend and often mandate that athletes be removed from the sport and be allowed to recover in a therapeutic environment, usually with specific rehabilitation services until both an adequate period of recovery has occurred and until the athlete demonstrates the ability perform the skills needed for the sport without symptoms. The specifics of these recommendations vary with the type (concussion, knee injury, back pain) and severity (strain, sprain, or tear) of the injury. There is an increased urgency in the sports world to closely following and even re-verifying the guidelines that are used for concussion care, in light of increasing evidence that there are significant short- and long-term devastating effects from multiple sports concussions. These same guidelines are also often applied to injured workers, especially if the job being performed requires significant physical abilities. In general through recent studies it has become clear that a return to full physical activity or active duty military status should be delayed until the person is able to perform all of the key elements of the activity and any symptoms are either resolved or easily managed. Although this may seem to make common sense, it's actually based on the notion that the brain needs to be given sufficient time to heal and return to normal functioning before it is allowed to take the body into a high level of performance where it could get itself re-injured. This is not only a self-survival strategy, but also a way to assure that the body heals to its maximum. Although this doesn't mean that the brain and body should be shut down and need to be completely immobilized, it does mean that the body and brain should be in a safe environment while healing and being asked to progressively increase their activity levels. So, although the military strives to prevent all levels of injuries to its troops, it is as important to prevent that second high-intensity exposure, as it was the first, especially if the first one hasn't healed yet. By definition, the more of these exposures that you are exposed to and the shorter the period of time in between exposures, the more likely you are to develop PDS and the more challenging your recovery pathway will be.

Two high-intensity exposures that occur close to each other in time is a common cause of PDS.

What About Treatments?

Failure to receive timely and appropriate treatment for a low- or high-intensity combat exposure is yet another likely factor responsible for PDS. Although this doesn't mean that everyone who receives these treatments will be successful or everyone who doesn't will develop PDS, these early interventions at least usually allow the body and brain to begin the process of recovery and allow you to respond more readily to future treatments. In fact, many of the difficulties experienced during wartime require a series of targeted treatments delivered over a period of time to return the body to adequate functioning, rather than just intense bursts of care. Fortunately, in the case of PDS, there are often a wide range of options as to how to best control symptoms and how to get your life back onto a productive path.

Unfortunately, if you are more than 6 months from your injury or deployment to home, a simple symptoms treatment approach may not be enough. If your exposure and/or deployment is within the past 6 months, there are a significant number of focused therapeutic interventions that are likely to work because we know that most of the elements that make up PDS respond extremely well in the first 6 months. Even so, it's still best to go through the entire regimen outlined in this book, regardless of how well symptoms resolve or how long you've had them, to both enhance your chances of success and to build your overall resiliency. On the other hand, if you are like most returning warriors, you are more than 6 months from your time of initial high-exposure or from your redeployment to home. In this case, while it is always worthwhile to enter into a traditional symptom-based approach, more likely than not, you'll want to truly take a deep dive into the comprehensive program of recovery outlined here.

 Early, appropriate treatment is useful for PDS, but often isn't the sole answer to lifelong recovery.

SO WHAT NOW?

What can a person with PDS do? Here's the good news, there's plenty that you can do to reclaim your life. The bad news, however, is that restoring your life isn't something that someone else can do for you, a pill can give you, or a check can provide to you. Granted that each of these things (a concerned person, health care treatments, Veterans' benefits payments) can play a small role in helping you to regain your life and we'll explore how each should be used to its fullest; however, the bigger message behind it all is understanding ways that you can take charge of what's going on inside you and you can learn to return to wellness. Like anything else, the recovery contained within this book is multistep; however, these steps tend to be fluid in nature, more ramp-like than stepwise, and more flexible than other common treatment regimens or self-help books. Understanding the concepts behind the specific exercises outlined is far more important than the exercises themselves. There are not really right or wrong ways to use the healing principles outlined; however, it's extremely important that you look at this as an approach to live your life and return to your optimal level of productivity, not as merely a treatment for PDS. The approach in this book will entail a series of exercises, treatment recommendations, and discussions that will help to focus you on the importance of keying in regaining your post-deployment functioning, while utilizing strategies to decrease PDS symptoms. This refocusing of your attention and sights from symptom resolution to the more productive goals of restoring physical and mental functioning, establishing a purpose for your day-to-day activities, identifying the most supportive environment to allow for your short- and long-term recovery, and to resolving to redefine your post-deployment mindset toward one of progressive healing and eventual wellness are the keys to success from PDS.

 Refocusing yourself away from symptoms and towards progressive wellness is the key to PDS.

So, PDS is truly the illness of war. There are many things that may predispose you to have gotten PDS and just as many factors from military theater and the post-deployment period that may have brought about and worsened your condition. We'll begin to look at treatments that are out there in the military, the Veterans' hospitals, and other health care centers across the country. Hopefully, there are some of these standard treatments that can help you. Then, we'll take you through a step-by-step program to help you get your PDS under control, begin the process of regaining your life, and over time getting you on the road to a lifetime of wellness. You have the ability to achieve all of this within you—you just need to learn how.

We are the knowing, not the conditions known.

—Ekhart Tolle

3

Military and Veteran Health Care Systems: A Traditional Approach

Victory is reserved for those who are willing to pay its price.
—Sun Tzu

. . . to care for him who shall have borne the battle and for his widow and his orphan . . .
—Abraham Lincoln, Second Inaugural Address
(inscription on VA Central Office Building, Washington, DC)

U.S. combat operations in Afghanistan, referred to as Operation Enduring Freedom (OEF), in response to the September 11 terrorist attacks began on October 7, 2001. On March 19, 2003, the United States became engaged in military operations in Iraq, referred to as Operation Iraqi Freedom (OIF), as part of the larger Global War on Terror (GWOT). These two wars combined have been the longest, continuous military campaign in the history of the United States, with more than 2 million troops deployed as of late-2010. Both wars have seen the widespread use of powerful explosive devices that employ creative detonation methods and carry devastating blast components. Nearly three-quarters of all military casualties in OEF and OIF have been caused by explosive weaponry. This has lead to a whole host of complex injuries, often involving multiple organ systems including the brain, a phenomenon called polytrauma. Compared to past conflicts, including the first Gulf War, there has been a marked increase in the level of disability of the wounded, the overall volume of traumatic brain injuries (TBIs), post-traumatic stress disorder (PTSD), amputations, pain, and, ultimately, the phenomenon of post-deployment syndrome (PDS). Fortunately, despite these tactics, the incredible ability of the U.S. military's trauma teams to rapidly treat, stabilize, and evacuate the severely injured out of the battle zone has resulted in a field survival rate of *greater than 95%*. This is compared with the 78% rate in Vietnam, which at the time was phenomenal. So, despite the large number of explosive injuries and the untoward effects of these blasts on the body, the cutting edge technology and systems of the military have allowed for an incredibly high survival rate. More than twice the wounded are surviving as compared to Vietnam—and 10 times more than in World War II.

> *Never in the history of the world has any soldier sacrificed more for the freedom and liberty of total strangers than the American soldier.*
> — Sen. Zell Miller (D-Georgia), 2004

As of October 2010, there have been nearly 45,000 reported casualties, including more than 2,500 moderate-severe traumatic brain injuries, 1,250 limb amputations, 150 spinal cord injuries (SCI), and 550 major burns. But, these casualty figures only include those service members who have had injuries bad enough to require emergent or urgent care and removal from the battlefield. The numbers of service members returning with symptoms and disability related to mild brain injury, combat-related stress, and musculoskeletal pain is far greater, in the hundreds of thousands. Intensive, standardized screening programs are in place worldwide in the Department of Defense (DoD) and Veterans Health Administration (VHA) clinical centers to identify service members who may be have had these injuries, but have not been initially diagnosed. These programs have identified a far larger number of individuals. Nearly 5% of all deployed service members and more than 7% of all service members who seek care at VAs have been exposed to a concussion or mild brain injury, with more than 100,000 of these injuries identified. Research reports that at least 10% of all deployed personnel are returning with pain-related conditions, which means that nearly a quarter of a million service members and Veterans are affected. Add to these numbers all of the service members and Veterans who are having psychological health issues, such as PTSD, anxiety, and depression, and the total jumps to as many as one half million of America's warriors who have symptoms of PDS, and who may be at risk to develop the full blown disability that often accompanies it.

> *Now that a lot of my buddies are home you can see how much trouble a lot of them are having. Sean was a rock in Iraq. I actually called him Irock. We only got rolled once. He's been trying to go back to school but he can't seem to hold it together.*
> —Cpl Tim Owen

It seemed like every other day one of the convoys got hit. That was probably the worst part. Not really fight'in. Just waiting to be blown up. They're some sneaky bastards.
— Marine Sgt Sean Waldrop

The uniqueness of the explosive blast injury has proven to be the most devastating injury seen in OEF/OIF. These injuries not only result from the secondary (shrapnel and other projectiles) and tertiary effects of the blast (being thrown from the seen, having flying objects hitting you, causing vehicles to crash), but also from the primary presence of an under- and over-pressure wave of energy from the blast itself. The combination of the physical effects from the blast and this pressure wave is felt to be the culprit behind the wide range of injuries and the challenging recovery patterns seen. The pervasiveness of blast exposures, especially in the form of improvised explosive devices (IEDs), have taken a particular toll on the parts of the service members' body that are least protected by body armor, namely the head, neck, and limbs. Despite high-tech helmets, the head and neck remain vulnerable to injury, and traumatic brain injury has been referred to as the *signature injury* of this war. And, although a single large blast can have devastating effects on the body and brain, the majority of the difficulties being reported are resulting from repeated exposure over a period of days to months. These multiple blasts can be of lower intensity or even at a relatively far distance away, but still their effects seem to add up. The cumulative physical, neurologic, and psychological damage that these repeated exposures are causing appears to be made worse by the everyday and everywhere stressors of military theater. These stressors include a wide range of factors including everything from poor sleep patterns and emotional stress from the dangers of the battlefield, to the limited leisure time activities present in the harsh environment, poorly balanced diets, and lack of structured exercise and relaxation time. This whole range of injury and stress factors are part of the whole host of things that are contributing to PDS. Add to this the challenge of making a definitive diagnosis and starting treatment in a war zone, which leads to significant delays in dealing with symptoms, and you can better understand why it has been so hard for the military and the VA to provide the much needed care.

They wrote in the old days that it is sweet and fitting to die for one's country. But in modern war, there is nothing sweet nor fitting in your dying. You will die like a dog for no good reason.
— Ernest Hemmingway

To try and meet the unique and pervasive challenges of these OEF/OIF injuries and exposures, there has been a massive effort by the VHA and the DoD—as well as hundreds of partners in the world of academics (major universities and medical centers) and the private health industry—to try and meet the problems head on. These efforts have been driven by all of the right reasons: the desire to maintain a fighting force that is battle ready, the wish to fully support America's warriors, an understanding of the price of freedom, the fear of creating an alienated generation of Veterans like the one that returned from Vietnam, and the strong outpouring of support that has come from the nation's population and its political leaders. As a result of all of these good reasons to provide state of the art care, the DoD and VHA have adopted a layered system of screening programs, evaluation protocols, and treatment paradigms that are all clued in to the wide range of issues that the returning service members and Veterans have. Although many have complained that it took too long to set up this care system or that there remain many gaps in the system that allow service members and Veterans to fall through the cracks, this massive effort represents the world's largest and most sophisticated post-deployment health care network in history. Literally tens of billions of dollars have been invested to create battlefield, military hospital, VA medical center and outpatient clinic evaluation, management, and ongoing care programs to meet a vast range of needs spawning from these conflicts. It has truly an impressive effort and resulting system of care and it is being updated and upgraded on a nearly monthly basis. Unfortunately, if you're reading this book, you, someone you know, or someone you care for has had some persisting difficulties despite the intricacies of the system that's been created and the immense amount of resources that have been brought to bear. So what now?

It may anger you to know how much time, energy, and resources have been spent developing and implementing this massive health care system and the benefits system that accompanies it. You may figure that it must represent yet another example of how your government has failed you, or of how unfair the system is, or of how unfair life can be. You may want to blame someone in the military, the VA, or the government for messing up or for wasting your tax dollars. You may have turned to this book as a way of finding a new solution, one that will make up for what you were cheated of. Or, maybe you think that this book will show you the truth about what was lacking in your nation's system of care and who to blame. Well, this book is the key to understanding the issues and is the key to your recovery and success, but there's good news and there's bad news about all this. If you want the inside scoop and the dirty little secrets that no one's had the guts to tell you yet, then read on.

Okay, so here's the good news and the bad news about this book and the military health care system:

The Good News: There are many great things embedded in the military and VA health system and this book will show you how to unlock them and help them work to your advantage.

The Bad News: There really isn't any deep conspiracy designed to cheat you of your health or your rights.

The Best News: This book will provide you with a whole slew of tools, techniques, and ways of helping to get control of the way the symptoms of PDS have affected you.

If you commit to taking on the mission of getting yourself back on the path of recovery, then you will improve, and we can help. That's the best good news there could be. It's also really good news that the health care funding, manpower, and drive are already in place. America has not let down its heroes, but instead has supported allocating what it takes to try and provide state-of-the-art care to its warriors. In fact, many of the things that can help you to get well and that can make your road to wellness easier to navigate already exist within this huge system of care. Perhaps not all of the philosophies of recovery or the approaches to wellness are exactly perfect for the complexities of your PDS symptoms, or to supporting your return to the fluid warrior you once were, but many of the lifelong resources you may need are there and many of the dedicated and well-trained clinicians who can assist you are there too. We're talking about services and clinicians that are specifically paid to see you and to get you well, not to make money for some organization. There's no middleman or stockholder making money off of your health. The only one who benefits is you (actually, it makes the health care providers feel pretty darn good also!). Many, if not all, of the unique services that can make your symptoms and your problems improve are already located within the walls of the military bases, the halls of the VA hospitals, the waiting rooms of the Veterans' centers and the offices of the community counseling centers. You have to know how to access and use these resources, and you have to know they exist. Even some of those dreaded benefits and disability forms that you have been completing for what seems like years can actually be used to your advantage. The real goal of this book is to show you a way to be able to take advantage of the *positive things* that all of these resources have to offer you. Many, many people who are suffering from the OEF/OIF wars are already very aware of the *negative things* that are out there, but as you try and journey to wellness can you find the positive effects, too? As two folks who have worked within this system, we have seen just how well aspects of the system *can* work for the wounded warrior when used the right way. We've also seen how things don't work out well, and we understand the issues separating these two possible roads. We hope to open your eyes to what role you and your approach to health can have in a positive outcome and, at the same time, we'd like to give you the tools to take advantage of them. Many of those tools are already inside you, waiting to assist.

One of the first steps to making the most of what the military health system has to offer is to understand how to get into it. Once you do that, it's important to know where to get seen, who to get seen by, and what to take away from it. Let's start with how and where to get seen. As a Veteran of the OEF/OIF wars, all active and former service members are eligible to receive health care at VA facilities for a period of 5 years post-deployment. Even if you're still in the military, you can be seen at one of the VA's specialized brain injury, pain, or PTSD programs. Sometimes these specialty centers are good ways to get to the bottom of your diagnosis. They may help figure out the problem and then refer you for care at a military or community treatment center close to your base or home. If you are diagnosed with a specific injury or difficulty from the conflicts, like TBI, PTSD, or pain, then you are eligible to receive a *lifetime of care* at a VA facility for that problem. Of course, if you are still on active duty, then you may wish to receive your care at your assigned military treatment facility. Or, you can use your military insurance (TriCare) at community health clinics and offices. If none of these situations fit you (e.g., if you've got difficulties as a result of an earlier conflict or from a nonmilitary cause), the DoD, VA, and many academic/private facilities still remain great resources to help with your difficulties. You may just need to help figure out what you're eligible to receive for free (in recognition of your service) and what may cost some money. Not sure what you're eligible for or where the closest facility is located? Then go to any VA facility and ask, or check them out on the web. All of these services shouldn't be ignored and we'll be identifying what things you can incorporate into the wellness strategies we show you.

 Find out where the closest VA facility is at www.va.gov.

So where should you go? In general, receiving your health care for the symptoms of PDS should be done at those centers where they are accustomed to caring for others with similar problems. No reason to reinvent the wheel. Just as the best place to receive an initial diagnosis and treatment recommendations for a cancer or a liver problem is at a major center that has seen lots of folks with similar issues—a major polytrauma, brain injury—a post-deployment center is the best place to start. Large military bases that have had high numbers of service members returning from the battlefield or one of the hundreds of VAs that have specialized programs in polytrauma care are usually better equipped, better experienced, and better able to make the right diagnoses, set up the right care plan, and arrange for follow through in getting the treatments you need.

 You can find great information at www.polytrauma.va.gov.

Even if the VA site you go to then refers you for treatments closer to your home or base, at least you have been seen by a team that knows exactly what to do and can set you on the right road. Although PDS and the other challenging conditions from the OEF/OIF wars are not the easiest things to understand and treat, when you've seen a few hundred or thousand folks with these kinds of problems, it's actually not nearly as tough as you might think. That's how specialists get to be called that, lots and lots of patients, time, and way too much reading. These specialty sites also have highly trained case managers (social workers or nurses) whose job it is to help you to navigate the system, get you correctly linked to resources (clinicians, medications, benefits), and then make sure you don't fall through cracks. Make sure you get linked in with one of these case managers. If you don't get assigned one, ASK FOR IT. If you want to find your way around the "complex city of medicine," you need a map, a really good map. Case managers are like city tour guides with the best darn maps around.

> *I don't know which is worse; going to Iraq or trying to get the Army to help me out with this. At first they tried to tell me there was nothing wrong with me. Then they told me I was just depressed and gave me some drugs. My sergeant was a total pain. In Iraq at least I knew who the enemy was.*
> —PFC Lori Stefano

So, you understand how to access the programs, you know you need to been seen by a specialists and get linked into the system; now what? The next step is making sure you have been seen or will be seen by the right people. Unfortunately, not every center

- has what everyone needs (or wants),
- is always able to figure out the best way to go, or
- can help you with all of your difficulties.

This doesn't mean that the entire system is broken or that you can't benefit at all from what they have to offer. Part of the strength of this book is to help you to find out (and understand) just what is wrong with you. This information can then be combined with your knowledge of what problems you are having on a day-to-day basis to try and put together a plan for recovery. To do this, the first step is making sure you have all of your records and you are getting them to the right people to review. In the right hands, these records can help to determine if you may need some new tests or studies. They can also determine if you've had all of the traditional treatments that can help you. Although just using this book alone can help you tremendously, its strategies can be even more effective if you take full advantage of the tremendous number of specialists and services that the military, VA, and community programs have to offer. Why is this so important and how can you know what the good elements of the system might be? It's important to understand that, despite what may seem like a daunting organization, the military and VA health care programs are made up of people who, for the most part, are really good people. These people, and in particular the clinicians (doctors, nurses, therapists, psychologists, social workers), are there to help people. They have trained for much of their lives to be of service to others. It actually makes them feel whole to make someone else well. Although they are getting paid to do this job, it is the job itself that ultimately drives them. There are much easier ways to make money with all of the skills they have. They stay around because they get a kick out of doing their jobs well and that means out of getting you better. So, if you can bring to them specific issues that they are able to understand and then treat, you will not only help yourself, but you are actually also helping them. So, regardless of what may have been your past experiences or beliefs, bringing an attitude of willingness to work together with the clinician is a good beginning. This includes trusting the clinician to be honest with you, to listen to you, and to be open with what you have to tell them. This also entails your willingness to fully discuss how you are feeling, how your body is working, and what you are seeing in your recovery. This mutual trust is the first step in helping to best understand what is going on with you, to better understand what may have happened to you, and to begin to identify the steps needed for recovery. Focusing your attitude to try and take full advantage of the knowledge, skills, and services that the clinicians can provide you is a key way to make the most of the health care system.

What a runaround. The VA is just a bunch of people doing nothing. I spent six hours over there and I got a foam roller. Everybody talks a big game and thanks me for my service. What a joke. How about disability check that's worth something. Now they are bugging me about my pain killers. Can't they get off my ass already and help me.
—Pft 2nd class Jimmy Freidland

Just because you have committed yourself to bringing honesty and trust to the clinical setting does not ensure that you will get fully better with all of the treatments or medications recommended, or that you will feel fully comfortable with the care delivered. It's likely that you may need to use the information contained in the upcoming sections of this book to help to work *with* these recommendations to improve. Just as gas sometimes works better with additives in it, so too many of the health care treatments that are the right answer for your symptoms may need an additive. This book is your additive. This does not mean that the clinicians or that the system are not trying to help you. Large health care systems and even solo practitioner clinicians are established to provide care that helps the majority of patients. Many of the problems seen as a result of the OEF/OIF conflicts are not typical and are not what most people have. They are not what are usually seen in these settings. They are highly complex, they are not straightforward, and they are not easily diagnosed or cared for by a clinician or a team that is not specially trained to deal with it. Even in teams that are specially prepared to diagnose and manage the major elements of PDS, sometimes they cannot completely eliminate all of the symptoms or sometimes they misinterpret or misread the signals. Treatments that work for 8 of 10 service members may do nothing for the other 2. If you're still having problems months (or years) after deployment, you may be like the 2 of 10 service members who need something more. This book is designed to help you, it's the something more that you need. But, it is not designed to work to the exclusion of the entire health care system. Rather, the goal is to use the techniques and systems that have been developed in this country in the past 100 or so years, to take into consideration the techniques and systems that have been developed in many parts of the world for the past 2000 or more years, and to blend these with the power of personal commitment to regain your wellness.

So here are some simple guidelines to use when visiting your clinicians office, when speaking with your DoD, VA or other benefits personnel, and when reaching out to other health care professionals for assistance.

1. Health care systems work best when you come prepared to communicate openly and honestly about your difficulties, in a way that the providers can understand. Find the most appropriate provider for your difficulties from the list here, so that they have the right frame of reference to help you.
2. Come prepared to a get the most from your visit. Write down, in advance, how things are going, what you have been doing to get well, and what problems still exist. Bring an accurate list of your medications and supplements. Bring a several day schedule of your routine, of your activity level, of your sleep pattern.
3. Commit to following your clinicians' treatment plans. If possible, try and see if you can get a single physician to manage

all of your PDS symptoms. If you cannot do certain things they recommend, let them know and see if there's another approach.

4. Work hard to understand what your diagnoses are, what the short- and long-term treatments are, and what the course of recovery should be like. This is a major step in recovery. Knowing what the future is likely to hold makes it less frightening and mysterious. The mystery of illness and injury is often the primary obstacle to healing. Understand the specifics of treatment so you can fully commit yourself to these treatments. Although not always successful when applied in isolation, these treatments are often part of the answers to recovery. Just as you went into a battle armed and prepared, arming yourself with knowledge is a vital part of achieving wellness.

5. Benefits are dispersed based on cut and dried formulas. Benefits personnel do not generally have any stake in whether benefits are paid out or not. They don't get paid extra if they give out or if they withhold monies form you. Be nice to them and have the information they need and you will find them to be amazingly helpful. There are pre-determined formulas and criteria that determine who gets paid what, when, and how often. The better you can answer the questions and fill in the blanks, the more likely you will get what is appropriate. Tell the truth about how you are doing, whether it's on your military post-deployment heath assessment (PDHA) or post-deployment health re-assessment (PDHRA) or your VA compensation and pension (C&P) examination. Heath case managers and social workers can help in extraordinary ways with this.

6. Creating a hostile environment is really not a way to connect well with health care providers. Getting angry, yelling at team members, being rude or sarcastic, or writing mean letters may make you feel better for a while, but really isn't a good approach to collaboration. Although congressmen and senators can occasionally make things happen for you, it usually is not a good long-term strategy either. You should be trying to develop life-long linkages with providers that will get you well.

7. Keep copies of all of your records in a neat and organized manner, such as in a loose leaf binder or on a CD-ROM, and make sure your clinicians have these records. Not every clinician can really benefit from all of your records, but try to get them into the hands of your primary care clinician and into your electronic medical record (in the military this record is called "Alta" and in the VA it's called "CPRS.") Try and keep a long-term relationship with only a few clinicians who can have copies of these records and can work with you on your care.

8. Do not shop for clinicians because you don't like what some say. A good clinician can only be effective if you give them a chance

to get to know you. A good clinician will be able to tell you the honest truth about how you are doing or what's wrong with you. The best clinicians can convey it to you in a way that you can accept, but you must give them the chance. One or two committed and well-meaning clinicians who can partner with you in your care is far better than a score of specialists and super-specialists who like to hear themselves think out loud. You are your own best therapist and healer, you just have to find the right clinicians to educate you and assist you.

9. Work with your clinicians to integrate all aspects of your health care and your life into a single system of living. Work with them to integrate your medicines, your therapy, your work, your family life, and all other aspects of who you are into a single process. The interrelatedness of everything can be made to work to your advantage if you are able to be aware of it. Work with your health care providers to realize this.

10. Going to see the doctor or therapists should not be your life's work or your hobby, *nor* is it a punishment. As long as it is helping you to more fully realize your warrior character, then it is a positive experience. As with other aspects of your recovery, you must embrace and commit to the therapeutic nature of this care. If there are aspects of the care that make it seem like punishment, then explore what those are and work to improve them. Good health care helps millions of people every year. Unfortunately, when it becomes nontherapeutic it can cause harm.

Applying these guidelines to your use of the DoD, VA, and private health care world is a good start in the often challenging world of organized medicine. Another important aspect of successes accessing health care and of using this book in an integrative style with clinicians, is making sure you are seeing the right clinician. But, it's hard to tell the players without a scorecard, so we'll see if we can help. Here's a list of the common types of clinicians that you might see and some pointers on what to expect and how to approach them.

Primary Care Clinician (PCC): Either a doctor or a specially trained nurse who has training on the general care of the body's systems and functioning. They see many patients and are asked to take into account literally hundreds of issues at once, usually in a brief period of time. Although they need to record all of the issues you may have going on, usually they can only really address one or two problem at a visit, and determine whether a simple fix can help the problem, a test is needed for more information or if they should have you see a specialist. They serve as the best central repository of information on your care and may also serve to help coordinate our care. Because they are looking at all aspects of your care and don't have a great deal of time to do so, they are really not the best choice for your definitive diagnosis or to make recommendations about your overall care for PDS. If you are having significant problems with PDS or have not done well in accessing the system before, you should ask your PCC to help you to see a specialist or a specialty team. The PCC's knowledge of brain injuries, pain, or most psychological issues is too general to manage your problems. If you are having only one small problem or have other non-PDS medical issues, then the PCC is your best option. It's important though to make sure your PCC is made aware of and is part of all aspects of your care, even if a specialist is actually doing most of your PDS care. Your PCC is your health care provider for life.

Physiatrist or Rehab Physician: They are specialty doctors with a focus on returning you to full functioning, rather than just treating medical disease. They usually have a good big-picture view of care, address things that are particularly important to you (everyday life, how you feel, sexuality, work, finances) and have specialty training in brain injury, amputation, pain, and many psychological disorders. They often work closely as part of a rehabilitation team with therapists, psychologists, and social workers to both make diagnoses and to make sure you are receiving the right types of care. These doctors are good providers to see for PDS and work well with your PCC and other members of your health care team. There are very few of these doctors in the military, but a large number in the VA and in the community.

Neurologists: Doctors who specialize in the diagnosis and care of disorders of the nerves and brain. Although great diagnosticians, who also do well with managing headaches and seizures, they are usually more focused on the tree than the forest and may miss how having had a concussion or PDS impacts on your overall life. They have limited specialty training with concussion, pain (except for headaches), or psychological disorders. Occasionally they work as part of a larger team of rehabilitation professionals and, when this occurs, they can be fair to good providers for PDS. There are a large number of these doctors in the military, but a smaller number in the VA and in the community.

Neurosurgeons: Doctors who are exquisitely trained in the acute surgical care of disorders of the brain and spine. Although they are the premiere clinicians for the surgical and intensive care management of problems with the brain and spine, they have limited skill in the typical problems in PDS. In general, they should not be involved in your care, unless you need surgery on your spine or brain for some other reason (let's hope not). There are very few of these doctors in the military and in the VA, but a larger number in the community.

Psychiatrists: Doctors who specialize in the care of psychiatric, psychological, emotional, and behavioral disorders. Although they have specialty training in brain injury and pain, this is not typically part of their core skills. They also are experienced in working as part of treatment teams, but usually in the areas of mental illness. They are the best qualified to make recommendations regarding the appropriate medications to use for mental illnesses, including depression, anxiety, schizophrenia, and related illnesses. They are good consultants to the rehabilitation team for psychological conditions that are interfering with most of your recovery. They are also the appropriate physicians to care for individuals who are suicidal. There are a large number of these doctors in the military, VA, and in the community.

Other Medical Specialists: You may have occasion to see other physician specialists in the areas of orthopedics (bone issues), otolaryngologists or ENTs (balance or hearing issues), ophthalmologists (eye or vision issues), or other areas. In general, these doctors are helpful for specific problems, but are not the best to manage the initial diagnosis or care of PDS.

Psychologists: Therapists with doctoral degrees in the field of psychology (human behavior) who specialize in the diagnosis and management of thinking (cognitive) and emotional (behavior) problems. They help to figure out what types of therapy (counseling, cognitive training, cognitive-behavior therapy, adjustment skills) would be most useful. They are the best ones to see when you need to have psychotherapy to help deal with emotions and feelings (see Chapter 8). Neuropsychologists have expertise in testing to find the specific problems you're having in these areas. They often work as part of a rehabilitation or mental health team. There are a fair number of these therapists in the military, and a large number in VA and in the community.

Rehabilitation Therapists: Therapists who focus on the different areas of functioning to help you regain your independence. This includes physical therapists (balance, strength, walking), occupational therapists (coordination, household skills, computer skills), speech and language pathologists (language and thinking skills), recreational therapists (leisure and community skills), kinesiotherapists (endurance training and wellness), blind rehabilitation specialists (visual deficits), and vocational rehabilitation therapists (work skills).

Case Managers: Nurses or social workers who can assist you to integrate all aspects of your care and to understand what your role is within the larger system of care. They also can assist you to understand what benefits you are eligible for and how to take full advantage of them.

The vast military and VA health care systems are there to serve you, although getting into and navigating the system can be a challenge. Even after you've identified what you're eligible to get, how to get into the system and who to try and see can still be frustrating. Appointments can be hard to get to. Some visits seem like a waste of time. Or, even if you've tried faithfully to make it work, you're still not getting better. Or even worse, you still don't know what's wrong. It may be that your diagnosis is hard to pin down because many of the conditions have nearly identical causes and very similar symptoms. After a few months (let alone years), many symptoms change or blend together. Just as it's tough to repair an engine that's been misdiagnosed for a long time or poorly cared for, it can be extremely difficult to fix problems in people that have been developing and changing for a long time. Even at the best automotive shop, not all vehicles can be figured out or brought back to mint condition. So what's left to do? Has your warranty expired? Are you a lemon? Should we look to sell you for scrap? As we've said, the decision to consider if it's time and if it's worth the effort of looking at this from a different angle lies within you. There are plenty of centers of excellence that are set up to try and help you, but they can't be helpful to you if you aren't what they are set up to help. Although you can complain or feel angry about how none of these places can help you, that really won't get you better in the long run (although it usually feels pretty darn good for a few minutes or so). The state of the matter is that we've got to help you to first get to a place and condition where you can be ready to be helped what this multibillion dollar system can fix. Think of yourself as an exotic American automobile (okay, maybe that's stretching it a bit, how about a vintage Pinto?) that's broken down and in need of an expert repair, but the problems are so challenging that none of the mechanics know how to help. What can you do? Well there is someone who can begin the process and who can help the mechanics get to work on you. Someone who understands what makes your engine run. That someone is you. You know about your body, your mind, and the problems you're having. You also are extremely motivated to get yourself well again. But, how can you fix yourself? You can't completely, but you can begin to make some changes jump start this process. We've got to first try some different strategies to get your body and mind in the right place to take advantage of all of the mechanics that the government has put into place to get you running well. These centers are actually quite good at what they do and can achieve what may seem like miracles. But miracles can only happen when the timing and setting are right. If you want to create those conditions, then turn the page and begin to the process.

4

A New Model of Wellness:
Rebuilding the Warrior

Look at every path closely and deliberately, then ask yourself this crucial question: Does this path have a heart? If it does, then the path is good. If it doesn't, it is of no use.

—Carlos Castaneda

In this chapter, we'll introduce you to some concepts and exercises that will engage your whole healing system, regardless of which symptoms of post-deployment syndrome (PDS) you may have. These concepts advocate a way of seeing your body, mind, and health that will inform the way *you* approach *your own* healing. At the same time, the exercises will suggest specific strategies to treat the symptoms you're having. It's important for you to feel better as soon as possible, so that you'll regain the ability to do more than just suffer and try and seek help for your suffering. More than anything, we want to give you the tools to help you get on with the business of creating an amazing life for yourself. In the middle of all this, we want to remind you that it is the quality of your involvement, of how you study, and of how you apply this material on a day-to-day basis that is most important in your ultimate success. This chapter will begin to outline the overall healing and integration process. We will introduce some of the large overriding principles of healing that are often overlooked in traditional clinical settings, where the focus is usually on specific symptoms or medical diagnoses. We will also reinforce the notion that this more traditional health care approach of individually addressing your specific conditions can be effectively applied, while at the same time reconnecting with what your inner strength has to offer.

Trauma afflicts both the mind and the body, never just one or the other. The body and mind are inseparable, so we want to introduce you to methods of healing both. When you are fully engaged in healing one, you are also healing the other. The sun of life and renewal can rise from either place, so when that sun rises in the mind it casts light into the body, and when it rises in the body it casts light into the mind. Bringing this light or awareness into how we think, feel, and move is what healing is all about. Despite what you might sometimes feel, you are not alone in this. The same issues and processes that we'll be exploring for you and to help manage PDS, apply to everyone else out there who is challenged with health problems. Everyone on the planet is engaged in healing, which can be looked at as a type of growing and coming to maturity. In the long run, true healing *is* coming to maturity. Your process of healing after trauma is just a million times more intense.

Whether your difficulties are the result of a blast-related concussion with ongoing thinking problems, persistent back or neck pain, the inability to find restful sleep, or emotional or mood disturbances from having been exposed to traumas on the battlefield, the common factor is how each of these injuries affect your brain's processing. The highest functioning component of your brain, what scientists call your *executive function*, is thrown off by these types of injuries, traumas, and persistent symptoms and is not working ideally. Your injury, trauma, exposures, and stressors have directly affected your ability to handle the world around you and the way your body integrates with that world. For some of you, it was a part of your brain that was never finely tuned to begin with. For others of you, it was working at the highest level. Your executive functioning controls your ability to see, understand, and plan your life. It handles way more than just getting up and moving through your life—it's truly understanding everything around you and fully living that life. It's what you need to be fully developed so that you can become your own best commanding officer. We'll be looking at ways to help better understand and control how your brain works with your body and integrates with the world, as well as ways to improve the way your body is functioning.

One of the most common things that is done to redevelop your executive function and to improve the way your brain works is to get to know some of the methods talk therapists use to help these problems. The most common therapeutic method used for this, especially after battlefield issues, is called cognitive-behavioral therapy (CBT). This approach entails examining your thinking abilities, seeing how you are applying them to day-to-day functioning, and then figuring out where they do not jibe with reality. CBT is a collaborative effort between the therapist and the client. CBT is based on the assumption that most emotional and behavioral reactions are learned. Therefore, the goal of therapy is to help clients unlearn their unwanted reactions and to learn a new way of reacting. It has proven to be *one of the most effective treatments for post-traumatic stress disorder* (PTSD) and can also help with brain injury–related cognitive and behavior issues. Although CBT is the most commonly used therapy approach, there are many, many others. We want to introduce you to some of them, so that you can find what works for you. Some involve learning to access your unconscious mind, such as eye movement desensitization and reprocessing (EMDR). Others are concerned with diving into the traumatic emotional experiences of the body and allowing them to play out, a method known as *somatic experiencing*. This process, introduced by Peter Levine, is literally learning to gradually release energy and emotions that trauma generates and traps in the muscles and brain. Another particularly accessible type of therapy, created by the spiritual teacher Byron Katie, involves a method and set of questions, called *The Work*, which can be very helpful in discovering where our belief systems are out of whack and are causing us suffering. All of these methods are about learning to see and live our lives intelligently. It's important to keep in mind that although each of these methods are best practiced with a trained therapist, it's still extremely helpful and important for you to understand the principles behind them. We explore them in further depth in Chapter 8.

In addition to taking input from many of these relatively recent discoveries of psychotherapy, we will also explore some of the innate patterns of our bodies and many of the longstanding lessons of ancient cultures. There are so many relatively accessible methods available to each of us that you can use to your advantage with only a small amount of instruction and support, which we'll explore with you. Some of the questions we'll be helping you with include:

- What patterns are already within each of us that can aid in our healing?
- How can we tap into the energy of these inborn patterns that exist within the fiber of our bodies, within our very movements, and within the patterns of our bond with nature?
- What can we do to restore the basic care of our bodies and our minds, so that some of these intrinsic energies may be enhanced?
- What role can diet, exercise, and sleep play in a return to health?
- How can creative arts and activities, such as journal writing, music, and sports aid in wellness?

Although many of these areas of self-healing have been recently recognized in our society, many of these simple resources have been known by ancient cultures for centuries and millennia. As a warrior yourself, it's important to recognize that there is a great deal to be learned from indigenous warrior cultures, including our own Native American one. For them, part of the path of coming fully home from the war was maintaining a bond with the community and becoming initiated into elderhood. Elderhood, or wisdom, is not necessarily the result of how old you are, but can be the result of your proximity to death. We want you to think hard about the possibility of becoming an elder. What does that mean? Remember, being an elder is not a function of how long you have been alive, but rather it is the result of how deeply you've looked into the face of death. Many of you have experienced things that have allowed you to have truly learned what it means to be alive. Many traditions advocate contemplating death as a way of learning to appreciate and cultivate life. Being an elder is about being in service to life. How can you use your experiences, many of them painfully traumatic, to help others around you? In doing this, not only are you continuing an ancient tradition, but you are also helping yourself. We more fully explore the uniqueness and strength found in being an elder and being of service in Chapter 11.

I want to help you. I want to help you because helping you seems like helping myself. I sense the frustration and suffering that goes on in you. I sense the pain, the confusion. The wishing things were the way they used to be. And you are trying. You want to be the full man you were. I believe that the stuff I have learned over my life, in and out of war, might be of some use to you. It will not take the place of the trained specialists you are working with, but I think it might offer a different perspective than you have right now. Maybe if we can shift the perspective we can create a little movement in the process, a movement up towards the light. I think that if we can just concentrate a bit on the light our world can become infused with something new. If our sense of possibility can grow. If we can feel like we are on to something. If we can forge ahead even when we don't feel like we are on to something. If we can study the movement of ourselves and discern which ways are toward the light and which ways are not. And even perhaps to think we might learn something from the dark.

There is an ancient Tibetan warrior training, Shambala Warrior Training, that espouses these 5 perfections. They have to do with seeing whatever our situation is, as perfect. They are:

- *This is the perfect time*
- *This is the perfect place*
- *This is the perfect teacher*
- *This is the perfect teaching*
- *This is the perfect student*

Sometimes a little shift in attitude is all we need to enter the stream of life.

—Letter to an Afghanistan Vet from a Vietnam Vet

Many of the things we suggest are in fact modern takes on ancient methods. Meditation and mindfulness practices have been around in all cultures in some form for thousands of years. Both religious and warrior cultures have long practiced some variation of these mind focusing and body steadying techniques. The most well known application of these techniques used by warriors is seen in the martial arts: Kung Fu, Karate, and Tai Quan Do. The most commonly used movement exercise internationally, Tai Chi Chuan, also applies many of these same principles. Tai Chi has been shown by modern scientific methods to be highly effective for a wide variety of ailments, ranging from poor balance to high blood pressure. Modern scientific research is finally starting to explain how meditation practices can help create health in our bodies, clarity in our thinking, and excellence in our lives. Even more importantly, neuroscientists are discovering that the brain is not fixed or permanently broken, but rather it is a dynamic, changeable life force. It is capable of regenerating and rewiring even when it's injured. That's called neuroplasticity. Researchers are learning how important meditation is in this process. We dive more deeply into this in Chapter 6, but for now, let's just say that every time you see our little sign from Chapter 1 (☯), stop, remember there is no hurry, enjoy a breath, and rest in this moment. This is the first step in meditation and in growing the strength of your mind.

> *I used to watch a lot of Kung Fu movies when I was teenager. I wanted to be able to fight like that so I took Tai Quan Do for a couple of years. My friends used to call me Ninja.*
>
> — Cpl Tim Owen

Creativity in all of its forms is healing. To that end, we will be advocating becoming involved in music, art, and writing. Something as simple as keeping a journal can help you to better understand where you've been, where you are, and where you are heading. Creative arts, such as experiencing or creating music or art, can be amazingly therapeutic. We'll even be looking at the power of sound alone to help healing. We want you to focus on anything and everything that brings enjoyment into your life. Linking into the beauty of nature, for example, is a key component of healing. When we are open to it, just being *in* nature is a tremendous healing force. The sun itself gives us vitamin D and warms our bodies and souls. If we had our way, all hospitals, VAs, convalescent centers, and warrior transition units would be located on the ocean, by a river, in the mountains, in a grove of maple trees or the bayou or the Utah national parks. Being in nature reminds us that whatever our particular life circumstances, we are part of a much larger process. The inner quiet that can come from just a little while in nature is highly conducive to the forces that lift us. When we don't have access to these large and majestic areas, we can take a short walk in woods near our homes, or a little park. If we are incapacitated or without access to nature, an African violet or some ordinary houseplant can remind us of it. The same life force that drives plants, drives us. We can grow things. The tiniest germinating seed can ignite a sense of wonder. Gardening takes one out of one's self and into the earth. When we pay attention, what rises up in the plants also rises up within us. Never underestimate how much nature and being with growing things can do for us. The companionship of animals, whether it's a dog, a cat, or even a horse, is without parallel. And here is the most amazing thing. We, ourselves, are nature. The processes that we observe in nature are observable in our own bodies. They are in our breath and life. A sense of connection goes a long way in ordering us. We look at this and identify some specific activities for you in Chapter 9.

> *We are all connected: to each other biologically, to the earth, chemically, to the galaxies, atomically.*
>
> —Neil de Grasse Tyson, Physicist
> Director, New York Planetarium

Admittedly, many of the ideas we'll be discussing are not always sentiments expounded on in the military; the military emphasizes different aspects of existence. But remember, it's not an "either/or" situation, you can have it all. The goals and directions of these activities are adding to the way you see things, expanding your notion of who and what you are. Recognizing the relatedness of all things forms a ground of support. We are not in this alone.

Some of what we will be doing might seem like Yoga, or Tai Chi, or other related movement disciplines. These, too, are ancient practices and in their original form reflect the eastern spiritual traditions from which they came. In the United States, over the past 30 years or so, they have become mostly secular mainstream fitness practices. In almost every town and city, yoga teachers and studios abound. You will find classes in Yoga or Tai Chi at your local YMCA and even in health care facilities or Veterans' Hospitals. If you already have a body/mind practice, or these or similar forms appeal to you, then by all means go ahead and pursue them. They will help you tremendously. If something feels right to you, and you can see some benefit, keep at it. The tricky part here is that although these forms of movement will aid your healing, as commonly practiced they tend to be more about fitness. They are predominantly for those who, on a health scale where 10 is fully fit, want to go from being a 6 to a 7, or from 9 to 10. They aren't routinely used by those with serious injuries or significant physical and mental health problems, who are trying to go from 3 to 4, or even 1 to 2. It's unlikely that a warrior who was hit by an improvised explosive device in Afghanistan, suffers from PTSD, has spent 6 months at Walter Reed, and is just getting home, is ready to join a bunch of spandex-clad fitness buffs in a Yoga class. But, we'll discuss how to make this transition smoother and more therapeutic.

In Chapter 5, we visit the traditional medical approach to care and give you the information needed to get the most out of your hospital, clinic, or doctor's office visits. Better still, how to integrate what you may have heard from your doctor or therapists at the hospital or clinic into these mind/body activities. Although the long-term goal is to have as little or no medications being used to manage the typical problems of PDS, sometimes they are much needed in the short-term or can help to synergize with the other remedies to get you where you want to go faster. So, we'll look at what medications are best for persistent sleep problems, for specific types of headaches, or for mood disturbances. How do you know when you really might benefit from a medication and when it's time to stop taking them? What are the expected side effects and which ones should you tolerate while the treatments are occurring? *None* of the mind/body treatments we'll be describing and taking you through *will work against* the traditional treatments or medications prescribed— actually, they are likely to make them work better.

In the last 50 years, there have been great developments in the art and science of healing. Some of it has been within the traditional medical structure and much of it outside of these walls. Most of what we are presenting comes from the recent discoveries about what a human being is and what methods can open our greatest potential. The bulk of the natural healing ideas in this book come from a work called Continuum: an innovative body/mind method that is quite simply about what type of thinking and what type of moving quickens the healing process and creates the most aware human being. Continuum is based on the fact that we, and all living things, are in constant motion and that we are fluid systems made mostly of water. Its fundamental premise is that when we become more fluid, and de-pattern our bodies and thinking, we become renewed and open for healing. You cannot write your name in water. It is new in every moment. Continuum exercises erase the history of trauma in the body and in the mind. They open you up to change and recovery. We introduce this here, but will cover this in greater depth in Chapter 7.

MOVEMENT AND FLOW

Life is movement. That means: you are movement. You are in a constant state of movement and, whether you are awake or even in the apparent stillness of sleep, there is breathing and every cell in your body is engaged in metabolic process. Even in death there is the movement of decomposition. At all times, something is coming, and something is going. One complete breath observed teaches us this. Health and wellness are a balanced flow between this coming and going. Healing is coming back into balance and flow. Movement is not only what you are but it is also how you are going to heal.

You've no doubt heard of the Golden Rule: *Do unto others as you would have them do unto you.* Sounds great—a noble sentiment that's perfect if what you like is what others like. But it makes the assumption that what you want is what others want, or that you know what they want. Who really knows what the best thing is for others or for you? Let's look at this through the eyes of your body. How can we know what is the best thing for your body? Is it always something that is in a textbook, in some specialist's head, or in a test? If we really think about it, your body intrinsically knows what the best thing is for it. Living organisms come equipped with built in sensors and mechanisms to detect problems and to correct them. Listening to what our bodies are telling us and taking advantage of these tools may be the challenge. When it comes to taking care of our bodies and our minds, we need to consider a different version of this Golden Rule, let's call it the Platinum version: *Do unto others as they would have done unto themselves.*

Do unto others as they would have done unto themselves. That's interesting. Now we have to look deeper, we have to walk in someone else's shoes; actually, in this case, it's getting inside of your own body. We have to make the inquiry: what does my body want? Let's not be too sure we really know. Some simple examples: I want to smoke a cigarette or I want another piece of cake. Is that what my body wants? I want to look like the young versions of Arnold Schwarzenegger or Pamela Anderson. Is that really what my body wants? Or does it want to experience fluidity, connection, strength, and ease?

> *I love gettin' drunk with my friends. I really got wasted at "The Happy Crab" the other night. It was a blast. The only problem is I don't remember most of it. I was sick as a dog and the headache I woke up with screwed me up for a day and a half.*
>
> —PFC Lori Stefano

In healing, coming to the body's perspective is essential. What nourishes it? We know it thrives on certain food and drink more than others. Peanut butter is better than battery acid. We know it prefers certain environments to others. Naked in Cancun is better than naked in Antarctica. But let's get more specific. Because the body is movement, when we ask the question, "What does the body want?" we are also asking "How does the body want to move?" Understanding what makes the body move (work) is also the key to what makes the mind move (work). Figuring this out is what this book is about.

There are some basic clues to discovering movement that heals.

- How does water, which makes up more than 70% of the body, move naturally?
- What do my senses tell me about the way I'm moving?
- Do some movements feel more nourishing and restorative than others?
- How do I participate with and encourage any movements that feel restorative?

In healing, these are essential questions.

Opening the Body by Encouraging Flow

It is helpful to think of the body as a moving river. If the current is fairly steady, and the water is clean, then the river is healthy. It can handle the minor and most of the major challenges that come its way. It is the nature of a river, and a body, to maintain its own health. But a river can lose this ability if there is chaos, or if it's obstructed or constricted, becomes clogged or dries out, or becomes polluted or stagnant. Physical and psychological trauma can bring about all of these conditions and profoundly alter the nature of the body. Pain, illness, and disorientation can be the result of these disruptions in flow. Observing and acting on the body *from the outside*—resetting a broken bone, sewing up a spouting artery, diagnosing problems by examining blood under a microscope, making sure that what we put into the body is clean and nourishing, even replacing organs—is an important way to help the body's river return to flow. These are the ways of traditional medicine. They tend to focus mostly on the external structures that form the body, more than the actual flow of that body; however, oftentimes that's all that's needed.

But there is another way of tending the health of this river: *from the inside*. Tuning in to and tending the quality of the body's flow from the inside is the other major way of healing. And here's where this gets really interesting, because this is quite literally restoring the flow of our body's cells that helps us recover. It's the natural or organic way to facilitate recovery. Because we are literally mostly fluid—more than

70% water to be exact—the more we move like fluid, the more we call upon that fluid to flow, and the more we activate our body's ability to heal, the better we will become. What is also important to understand is that when we work with the body in this way we are simultaneously working with the mind. *There is no dividing line between the body and the mind.* The mind has been orchestrating the development and functioning of the fluid body since the very beginning. Every movement that your body makes is reflected in movement in the circuitry of the brain. Creative fluid movement in the body equals creative fluid movement in the brain.

We'll talk a lot more about this, but for now, think of your body and your muscles as thick water. Other parts of your body, the tendons, the ligaments, and the connective tissue are also just variations on this thickened water. Even bone is about 22% water. In most cases the better hydrated (or more fluid rich) we make these tissues, the better they will function. When you start exploring all the different shapes that this thick water can take, especially if you are moving in a fluid way, you are increasing flow and bringing nourishment to all the little hidden, tight, dense, dried out, damaged, and stuck places in your body. Movement like this literally washes the inside body clean and keeps things fresh. In short, it heals. What's more, because you are paying deep attention to how all of this feels, your brain is completely involved and activated as well. Your brain is growing connections. Your entire being (mind and body) is becoming one with the fluid nature of life itself. We are going to show you a process of:

- Slowing down
- Opening up your attention and awareness to use your brain more fully
- Learning to enjoy the flow of your own breath
- Seeing what it's like to fully feel your body and it's movements
- Maintaining curiosity about this process
- Being creative with how you use your mind and body
- Exploring movements that are fluid in nature

If you take this process seriously, and pursue it rigorously, it will unscramble your system, bathe you in the elixir of life, and make you new again. No joke, you will be amazed.

Water . . . It swirls, and flows, and curves, and spirals, and waves, and undulates, and splashes, and mists, and waterfalls, and rains, and evaporates, and jets, and dissolves, and Heals.

At first I thought these exercises were dumber than dirt, but I said what the hell, the other guys were doing it, and so I gave it a shot. I think it was the third time I did it I actually started feeling good and I was really surprised at how much more relaxed I felt when we finished. The music was a little weird but then I started liking that too. Now I do it all the time. It has made a big difference in all the shoulder pain I had. It's one thing, along with the breathing, that really helps me get to sleep. And if I do wake up I just do some more.
—Cpl Leon T. Church

Sensation

To begin the task of self-healing, we must first listen to and understand what the body is telling us. We must learn to listen at the silent wordless level where we aren't making any judgments good or bad about what we are feeling. We must recognize that the body speaks to us through sensation. In fact, that is how the whole world speaks to us. In time, we become more fluent in the language of the body. We begin to notice that sensation is always changing and does not stay the same for very long. Now we can begin to experiment with, and see, how different types of movements affect us. We can tell what type of movement is best for us: what type of movement heals us.

Self-exploration
Feel into you body right now.
How are your feet?

Your hands?
How is your breath?
How are you sitting?

Let's make one thing perfectly clear: this is NOT about just "going with the flow." That will take you right down a storm drain. This is work. It is concerted effort to see clearly where you are, learn these principles of healing, understand where you want to go, and then exercise your power to coax and create the flow necessary to take you there. In all of this, you have to keep an open and flexible mind. There is a constant juggling between focusing on where you want to go and focusing on where you actually are. The paradox is that focusing on where you are *is* the way you get to where you want to go. You also have to realize that what you have in mind may not be what the universe has in mind. Your body may not look or act the way you want it to. Just because you want something doesn't mean you get it. You may be experiencing a lot of suffering, the speed of your healing may not be to your liking, and even learning this process may be difficult but, understand that as Byron Katie writes, *If you argue with reality, you lose. But only 100% of the time.*

Acceptance

Acceptance is a major part of creating flow, because resistance constricts and dams it up. Cussing out your situation gets you nowhere. This is about working with the flow that is present right now and then helping create an optimum flow. We also run into trouble when we try to force flow. This is about using your power of awareness to see what type of movement is necessary to encourage flow and then gently coaxing that movement into being. There is a higher river within you. Your job is to learn to merge with it.

Starting Where You Are

In many ways, we are not interested in what is "wrong" with you. It may actually be that what is "wrong" with you is the mechanism that catapults you into a more vibrant and creative life. Yes, even if you've lost your legs or have some other severe condition. How can that injury or illness be used to motivate or even direct you toward a new, better existence? We don't know. We can't be sure. We do know that healing can be unpredictable and that what we consider of utmost value can change. The thrust of this book is to find movement in the body and mind that facilitates your own *evolutionary* process. That's why we are interested in "starting where you are." If you can't move your right arm, we are interested in your left. If you're paralyzed from the waist down, we are interested in the waist up. If you are irritated when in traffic, we are interested in how you are when sitting by a mountain stream. We want to help you cultivate the things in your life that are most enjoyable. This is about creating what you *do* want as much or more as it is getting rid of what you don't. We encourage you to ask this particular question daily, even hourly:

- What is alive in me right now, and what can I do right now to feed that aliveness?

We believe that questions set us in motion. They engage us. They help us learn. Again and again we stress that it's what you discover, for yourself, that is important.

- Does the idea of self-discovery appeal to you?
- Where do you think there is more learning: being given the answers,or finding them yourself?
- Which generates more strength?
- What puts you more in charge: receiving answers, or coming to them yourself?
- Is it possible, that if you think long and hard, that *you* actually know best what's best for you?

Please enjoy a few breaths and ask your self, how does all this talk about questions makes you feel right now?

THE SOLID WARRIOR

The solid warrior knows how to fight. Solid warriors know how to push forward and make things happen. They know how to withstand the pain it takes to accomplish a mission. They break through and always do their best. The solid warrior wins the battle.

> *Unless you do your best, the day will come when, tired and hungry, you will halt just short of the goal you were ordered to reach, and by halting you will make useless the efforts and deaths of thousands.*
> —Gen George S. Patton

> *People sleep peacefully in their beds at night because rough men stand ready to do violence on their behalf.*
> —George Orwell

All of us who value freedom and a peaceful way of life are indebted to those American warriors who have been willing to fight for it. And all of us, even those who have not been in the military, need access to at least the spirit of this type of warrior on occasion. She or he gets things done. The solid warrior will not be stopped and never admits defeat. They kick ass.

The solid warrior's muscles are hard, dense, and thick. Bulging, shortened muscles are good for powerful explosive activity. This warrior's muscles are themselves a type of armor. Training these types of muscles involves exertion to failure, or damn close to it. This warrior's maxims about growth and fitness are *"no pain, no gain"* and *"pain is weakness leaving the body."* Will and force are the operative principles of the solid warrior. They suck it up and drive on. Their training involves repetition and pushing through and they have bodies efficient for getting from point A to point B. They are constantly attuned to the threats outside, and are forward oriented, because the battle is right there in front of them. These men and woman eat adrenalin and velocity for breakfast. They are ready right now for whatever. They are hair triggers. In short, these warriors are unstoppable machines. You want them on your side and you do not want to fuck with them.

> *In battle, the guy who wins is the guy who gets violent fastest.*
> —Brendan O'Byrne
> from Sebastian Junger's *War*

People join the military for all kinds of reasons and we are aware that you may not aspire to be this kind of warrior. You may not think of yourself in these terms at all. But we wanted to define this traditional warrior and the nature of his or her body so that we could discuss a different kind of warrior—the one we are recommending you learn about in order to accomplish your new mission of healing.

THE FLUID WARRIOR

The fluid warrior has a body of supple elongated muscles; more like swimmers' muscles. These warriors have tremendous physical and mental flexibility and can move with ninja-like stealth. They have a highly refined sense of inner sensation and are as attuned to what is happening within themselves as to what is happening without. Listening, balancing, and creativity are operative principles. They are interested in the art of attention and their training regimen requires deep inner listening and involves nonrepetitive and nonmechanical movement that imitates the way of water. Fluid warriors create harmony in the world by creating harmony within themselves. Much of the rest of this book is about defining and creating the fluid warrior and, if you need to heal, this is your model.

The bodies and minds of these two warriors complement each other, but they are as different as stone and water. They have different functions. The body adapts and becomes what it needs to become to accomplish the task at hand. It's a good thing. If you fought in Iraq or Afghanistan you have probably had the muscles of a solid warrior. And thank God. You certainly don't want guys with swimmers muscles trying to hump an 80-pound pack for 10 miles up the side of a mountain, dig in, get in a firefight, and then fight hand-to-hand with the Taliban. There's no water in the desert and . . . the fluid warrior would be toast.

Both these warriors are dedicated to the mission, but their attitudes and methods differ greatly. One becomes the hardest thing in order to drive forward and break through, accomplishing through overcoming. The other softens and becomes like water in order to dissolve barriers and allow a natural flow to emerge. Like water, the fluid warrior is strong and indestructible, and gets his or her way over time by yielding. One honors the mission by carrying out orders given from commanding officers. One honors the mission by tapping into the source—recognizing that change is a constant and that constantly listening and readjusting is required to know how to accomplish the mission. One takes orders from without and makes them his or her own, and one takes orders only from within. We think you'll find our discussion of the solid and fluid warriors' approaches to life, learning, and evolving, a pivotal one.

This chapter introduced the need for encouraging fluidity in our bodies and minds. We highlight that there is no strict traditional or non-traditional approach to recovery. Each of you must find your own way. Listening and responding to our body's deepest desires is the key to healing, but we have to make sure we are also giving ourselves the tools to hear these answers. We have identified a goal to achieve: becoming a fluid warrior that can overcome PDS by adjusting his or her body and mind to the challenges that are facing it, not by banging up against the wall that has been formed. These are guiding principles on the road to wellness. Now let's begin the long journey down that road, by taking specific symptoms and difficulties and going through a detailed program of healing.

Change is not only possible, it's inevitable.

5

First Step: Understanding Your Body's Symptoms

Now that we've given you some perspectives on post-deployment syndrome (PDS) and the range of recovery strategies, let's drill down to the specific diagnoses associated with PDS and the common symptoms that accompany them. It is extremely important that you continue to remember that the keys to success in overcoming PDS begin with:

- an understanding of the complex causes that have brought it about
- a realization that you must lead your own course of recovery
- an acceptance of overcoming PDS as your primary mission
- the vision that your body and mind are not only an intertwined system that has been impacted by PDS, but also a vital resource that you can be taught to tap into as you recover

With this in mind, let's take a look at 10 of the most common symptoms that make up PDS and get a better understanding of what they mean, why they are occurring, and how you can reduce or even eliminate them. We'll also highlight how many of these symptoms are interconnected and may actually cause or worsen each other. The whole time that we are working to relieve these symptoms, we'll also be reminding you that our goal is to move beyond these symptoms toward the underlying difficulties (or diagnoses) that you are experiencing and to bring you back onto a path of wellness. In this chapter, we explain what the most common diagnoses and symptoms that accompany PDS are, give you some idea of the typical traditional medical treatments (medications, physical and occupational therapy, cognitive training, psychological counseling services), and begin to introduce the concepts that will be important in you taking over for your recovery from these problems.

Healing is the intuitive art of wooing nature.

—W. H. Auden

The numerous factors that contribute to PDS, ranging from concussive blasts to physically stressful living conditions to the emotional trauma of war and death, can result in a variety of medical and psychological conditions of diagnoses. Interestingly, even though many service members may be diagnosed with differing conditions, almost all of them share a similar smaller group of symptoms. Although not everyone will share all symptoms, most folks will have some, if not all, of the top 10 listed. The 10 most common post-deployment symptoms are:

- headache
- sleep problems (insomnia)
- dizziness, balance, and coordination difficulties
- tinnitus (or ringing in the ears)
- light sensitivity and vision disturbance
- depressed mood
- irritability with low frustration tolerance
- fatigue
- memory deficits
- attention and concentration difficulties

Even though we'll be using the term PDS to describe your difficulties, many of you will have been labeled with some other diagnoses. Don't worry, your health care providers were not wrong when they made their diagnoses. There are a whole host of conditions that contribute to PDS—remember PDS is a syndrome or collection of interrelated symptoms. The best way to treat such a syndrome is to understand the nature of the conditions that have contributed to that syndrome, to see what the typical symptoms are, and to use a holistic, interdisciplinary approach to take all elements into consideration. Just as there are a number of common symptoms in returning warriors from Operation Enduring Freedom/Operation Iraqi Freedom (OEF/OIF), so too are there a common set of diagnoses that are seen as the underlying causes for these symptoms. These symptoms and diagnoses all contribute to the syndrome of PDS. The five most common diagnoses from the wars of Iraq and Afghanistan, as well as in most wars, are

- traumatic brain injury (TBI)
- post-traumatic stress disorder (PTSD)
- depression
- chronic pain
- generalized anxiety disorder (GAD)

We look at these symptoms and diagnoses and try to give you a better feel for what they are and what they mean. For some of you, just knowing this diagnosis will be a relief to you. For others, knowing about these diagnoses will be more of a burden. Usually, regardless of the diagnosis, these symptoms respond well to the same types of care, so it's okay if you don't want to know every detail or can't figure out exactly what's wrong with you. Even if you feel better knowing the specific diagnosis, just focusing on the diagnosis and not truly attending to the symptoms is not usually a good approach to overall care. So, regardless of how you've been labeled, even if you're one of those folks who have a whole bunch of diagnoses that may make recovery and treatment difficult, the approach to the symptoms that we help you with will not change. We focus on strategies to help enable your body and mind to be ready to address any symptom. Often, the way you treat one symptom may actually help treat several.

TRAUMATIC BRAIN INJURY

A TBI occurs when a physical force causes

- your head to either move rapidly one direction and then to either stop suddenly or to move rapidly in the reverse direction (often labeled as *whiplash*)
- your head to be move rapidly and then be hit by a still object, like the ground or a wall
- an object, such as a stone, fragment, or bullet, to impact your head rapidly
- your head and brain to be exposed to a blast wave

One or several of these scenarios are often enough to cause your brain to be injured sufficiently to temporarily or permanently stop it from functioning normally. When this happens, you may become unconscious or you become confused. When this happens, you may be termed as having had a TBI. Usually this period of unconsciousness or confusion lasts for only a brief period of time, perhaps seconds or minutes at most. Even with this brief malfunctioning of your brain, the symptoms from the injury (dizziness, headache, thinking difficulties, mood disturbances) may persist for weeks or months. If you have been unconscious or confused for 30 minutes or less, clinicians call this a mild TBI. Another term for this is concussion, although some reserve that for brain injuries that occur from sports. Many of the symptoms from a concussion may not be initially seen for 24 to 48 hours, or until after the "shock" of the battlefield or injury has faded. Some of the symptoms may not be fully noticed for 2 to 4 weeks, especially if you are highly focused on your current mission in the battle zone. If you were unconscious or confused for longer than 30 minutes, then you have had what is called a moderate or severe TBI and would have been urgently seen in an emergency room by a neurosurgeon or trauma surgeon. You may still have many of the symptoms of PDS but, because your actual brain injury was much more severe, it may take longer for you to heal. Because most periods of unconsciousness from mild TBI are very brief in duration and typically don't require medical or surgical care, it is unlikely that you were urgently evacuated from the battlefield or perhaps even seen by a medical personnel. Most people who have a concussion never see a doctor and never get a computed tomography (CT) scan of their brains. Actually, most folks will be totally well and back to normal in 2 weeks or so. In fact, the chance for nearly full recovery from a concussion in the civilian world is 97% after 1 year and nearly as high in the military. These are the lucky ones—those whose bodies and minds can reintegrate and establish a successful recovery. If you aren't one of the lucky ones, particularly if your injury was in the context of a military event, then it's likely that you have the added layer of complexity that we've been talking about, PDS. Rehabilitation physicians or physiatrists who specialize in brain injury care are the most appropriate health care professionals to see if you have persistent difficulties after a concussion, including PDS.

POST-TRAUMATIC STRESS DISORDER

It is entirely normal for a person to be acutely traumatized by an extreme event that they experience, witness, or are somehow involved in. In fact, it's almost abnormal to be unaffected by this kind of exposure. These events can range from unexpected deaths, physical injuries to you or to others around you, destruction of buildings or property, or simply the knowledge that you were somehow close to or even responsible for any of the previous events. Although it may be relatively easy for you to imagine the emotional turmoil that witnessing the death or severe injury of someone else or your own near-death or injury can cause, it is also important to realize that being the person who may have directly or indirectly caused such an injury (by your action or inaction, your position in the military, or by your orders) can also be quite traumatic. This same emotional trauma can also accompany the destruction of buildings or property. For the vast majority of people, there is a period of time after the event during which the following occurs:

- frequently remembering or even reliving the trauma
- thinking back on the person injured
- finding it difficult to associate with anything that reminds you of the event or the person injured
- developing physical difficulties (dizziness, insomnia, poor appetite, pain, fatigue, and memory problems) from the stress of the event

These are *normal* responses to stress. Usually these responses are intense at first, but then begin to fade over a period of days, weeks, or months. This period of time is usually called the *acute stress response* and may last as long as 3 months. Such a period accompanies almost all service members who have been in military theater, even if they haven't been directly exposed to trauma. Just the day-to-day low level stressors of the military theatre bring about this response. However, when these thoughts don't gradually improve, the physical symptoms persist, and it gets more and more difficult to lead your life, then this condition moves into the range of abnormal and is labeled as PTSD. Most experts report that 5% of all civilians and 30% of all service members will experience PTSD over the course of their life or military career. Others have reported the incidence to be significantly higher in the military setting. Some have taken to labeling this phenomenon as *post-traumatic combat disorder* for members of the Armed Forces to identify that there may be difficulties in readjusting to normal life after just being in the combat arena, even without a specific traumatic stress event. Although any of the symptoms listed for PDS can come about from PTSD, the specific hallmarks of this disorder include:

- frequent reliving of the event or battlefield conditions
- hypervigilance to one's environment in an attempt to avoid further injury
- recurrent nightmares

Although alcohol, marijuana, or other drugs may seem to help you to calm down or deaden the symptoms (flashbacks, nightmares, stress), they actually work against you by negatively affecting your mind (and body), and will make the problems worse. As with concussion, most people will overcome PTSD, often with the assistance of specific counseling strategies and medications. Again, these are the lucky ones—those whose bodies and minds can reintegrate and establish a successful recovery. If you aren't one of these lucky ones, then it's likely that you also have the added layer of complexity that we've been talking about, PDS. The most appropriate initial health care specialist to see if you have ongoing difficulties with PTSD or other stress disorders is a psychiatrist. You will also likely see a psychologist as well to assist you with counseling and therapy needs.

DEPRESSION

The most common psychologic health condition seen as a result of the OEF and OIF conflicts is depression. As with acute stress reactions, it is common for people who have had significant changes in their lives, who have suffered losses, and who have persistent difficulties in returning to their normal level of functioning to have accompanying sadness, depressed moods, and even despair. These fluctuations in mood are typically short-lived, resolving as new things occur in your life to distract or inspire you, stabilizing with the passage of time, or improving as you seek comfort in your family life or work. Sometimes this is called dysthymia or minor depression. Even simple or more complex grief over loss can look like this at first. A depressed mood is labeled as *major depression event* when it persists at least 2 weeks. A person may be diagnosed with major depression who has one or more of these events that are accompanied by a range of symptoms, including:

- sleep disturbance
- change in appetite
- fatigue
- inability to feel pleasure
- excessive crying
- feeling of worthlessness and guilt
- thoughts of suicide

As with PTSD, alcohol or drug use can worsen the symptoms, the intensity, and the depth of depression. A number of strategies have been shown to improve depression, including normalizing sleep patterns, receiving counseling, learning coping strategies, taking medications, and participating in regular aerobic exercise. These simple and relatively well tolerated approaches work well when used soon after the symptoms begin. Most people have had a mild degree of dysthymia when faced with life changes or tragedy. However, in the face of the complex post-deployment issues seen with OEF/OIF and when other conditions are co-occurring, major depression can be difficult to overcome. The multiple symptoms that are likely to occur with persistent depression, particularly when compounded with PDS, require more integrative solutions for effective treatment. The most appropriate health care specialist to see if you have ongoing difficulties with major depression or similar mood disorders is a psychiatrist. Again, as with PTSD, you will also likely see a psychologist as well to assist you with counseling and therapy needs.

CHRONIC PAIN

The heavy physical demands that are required of modern warfare are often more than the body, even the highly fit body of the solid warrior, can withstand. The body is even more likely to give out and fail when there are additional pressures on the body brought on by the common stressors of military theater, such as

- poor sleep patterns
- less than optimal food quality and quantity
- limited regular physical exercise
- emotional disturbances (e.g., depression, anger, fear)

Fortunately, most physical failures of the body are short-lived and temporary. The body's connective and muscular tissue have amazing regenerative and restorative powers. Almost all service members in combat are able to tolerate high physical loads and stressors on a regular basis. Despite this, conservative estimates are that at least 10% of all deployed service members have evidence of musculoskeletal difficulties that are likely to persist. When these persistent injuries result in painful limitations that are still there 3 or more months after the actual injury or period of overuse has ended, we term this chronic pain. Sometimes chronic pain can cause you to have accompanying psychologic issues (depression, anxiety) and maladaptive behaviors (seeking excess medications, not wanting to work, amplifying your symptoms) that lead you to develop what is called *chronic pain syndrome*. When this happens, you may see a multiplying of symptoms with increasing difficulties on attempting to return to a productive life. Whereas acute pain from injury has the protective role of reminding our bodies to stop doing something or to avoid it in the future, chronic pain represents a breakdown in what is normal for the body. With chronic pain, even in the face of no actual persistent threat to the body present, pain persists. No matter how hard your health care providers may look for a source of your pain on tests and examination, they won't find one. The so-called pain generator exists within your body's memory, not in some physical structure. Again, excessive alcohol or cigarette use can worsen symptoms of chronic pain by affecting or even damaging your brain and nerves.

The good news is that many people are able to remain physically active despite their pain and over time can resume relatively functional lives. As with the other common diagnoses of the OEF/OIF conflicts, counseling to teach adaptive techniques and pain management strategies along with simple medications can aid in this return to normalcy. Unfortunately, a small percentage of folks with chronic pain do not have positive recoveries, particularly those with other confounding diagnoses. These folks are more predisposed to develop the range of symptoms we've outlined for PDS and require additional strategies that employ care of both the mind and the body. The most appropriate health care specialist to see if you have ongoing difficulties with chronic pain are rehabilitation physicians or physiatrists. You will also likely see a psychologist as well to assist you with counseling and therapy needs.

GENERAL ANXIETY DISORDER

Each of our lives is filled with countless conditions and events that can provoke anxiety or worry, but most of us are able to deal with these happenings and to adjust our level of worrying accordingly. It's part of being a well-adjusted human being living in a stressful society. Even in a battle zone, most of us are able to control our worry and anxiety, despite the amazingly high level of stress involved there. GAD is diagnosed when we have uncontrollable, often irrational, and clearly disproportionate, worry about these everyday things. This high degree of worry interferes with daily living and functioning, such that everything becomes a crisis or an impending disaster. Many feel that features of GAD may be present relatively early in life, but it requires a significant life stressor to bring it to the surface. Although military deployment may actually allow us to downplay many of the day-to-day happenings in civilian life, the stress of the military theater and the transitions of the post-deployment period may be the factors that bring out GAD. Excessive alcohol or drug use can compound the effects of these stressors. A diagnosis would be made if you are experiencing any of these symptoms consistently for 6 months:

- anxiety
- insomnia
- irritability
- numbness of the hands and feet
- restlessness
- headaches
- bouts of difficulty breathing
- nausea
- muscle aches
- hot flashes
- rashes

Once GAD is diagnosed, there are a number of education and counseling techniques, like cognitive-behavioral therapy, that have been shown to work to help you to better deal with anxieties. A number of medications have also been shown to help alleviate the issues. Unfortunately, individuals who have additional diagnoses, such as TBI, PTSD, depression, or pain, may have a more challenging time in resolving symptoms and returning to full activity. Again, understanding how these elements of PDS interplay is the first step in applying healing principles to aid recovery. The most appropriate health care specialist to see if you have ongoing difficulties with GAD or similar anxiety disorders is a psychiatrist. You will also likely see a psychologist as well to assist you with counseling and therapy needs.

*A good traveler has no fixed plans
and is not intent upon arriving.
A good artist lets his intuition
lead him wherever it wants.
A good scientist has freed himself of concepts
and keeps his mind open to what is.*

—Tao Te Ching, Chapter 27
(translation by Stephen Mitchell)

COMMON SYMPTOMS AND TREATMENTS

Although formal diagnoses and the testing needed to make them are important in order to rule out other sources of symptom, enhance our understanding of the underpinnings of our difficulties, and allow us to target most treatments, many people are more focused on actually treating their symptoms. Even if the actual scientific cause of the symptoms may be somewhat unclear, realizing that the symptoms you are having are typical findings in PDS and not evidence for some other undiagnosed condition, is often reassuring. Importantly, understanding this concept and being reassured are the first steps to beginning the healing and recovery process. So, let's take a look at the 10 most common symptoms that are seen with PDS, try to get a clearer appreciation of what your symptoms mean, and understand what the common traditional approaches to their treatment are.

Headaches

Headaches of some type are reported by 75% of all Americans each year and 1 in 10 people will be incapacitated by one of these headaches annually. In fact, nearly 96% of people will have at least one significant headache during their lifetime that severely limits their ability to function. Along with back pain, headaches are one of the most common reasons people go to see their doctor or go to an emergency room. Not surprisingly, headaches are the most common condition reported after a concussion, occurring in 90% of warriors with blast-related concussion. They are also an extremely common symptom of all people with PDS and are also seen with PTSD, depression, and GAD. This is true whether the injury occurred in the military theater or civilian life. In most people, these headaches will lessen in intensity and frequency after a few weeks and with simple treatments. As you will see, there are a whole bunch of headache types from multiple sources that can be seen both civilians and warriors. Learning about the different types of headaches may help you to better understand what's going on with you and to best tailor your initial treatments from your health care provider. Neurologists are usually the most appropriate type of physician to see if you have headaches that are difficult to diagnose or treat. Some of the basic approaches to headache care, and pain care in general, include

- normalizing sleep patterns
- maintaining a balanced diet (e.g., avoiding some foods may make a headache worse, such as chocolate)
- using a daily relaxation regimen
- performing neck and shoulder stretches
- performing exercises to optimize your posture and the way your body moves
- having a daily focus or purpose (e.g., working, volunteering, or doing a hobby)

The more you know about your headaches, the more you know about what things may be recommended, and the more you take charge of your headache by getting engaged in getting it managed, the more rapidly you will get well.

A headache that begins within 2 weeks of a concussion is considered to be directly related to that concussive injury and may be called a post-traumatic headache or PTHA. If it continues for more than 8 weeks, it is considered a chronic PTHA. Chronic headaches may occur in nearly 50% of service members and Veterans after a military concussion. These headaches are often broken down into specific types to help focus treatments. The common types are

- tension
- migraine
- mixed (migraine + tension)
- cervicogenic
- cluster
- neuropathic

There are a number of things that you can do to help to prevent, treat, or manage headaches. Knowing your headache type can also help you to focus on ways to best control all elements of your life that can help you get well.

Tension headaches are the most common headaches seen in civilians or service members who have *not* had a concussion. They can also be seen in nearly 25% of military injured service members and Veterans. Tension headaches tend to be

- on both sides of the head
- nonthrobbing in nature
- mild to moderate pain intensity
- usually steady in pain intensity
- not aggravated by normal physical activity

Migraine headaches are common among people who have also never had a concussion. Over 10% of healthy people have at least one migraine headache a year. Migraine-type headaches can also be seen in up to 25% of people who *have had* a concussion and are then called post-traumatic migraines. Migraine headaches are believed to result from pain receptors within the skull located in the tissues just above the brain, called the meninges, and the veins within the skull, called the dural sinuses. These pain receptors are also linked to other receptors across the muscles and nerve tissues of the face, head, and neck. There's even some evidence that there may be contributions to the headaches from deep structures in the brain called the brainstem and that some people have a genetic predisposition to get these headaches. Migraines

- usually begin during the daytime
- rarely occur at night or overnight
- begin gradually with a mild, dull, deep, steady pain that may be across the entire head or in a specific area
- usually affect the front of the head and eyes
- usually evolve to an increasing amount of severe, throbbing pain

Some migraines may be preceded or accompanied by an *aura* or strange sensation. Auras are usually visual, but can also be sensory, motor, or verbal disturbances. Visual auras are most common and can include a flash of light (scotoma) or light sensitivity (photophobia). Auras can also be a strange smell, a feeling of nausea, sound sensitivity, numbness, or weakness. These changes are felt to be due to periods of decreased blood flow to parts of the brain from the headache. Auras occur in about one in five people who get migraines. Rarely, migraine may be associated with a feeling of intense pain or hypersensitivity of the skin associated with even the lightest touch. A number of things have been shown to make migraines worse. Some medications (risperidol, nitroglycerin) can bring on migraines. In some people, too rapid weaning away of steroid medications can bring them on. In women, menstruation can contribute to a migraine headache. Although it can often be difficult to tell which headache type you are having, the following features may be more indicative of a migraine:

- nausea
- excessive sensitivity to light
- extreme sensitivity to loud sounds
- exacerbation with physical activity
- foods that trigger the headaches

Cervicogenic headaches may be *very common* after a concussion, as the neck and shoulder muscles are often injured, a condition often called whiplash. Although elements of a tension or migraine headaches may be seen, cervicogenic headaches will usually have

- specific soft tissue (muscle) factors of the neck that initiate or worsen the pain
- an association with prolonged postures or certain movements of the neck
- initiation with pushing on or moving a specific location of the neck
- pain that radiates upward from the neck to the head
- pain may arise in the muscles of the skull itself

Cluster headaches are uncommon, occurring more in men than women, but have very specific symptoms. These headaches

- are severe in intensity
- last 15 minutes to 3 hours in duration
- have pain limited to one side of the face, usually around the eye, just above the eye, or over the temple
- are accompanied by autonomic phenomena on the same side as the pain

The autonomic phenomenon that accompany cluster headaches include

- nasal congestion
- rhinorrhea (runny nose)
- tearing of the eyes
- color or temperature change of the skin (usually of the hands or feet)
- a change in pupil (the dark part of the eye) size

Many people will confuse these cluster headaches with a sinus infection or sinus headache; however, true sinus infections are actually very rare. In a true sinus infection you will have actual pus coming out of your sinuses and a fever.

Neuropathic headaches are almost always associated with the hypersensitivity to the normal stimulus of the face or hair. This allodynia (which means "other pain" or pain that comes from an atypical or usually nonpainful source) may occur anywhere on the body, but is typically limited to the face.

A chronic daily headache is one that really doesn't easily fit into any category and may not have a clear source; however, they may be seen after a concussion. These types of headaches will occur for more than 15 days per month for at least 3 months. Up to 5% of adults worldwide have chronic daily headaches.

A primary exertional headache occurs only during or immediately after physical exercise. This type of headache

- tends to occur on both sides of the head
- is throbbing in nature
- may last anywhere from 5 minutes to 2 days
- may be associated with an abnormal blood vessel within the brain

Cerebrospinal fluid (CSF)–related headaches occur when a person has a CSF leak, whether from spinal surgery, a spinal tap, or from a moderate or severe brain injury with a skull fracture. These headaches are extremely rare after concussion, but can accompany even a mild skull fracture, so be alert to this. CSF-related headaches

- are intense in nature
- may be throbbing or dull in character
- will be relieved by lying down
- are made worse with cough or bearing down as if to have a bowel movement
- may develop into chronic daily headaches or exertional headaches, if they don't improve

There are a number of treatments that have been shown to improve headache pain.

A neurologist is the best type of medical specialists to see if you have persistent headaches or headaches that are difficult to treat.

Obviously, preventing headaches is one of the best ways to improve the pain. Before a headache starts, it's important to know all of the right things to do and what to avoid, so make sure you are prepared. If you get a new injury to your head or neck that causes a headache, you need to make sure that you haven't significantly damaged your skull (this is really unusual) or neck, so you should see your physician. Once you've been cleared as not having fractured anything, it's time to get moving. If you've just injured yourself, it's important to know that immobilizing your head and neck after a headache, such as with a neck brace or collar, for more than 1 to 2 days is never the right thing to do. Although it may feel good for the first day, it will absolutely *slow down* your recovery. So if you've gotten used to wearing such a brace, it's time to gradually wean yourself away from it, either with the help of a therapist or by putting yourself on a specific weaning schedule. After a new injury, putting some ice around your neck for the first 8 to 12 hours and limiting any sudden movements for the first 24 hours while resting the tissues is a good idea.

The following day, however, it's important to begin warming up your head and neck muscles and getting moving. This can be facilitated by reducing the pain and relaxing your muscles, which can be accomplished by the breathing and movement exercises that follow. See the next several chapters for whole sets of these exercises. Simple over-the-counter (OTC) medicines that can be used for the first week or so to reduce pain include acetaminophen (325-mg tablets, one or two tablets every 6 hours) or ibuprofen (200-mg tablets, one to two tablets every 6 hours). Just as the bottle says, don't take these medicines at all if you've got an allergy or have had some bad reaction to them before, or for more than 2 weeks without discussing it with your health care professional. Although a structured program of physical therapy may not be needed by most folks, it can be very helpful and be just the right jumpstart that you need. It may help to have someone assist you with gently mobilizing your neck for the first few weeks. This movement should be increased almost daily to get your neck and head back to normal rapidly.

In addition to the complete wellness program outlined in this book, there are certain medications and treatments that are used to prevent headaches.

Migraine headaches may often be prevented with the use of two different types of prescription medications:

- antiepileptics: medications often used to treat seizures
- beta-blockers: medications for high blood pressure

These medications must be taken on a daily basis to be effective. Some people also seem to respond to using regular injections of Botulinum toxin. Botulinum toxin is a derivative from mushrooms that can weaken muscles around the neck and skull and prevent them from generating pain. This treatment will last about 2 months between shots.

Tension headaches that are infrequent or have just begun may be prevented by using caffeine; however, too much caffeine may have systemic side effects (jitteriness, heart palpitations, insomnia) that prevent its usage. Simple OTC medications like acetaminophen (325-mg tablets, one or two tablets every 12 hours) or ibuprofen (200-mg tablets, one or two tablets every 6 hours) may also be effective. If these headaches persist (become frequent, episodic, or chronic), then the class of medications called tricyclic antidepressants may be a better choice. Nortriptyline or protriptyline are the two most commonly recommended due to their rare side effects. Other prescription medications, including some of the newer antidepressants called serotonin-norepinephrine reuptake inhibitors (SNRIs) and anticonvulsants (such as topiramate or gabapentin) may also have some effects. Also, a number of nonmedication therapies, usually delivered by a psychologist, may be highly effective. Examples of these include behavioral therapy, cognitive-behavioral therapy, relaxation training, and biofeedback.

Cluster headaches have been shown to respond well to preventive treatment with calcium channel blockers (often used as blood pressure medications, such as verapamil), corticosteroids (strong anti-inflammatory agents), lithium carbonate (a mineral salt that is used for manic depression), and anticonvulsants (such as topiramate).

Exertional headaches can usually be prevented by taking nonsteroidal anti-inflammatories (NSAIDs), such as ibuprofen, before exercising or immediately upon completion.

If your injury was some time ago and the preventative steps and medicine haven't worked or you've been having intermittent headaches, it's still important to remember the basics of pain care: sleep, eat, relax, move, focus. You may also want to know about some of the other medications used.

Migraines should be treated at the first sign of coming on, using *abortive medications,* to rapidly prevent them from getting worse. The ones that work the best are known as the triptans—these include sumatriptan, rizatriptan, naratriptan, zolmitriptan, eletriptan, almotriptan, frovatriptan, and avitriptan. Usually one of these triptan medications works so well, that all other agents are rarely needed. But there are some conditions that might not allow them to be used, such as having

- a basilar (base of the skull) migraine
- a history of stroke, heart disease, or poorly controlled high blood pressure
- taken another type of migraine headache medication (ergotamine) in the past 24 hours

The other abortive medication type that may be used are the agents known as ergotamines. There are also other medications that are used;

however, these are more for persistent pain not relieved with the abortive agents, such as various opioids, acetaminophen, and anti-inflammatories. In general, opioids and medications that combine multiple types of medications should be avoided because they are rarely effective and may actually transform episodic headaches to the chronic form.

Cluster headaches have been shown to respond well to abortive treatment with supplemental oxygen (given by face mask), triptans, ergotamines, lidocaine (given by vein in an emergency room), and octreotide.

Insomnia

Sleep disturbances, usually too little sleep (called insomnia), are extremely common during and after a period of deployment. In people without any other conditions or diagnoses, sleep cycles may remain altered for up to 3 months after return to the home from the combat zone. Similarly, alterations in sleep may accompany a large range of medical diagnoses, including those commonly associated with PDS. Importantly, poor sleep patterns alone can cause or worsen problems with headaches, pain, dizziness, mood disturbance, anxiety, and attention, concentration, and memory difficulties. So, improving the quality and quantity of sleep is essential for overall recovery. Although each person varies in the amount of sleep required, most researchers agree that it is optimal to have at *least 7 hours* of uninterrupted sleep daily in order to restore and maintain health. In addition to this critical duration of 7 hours needed to allow the body and mind to recharge, it is also important that the sleep be relaxing and truly restful. This includes adequate periods of both fully relaxed nonrapid eye movement sleep phase (usually 75% of sleep), which contributes most to the bodies regeneration and recovery and the active rapid eye movement (REM) sleep phase (the other 25% or 90 minutes or so of sleep), which helps the mind to process the events of the day. A healthy night's sleep will usually include up to five phases of relatively brief, but intense REM sleep, totaling nearly 2 hours per night. The keys to normalizing sleep, regardless of the causes include:

- making sure that there are no medically treatable conditions that are preventing normal sleep (such as sleep apnea), by seeing a physician specializing in sleep medicine
- attempting to perform at least 45 minutes of exercise daily, but making sure it is completed at least 2 hours before going to sleep
- refraining from eating or drinking for at least 2 hours before sleep
- using the bathroom no less than 30 minutes before sleep

- avoiding any dietary stimulants (caffeine, energy drinks) or to-bacco products at least 4 hours before going to sleep
- spending the last 30 minutes before going to sleep in a dimly lit room with limited stimuli (no television or reading), perhaps listening to soothing music or meditating
- avoiding daytime napping
- remaining on a regular schedule of sleep and wake

The elements of sleep care are usually referred to as sleep hygiene. Maintaining good sleep hygiene is absolutely vital to the short and long-term recovery from PDS.

Although the mainstay of traditional treatment for sleep entails focusing on sleep hygiene, there are some medications that can provide assistance with insomnia on a short-term basis. Similarly, there are some medications (both OTC and prescription) and supplements that should be avoided because of potential side effects. The three most commonly prescribed medications for disturbed sleep from PDS include trazadone, zolpidem, and eszopiclone. Each of these agents is nonhabit forming, rapid onset, and has limited or no hangover effect the next morning. Although many people do use them for long-term needs, their effect often wears off after a few weeks of regular usage and it is not recommended to use them long-term. Some people have also had good results with the usage of prazosin for PTSD-related nightmares with secondary improvements in sleep. Risperidone has also been used for this with fair to good effect. Medications to avoid with PDS-related insomnia include benzodiazepines (Valium and Valium-like medicines) or benadryl (which is in many OTC agents) because these can cause prolonged sedation and cognitive slowing. In addition, the benzodiazepines can be habit-forming. Although many herbal and other supplements have been promoted for assisting in sleep, the lack of careful regulation of the quality and quantity of substances in these (particularly the fillers used) makes them a poor choice with high potential risk.

Dizziness, Balance, and Coordination Difficulties

Balance and control of your body movements is controlled by the back part of your brain, called your cerebellum, working together with your midbrain connector (thalamus) to the motor centers of the gray matter (motor strip of the frontal lobe) and the body's nerves and muscles. All of the brain's actions and coordination of movement can only be performed with input received from:

- your feet and legs
- your eyes
- sensors in the neck tissue
- equilibrium organs of your inner ears
- other coordinating centers within the brain

Whether it is a direct injury to one of these structures, minor difficulties with a few of them or simply altered connections within the brain, even small problems anywhere along the system can cause significant difficulties. Usually, true problems with dizziness result from trauma or bleeding to the inner ear organs known as the labyrinthian system, although damage to the brainstem structures can also cause *vertigo* or dizziness. These types of injuries are quite common after even minor concussions and may persist for months after injury. But, balance and coordination difficulties can also be related to:

- an injury to or other abnormality (tumor, mass) of the brain
- acute or chronic pain of the head or spine (especially the neck)
- any abnormalities of vision or hearing
- inner ear infections
- many psychologic conditions
- heart conditions
- medication side effects

Physicians with special expertise in this area of medicine include rehabilitation physicians, neurologists, and ear, nose, and throat specialists (otolaryngologists). In addition to specialized testing techniques to assist in clarifying the factors contributing to the imbalance, there are some therapeutic interventions that may be provided (such as the Liberatory technique) to facilitate recovery. After other treatable diagnoses are excluded, a key to improving all aspects of balance, including dizziness, is a rapid return to mobility. It is vital to reintroduce the body and mind to movement early in the course of recovery, before the abnormal feelings become ingrained as the "new normal." For most, this may be done by gradually, but progressively, increasing time out of bed, time standing, time walking, and time being highly active. For those who are unable to move along this pathway, structured programs of physical reactivation or balance retraining may be needed through physical therapy programs. Unfortunately, there are no medications that have been shown to improve dizziness or balance, although occasionally mild sedatives (benzodiazepines, meclizine) may be tried if nausea, anxiety, and fear prevent progress.

Tinnitus or Noise Sensitivity

Trauma to the nerves of hearing and the parts of the brainstem where they originate can cause persistent but abnormal activation of these nerves and produce an intermittent or constant humming noise, called tinnitus. Although seemingly minor in nature, tinnitus can actually be life-altering in effect and can have the same impact on the psychologic functioning as chronic pain can have. In fact, tinnitus is one of the top three causes of disability among Veterans. More readily treatable conditions that can cause tinnitus, such as some inner ear infections, a mass or tumor of the brain, or excess use of aspirin, should always be ruled out. Natural recovery from tinnitus is typically completed in the first 3 months after injury. Although a vast number of interventions have been tried, the best results have been accomplished by using a small, within-ear white noise generator to override the signal in the ear and brain and behavioral strategies to tamper down the sound. No medications have proven effective in treatment of tinnitus. Physicians with special expertise in this area of medicine include rehabilitation physicians, neurologists, and ear, nose, and throat specialists (otolaryngologists).

A similar effect as tinnitus occurs in individuals who develop hypersensitivity to sounds (hyperaccussis) following physical or psychological trauma. Although the mechanism of injury is not as clearly understood, the effects on daily life and functioning can be equally devastating. Fortunately, there appear to be better short- and long-term treatments for hyperaccussis. Because the hypersensitivity is usually not an abnormality in the conduction of sounds into the brain, but rather a difficulty within the brain in interpreting and modulating those sounds, controlling the intensity of sounds delivered through the ears an be effective. Thus, the use of sound blocking headphones can be initially used to greatly reduce any sounds. The sound blocking ability of these headphones is then gradually reduced to progressively introduce more and louder sounds to the brain over time. When used in concert with behavioral techniques to help control your responses, these headphones can be gradually eliminated. Again, no medications, surgery, or other involved treatments have been shown to be effective.

Light Sensitivity and Vision Disturbance

Just as an injury to the brain—particularly one that affects the pathways connecting the frontal lobes to the rest of the brain as occurs with the most common types of concussion—can cause hypersensitivity to sound, hypersensitivity to light (photophobia) is also common acutely. This is fairly common in the first several weeks after a mild TBI, but tends to resolve by the first month. Photophobia is exacerbated by the co-occurrence of headaches and other types of pain, hyperaccussis, dizziness, stress conditions, and anxiety. Although often initially treated appropriately by avoiding bright lights (sunlight outdoors and fluorescent lights indoors) and the use of sunglasses, long-term treatment with these techniques is not recommended. Avoiding bright or sunny environments, keeping lights off, or wearing sunglasses indoors are not conducive to a return to normalcy and full activity. Progressively exposing yourself to an increasing amount light and using behavioral techniques to deal with any associated pain or emotional distress are vital to correcting the problem as soon as is possible. Although it is also essential to make certain that there are no easily treated disorders of the eyes, such as a localized eye trauma, irritation, or infection, there are few causes of photophobia that are not easily managed with behavioral techniques. Ophthalmologists (physicians who specialize in disorders of the eye) and neurophthalmologists (ophthalmologists with subspecialty skills in vision disorders originating from the brain) are the appropriate types of physicians to see for a comprehensive evaluation. Other visual difficulties, such as blurriness and double vision, are also most commonly related to an injury to the brain. These types of injuries are not often improved with regular glasses, but occasionally there are specialized lenses called orthoptics (prism lenses for blurriness, translucent lenses for double vision) that can be helpful. Additionally, vision rehabilitation techniques can be of benefit. Within the VA setting, there are vision therapists who are specially trained to work with all of these conditions. These specialty lenses and services are best coordinated under the supervision of a rehabilitation physician.

Depressed Mood

As described previously, it is normal to experience mood fluctuations associated with life changes, stress, or sad events. In fact, more than 50% of Americans annually report an episode of depressed mood lasting at least 24 hours. The likelihood, frequency, and intensity of these episodes significantly increases following with PDS. Fortunately, time will "heal" the vast majority of these episodes and, unless they are impacting your day-to-day activities and function, there is little that needs to be done for them. On the other hand, there are strategies to reduce the frequency and severity of these episodes that may also help to decrease the chances of developing full-blown major depression. Engaging in regular aerobic exercise, eating a balanced diet, practicing relaxation activities, avoiding tobacco products, minimizing alcohol use, and maintaining productivity through employment, volunteerism, and hobbies are all important ways to reduce emotional fluctuations. When a depressed mood significantly impacts your life or if it has become true major depression, then more formal treatments are needed. Cognitive-behavioral therapy and other types of psychological treatments are the mainstay of care. When secondary conditions, such as concussion, PTSD, or pain, are present, it is extremely important to work with a psychologist who has specialty training and experience with these diagnoses, along with depression. In addition, many individuals benefit from a course of a prescription antidepressant medication. There are many different types of antidepressants (selective serotonin reuptake inhibitors [SSRIs], SNRIs, tricyclic antidepressants [TCAs]) that have been shown to work for major depression, but the correct one must be chosen for you based on your diagnoses, age, specific symptoms, and reaction to potential side effects. A psychiatrist is the most appropriate physician to work with to help make this decision. It is important to realize the following about antidepressant use:

- for the first 3 to 5 days after beginning an antidepressant it is common to have neurologic symptoms, such as dizziness, drowsiness, mild confusion, and poor appetite
- it takes at least 2 weeks for an antidepressant to have any meaningful effect
- an antidepressant should be tried for at least 6 weeks before changing the dose
- it is best to be on a higher dose of one antidepressant than low doses of two or more antidepressants
- when antidepressants are being used, they should be continued for at least 12 months (even if all symptoms resolve), otherwise the likelihood of getting repeated episodes of depression are much higher

Irritability with Low Frustration Tolerance

The most common behavioral symptom seen acutely after a concussion is an increase in irritability. Although this is primarily related to an inability to filter the many stimuli in the environment resulting in a low frustration tolerance, there may be other factors that contribute to this irritability, including

- acute or chronic pain
- insomnia
- hyperaccussis
- light sensitivity
- anxiety
- repeated alcohol or illicit drug usage

As with all symptoms of PDS, following a routine of healthy, active living will help in reducing irritability. This includes engaging in regular aerobic exercise, eating a balanced diet, practicing good sleep hygiene, avoiding tobacco products, limiting alcohol intake, and having a focus on productivity through work, volunteerism, or hobbies. Irritability may be limited to only truly stressful conditions at home or at work, but more commonly may be brought on by normal day-to-day occurrences and situations. Although avoiding high-stress situations may be possible, this is a less practical option for everyday living. Approaches that are more realistic include understanding which elements of situations are most irritating and learning techniques to deal with them and informing your family and coworkers how to most effectively interact with you. Psychologists are specifically trained to assist you in learning about how to handle your low frustration levels, to teach you specific techniques to more appropriately deal with challenging social and professional situations, and to teach you to overcome some of the internal drives that are causing this irritability. Rehabilitation physicians and psychiatrists are health care professionals who can work with you to identify potential medications that can also reduce your irritability. Unfortunately, these medications work best when taken on a regular basis, not just when you think you may become irritated, to allow for a stable dose of the agent to be in your bloodstream. Thus, you must regularly take these agents at least once or twice daily. Some of the more commonly used prescription medications are from the same anticonvulsant, antidepressant, and anxiolytic classes discussed previuosly.

Fatigue

A low energy level, poor exercise tolerance, and overall fatigue are common findings of PDS. They are also commonly seen with each of the five major diagnoses that often accompany PDS, as well as a large number of other physical and psychological complaints. Although the underlying cause of fatigue can be related to medical conditions (anemia, infection, endocrine, medication usage), there can secondary complications of TBI (hydrocephalus) or psychiatric disorders (depression)—fatigue is typically multifactorial, so it will require multiple types of treatments. A primary care health care provider is the best person to start with to evaluate for any medical conditions that might be contributing to your lack of energy. The aforementioned attention to the basic tenets of health living (exercise, rest, nutrition, eliminating tobacco and alcohol, productivity) continue to be a key component of focus in treating fatigue. Although it may be tempting to use caffeine-containing drinks, high glucose energy drinks, or OTC agents that have stimulant effects to try and jump start your life, these treatments often leave you feeling more lethargic once the active ingredients have worn off, can negatively interact with your medications, and can have side effects on their own. Frequent use of these types of supplements is almost always bad for you, whether it be from the excessive dosing of caffeine, the high calories of energy drinks, or the unknown compounds found in most OTC supplements. Psychiatrists are also key health care providers to provide both assessment and treatment recommendations. Many of the antidepressant medications that are used have the quality of activating the body and mind, so they are also effective to provide the much needed energy boost to overcome fatigue. A more focused medication for fatigue is the stimulant agent methylphenidate (Ritalin). Methylphenidate and the other related neurostimulant medications are safe, time-tested agents with a number of medical indications that have been in use for over 30 years. Although they serve as only one element in the overall treatment of PDS, they can provide the short-term (6–12 week) boost that may be needed for you to feel the effects of some of the other treatments recommended in the following chapters. Methylphenidate is a very simple and nonreactive agent, so it may be especially useful for you if you

- have had an extended period of illness
- have other medical conditions that may limit using certain medications
- are on other medications that can have interactions

It is also extremely inexpensive and easy to use. It is a closely regulated medication, due to its abuse potential (particularly by students seeking to use it to stay awake for studying), so you must work closely with your physician to use it.

Memory Deficits

The term *memory* is often used to describe a number of interrelated thinking skills that describe how new information is perceived, processed, encoded, stored, and then retrieved when needed. The initial perception task involves being aroused or alert enough to be aware of the information, then being able to attend to it, then to concentrate sufficiently on what it is to understand it. Once adequate attention and concentration has been applied to this information, it can then be understood and processed in such a way so that it can be appropriately encoded for appropriate storage. In most cases, this storage is usually only for a short period of time (hours to days to weeks) and then the information is forgotten. On occasion, the information is deemed important enough, or some association to the information is important enough (a new career, a new home, a wedding, a traumatic injury, a death) for it to be stored for much longer. The final step in the memory process entails being able to retrieve the information accurately and in a timely fashion when appropriate. In PDS and the five common diagnoses associated with it, the major obstacle in this memory process is the initial one of attention and concentration. Without the ability to adequately attend to information (a list of items, someone's name, an appointment) initially and then in a sustained way (concentration), there is little opportunity for information to be perceived appropriated, encoded, or stored. Recommendations to improve this initial part of the memory process are discussed in the attention section. The next most common challenge for individuals suffering with PDS is being able to concentrate adequately to retrieve stored information. So you may have used a number of techniques to get new information into their short-term memory or you may have a long-term memory that you developed years before you had any difficulty, but you are still not able to recall this information because you lack this retrieval mechanism. The good news is that this retrieval problem is almost always again related to poor concentration and not a true brain level retrieval issue. The actual ability to lay down new memories or retrieve short- or long-term memories is almost never impacted by PDS, concussion, PTSD, pain, depression, or anxiety, merely the attention and concentration needed. It almost always takes more severe brain injuries and other significant disorders of the brain (seizures, tumors, dementing processes) to directly impair the actual memory encoding, storage, and retrieval. For individuals with these types of injuries, a neurologist is an appropriate health care professional to see for an evaluation. On the other hand, for individuals with attention and concentration difficulties, a rehabilitation physician and team members (psychologist, speech and language pathologist, occupational therapist) are the best choice to help develop strategies to overcome these difficulties.

Attention and Concentration Difficulties

As noted previously, the attention and concentration difficulties that are commonly associated with PDS and the related diagnoses can significantly impact your ability to think in many ways, including your memory. Simply put, the information that is all around you (someone's name, a chore, how to do your job, what you're supposed to be doing) cannot make it past the basic intake phase of your brain or you can't stay focused enough to use your retrieval mechanism to pull it out. You can assist the brain to overcome this in several ways, including

- eliminating any other source of information from distracting you
- making sure that you are in a quiet, well-lit space when you take in new information
- focusing on only the information at hand
- using cues to highlight the information, such as
  - saying out loud what you see
  - repeating instructions out loud
  - writing the information down
  - asking a person you're with to clarify the information
- re-reviewing the information several minutes later to help during the encoding process
- designating key times throughout the day (say right before meals and going to bed) to review all that you have been exposed to that day or the one before
- choosing a quiet environment in which to retrieve information from your memory
- organizing yourself by consistently using an indexed notebook, personal digital assistant, or cell phone program

Establishing these techniques and systems is not something that is easy or that comes naturally, so don't be frustrated by the need for them. If it was intuitive, you most likely wouldn't need them, so it makes sense to work with a professional to assist you. Psychologists, speech and language pathologists, and occupational therapists are the common rehabilitation professionals who can help with these issues. In addition to using these techniques and practicing good brain health (exercising, eating good nutrition, having good sleep hygiene, eliminating tobacco and alcohol, productivity), certain prescription medications have been demonstrated to improve attention and concentration. Unfortunately, these agents only work when they are regularly taken because they have limited carryover effect. However, hopefully they will provide a short-term boost while these other strategies are kicking in. These medicines are the stimulants (methylphenidate and related agents) and activating antidepressants (SSRIs, SSNIs) that have been described previously. These types of medications are most commonly prescribed by rehabilitation, psychiatry, and neurology physicians. There is no proof that herbals and other OTC supplements truly enhance attention and concentration and the risk of harm from the additives (fillers) in these agents makes their usage risky.

We outlined a lot of information about the different aspects of PDS in this chapter. Most likely, much of it relevant to the problems you've been having. In some cases, some of you haven't been seen by the right health care professionals or tried many of these traditional approaches to care. Clearly, we've only covered some of the basics in each area and a specially trained professional to give you the full range of information and get you started in treatment makes a lot of sense. For others of you, you've seen plenty of health care professionals already and have had more than your share of treatments without full success. Regardless, we highly recommend that you seek traditional health care explanations and solutions for your difficulties. Why? *Because the services and expertise these professionals provide works.* Plain and simple. Through basic, good medical care thousands of individuals have been returned to health. But, in addition to making sure you are getting this care, we also encourage you to read on and to find elements of our program that help you get *even better.* This program will complement and supplement the traditional health care programs that are available. How do we know? Because we have been practitioners of traditional health care for more than 20 years and we have found that patients who have the best success are the ones who *do it all.* Read on and see what you can add to your current recovery program.

> *I feel that as much as anything, it's my job to educate these guys. If they really understand what's going on and what they need to do to get better, they are much more likely to follow through. I know all about medicine, and I know I'm helping in some ways, but if I could just get them to really listen to me, and do what I say . . . that would make all the difference.*
> —Jeff Richards, MD
> Veterans Administration Medical Center

6

Second Step: Discovering Your Strengths and Resources

To be a warrior is not a simple matter of wishing to be one. It is rather an endless struggle that will go on to the very last moment of our lives. Nobody is born a warrior, in exactly the same way that nobody is born an average man. We make ourselves into one or the other.

—Carlos Castaneda

You've begun to understand the nature of post-deployment syndrome (PDS), the impact that the stressors of battle and of life have had on you, the effects of your injuries, and the types of symptoms and diagnoses that you have. You've begun to understand the importance of full engagement in this new mission, this mission focused on a life of wellness and productivity. You're ready to take on that mission. However, the best warriors know they need to prepare for the mission, to have the right equipment and supplies, and to know what to do. Over the next several chapters we help you to understand what those needed elements to achieve success are. Many of them are things that you've already learned in the military, but perhaps need a refresher course on their importance. Things like good nutrition, regular exercise and activity, a structure to your day and your life, and a strong focus on finding purpose and knowing your goals. We give you some specific ideas about how to go about this. But, we also provide you with some additional tools to get the job done. We introduce you to techniques that will let you once again fully use the power of your body and mind. Rediscovering these strengths will allow you to once again feel like a warrior and to once again be on a mission.

In this chapter, we introduce you to the following strengths and resources:

- Breath
- Illume
- Questions

- Mindfulness training
- Focused awareness
- Alternating awareness
- Expanding awareness
- Open awareness
- Continuum movement

We give you some simple exercises to begin to understand and master these techniques. We then begin building and expanding on these techniques in later chapters as we develop the full program of wellness.

BREATH

Before we embark on the journey of self-discovery to identify your strengths and resources, let's go to your most immediate resource to prepare you for the reading to come. This first readily accessible resource is your breath. It will serve as the core strength for each of the advanced therapeutic sessions in this book. Although we tend to take breath for granted and really only think about it when we are ill or short of it, breath is one of our body's greatest strengths. In the upcoming chapters, we take you through a number of breathing exercises to show you how to tap into this strength. Breath provides life sustaining nourishment to our bodies and our cells. Appreciating, monitoring, and regulating your breath can be also used to help access how you are doing, to help to restore normalcy to your systems, and to open up your senses to awareness. Each of the steps of recovery and specific exercises that you will be doing should begin with a breathing exercise. Spend a few minutes with Exercise #1: Breath.

Exercise #1: Breath

- Take a breath through your nose. Feel the fluid nature of your body interact with the fluid nature of air.
- Take another easy, full breath: slow enough to allow yourself to bask in the enjoyment of it.
- And now, become curious about your breath—play with it, lengthen it, vary it, make it audible. Experiment with it the way a musician might improvise on a musical theme.
- Enjoy the process in a self-guided investigation. Cultivate a sense of wonder about this astonishing life-giving event that is literally occurring right under your nose. Be nourished by this breath you're taking right now. This is your most immediate resource.

ILLUME

Learning how to participate with your own healing means first and foremost identifying your resources. As we've been saying all along, that starts with remembering that *you* are your most precious resource. How do you tap in to this inner resource and how do you use it to help yourself become well?

Modern soldiers know that *illume* (short for illumination) is the light, usually the moon, that makes night vision goggles work. It gives you the ability to look into the night landscape, to scan it for details. It is a particular type of seeing that gives the soldier a decided advantage over the enemy. The landscape we are interested in knowing the details about is the one that is directly inside of us. We are interested in developing a type of refined vision for looking into our own bodies and into our minds. In that regard, *illume is our most essential resource.* In a very real sense, the amount of inner illume we have is equal to how awake we are.

We propose that learning how to increase this internal illume, or learning to truly wake up to ourselves, is the foundation for all self-directed healing. It aids in working with the body and it aids in working with the mind. You'll see this in both the movement exercises and the movement techniques we'll give you. It is the foundation for the work of restructuring thinking pursued in psychotherapies, such as cognitive-behavioral therapy. It also increases our ability to heal our own bodies, by illuminating the type of movement that brings about flow. In some ways, waking up means that we first consider the possibility that we might be asleep; that we might not fully understand what's really going on. It's recognizing that what we *believe* is true, may not actually *be* true. That what is occupying our consciousness is not the whole picture. Waking up has us looking deeper. It doesn't assume anything and it puts us in touch with the sensations of the moment. That's where the difficulty may come in. Sometimes what we are feeling inside is too painful to look at with our minds. We may not always be able to say that or know that, but we can often feel it. Looking within accesses aches, pains, feelings, and memories we'd rather forget. But, waking up can mean that, despite being in the midst of a battle, whether on the battlefield or in your life, and being aware of and feeling everything, good and bad, that's happening around and within you, you are *still able to have a part of your mind seeing it all from a high place.* Developing and using this skill of seeing things from the 30,000-foot level, which is a component of executive function, is a key to wellness. It's the skill that field generals develop whether they truly are seeing the battlefield from 30,000 feet or if they're just looking out over a desert. Thus, just like in war, increasing illume in life makes you more skillful and more able to overcome obstacles.

The last thing I want to do is think about what I saw over there. And I definitely don't want to talk about it. But it keeps popping up no matter what I do. I'm on edge all the time. I almost punched a guy out who bumped his grocery cart into me the other night at the store. The look on the guy's face was scared as hell. I walked out and spent about 10 minutes in my car just sitting there calming down. God, It's been two years since I was over there. How the hell do I get through this?

—Cpl Tim Owen

QUESTIONS

A key to taking on and completing any mission is clearly understanding your objectives. Understanding where you are right now, what steps are needed to move ahead, and where you want to go. Without this, all of your effort and passion, all of the good intentions of others and all of the time and resources invested will never get you there.

One day Alice came to a fork in the road and saw a Cheshire Cat in a tree. "Which road do I take?" she asked. "Where do you want to go?" was his response. "I don't know," Alice answered. "Then," said the cat, "it doesn't matter."

—Lewis Carroll

But it does matter, doesn't it? It does matter which road you take. And, it's critical that you have an idea where you want to go. One way to turn up the light and power of the mind, so as to increase illume, is by asking and pondering the right questions. As your mind works to answer them, they mobilize attention. They engage the imagination. That generates energy, the energy to see. Whenever you ask a question, sit with it a while. It's a great time to try writing things down, maybe keeping a journal, which we discuss at some length later in the book. When you have identified a question, give it some time to work on you before an answer floats to the surface. Don't be content with the first thing that shows up. Spend some time with Exercise #2: Questions.

Exercise #2: Questions

Here are a few questions that you might find interesting. Again, really take your time with them. Read one question, put the book down, and think about it, perhaps write down some ideas or even more questions.
- What would healing look like for me?
- What is my idea of a full and healed life?
- What does the life I'd like to create look like.
- How can I learn to cope with what has happened to me?
- What can I do to move forward?

Although there are many questions to be asked, there is a root or essential question that you should be thinking about now, and then returning to as you progress in the program:

What state of mind is most helpful for healing my body, my mind, and my life and how can I create it?

As you work to answer this ultimate question, it will influence the answers to all the rest.

Answering this question leads us to a basic training of the mind. This basic training increases illume and allows you to engage in the self-directed healing practices that follow.

Training the mind makes training the body look like child's play
—Andrew Weil

MINDFULNESS TRAINING

Mind is a process of regulating the flow of energy and information.
—Daniel J. Siegel

This process of awakening, of bringing light into the mind, has been called meditation, contemplation, introspection, prayer, reflection, and mindfulness. Researchers like Jon Cabot-Zin and the medical community usually refer to it as mindfulness training. We will use any and all of these terms. There are countless books of both religious and secular nature from many traditions and thousands of years dedicated to this subject. Your religion is your business, this section isn't about that. Suggesting ways to use some of these practices to help you heal is our business. Here, we will introduce you to a few ideas and techniques that we think are appropriate to the mission you have before you.

Some days I can't think straight. No use me doing anything. Might as well just stay in bed.
—Cpl Leon T. Church

First let us say this: meditation is not fluff. It's as real and as scientific as taking a pill, getting a shot, or having a surgery. It is both a solid warrior *and* a fluid warrior skill. It has been proven to help with all manner of psychological, physical, and medical difficulties. Here is just a short list of what meditation will do for you.

- Calm you down
- Relieve anxiety and stress
- Lower your blood pressure
- Reduce pain
- Improve focus and concentration
- Decrease depressed mood
- Improve your sex life
- Relax muscles and tissues
- Allow you to think clearer
- Make your relationships more harmonious
- Create appreciation and gratitude
- Improve your life in general
- Create profound physical changes in the brain

Recent research has confirmed, for example, that *prolonged mindfulness practice actually thickens the tissue in the area of the prefrontal cortex.* This vital area of the brain directly behind the forehead really gets thicker. Just as biceps muscles get thicker when you do curls or the skin on your fingers gets thicker from playing the bass. Just from focusing your attention on yourself, there is a measurable increase in the area of the brain attributed to your executive function—your illume—*your personal commanding officer*. What's more, mindfulness practice actually thickens and extends fibers that join the upper and lower part of the brain. These connections of white matter in the middle of your brain can help to control your behavioral swings that in the past have given you overly emotional and crazy responses. When it comes to overcoming the behavioral issues associated with post-traumatic stress disorder (PTSD) or concussion, this is extremely important. Have you ever experienced the difference between a commanding officer or boss who is a blithering idiot and one who is cool, calm, and collected? Ever notice how the focused leader with a clear vision and direction moves the mission easily and efficiently forward? Which would you rather have running your body and actions, the out of control moron or the focused, born leader? Would you like to be more in control? Do you want to improve your brain? We sure do.

Through mindfulness practice, we become aware that our whole body, as it speaks to us through sensation, possesses a profound intelligence. It is instructing us all the time. It is telling us what to do to heal it. This intuition is a powerful resource. The more we listen, the more we hear. Even in the midst of pain, which is one of the many ways the body speaks to us, our body's voice can help us come to a perspective and course of action that is most beneficial. It can help us *see through* feelings of anger, depression, or anxiety. It answers such questions as:

- Do we need rest, or work, or play?
- Do we need quiet or arousal?
- Are we hungry, thirsty, or have we had enough water?
- Which food or drink is really good for me?
- Do we need solitude or companionship?
- With whom should we spend our time?
- What do we need right now?
- Do we need to anchor and stay on task, or to let go and be spontaneous?
- What does my body's intuition tell me about a decision I have to make?
- What's really causing this anxiety or anger?
- What do I need right now?

These questions can only be answered in the present moment by each of us individually; however, by looking deeply within the body we can learn to answer them and to care for ourselves.

Mindfulness practice is about slowing down, seeing, drawing power from an inner resource, and learning to rest. It's about recognizing that sometimes there's nothing better, nor more important to do, than to stay put and enjoy your breath. Everything is okay just like it is. There is no goal other than being in the moment. It can be a kind of ultimate rest, although it's amazing how much effort this ultimate resting can take. Let's be clear about one thing: seeing, increasing illume, waking up, meditation, mindfulness, or whatever you want to call these practices we learn, *does not mean there is no pain or suffering.* Sometimes it may even mean that temporarily we experience more pain. Being asleep is easier in the short run. That's why we drink or take pills. It's why we avoid feelings. It's why we miss doctor's or therapist's appointments. It's really hard to just stop and look within yourself. It requires such fierce commitment that getting there is the work of a warrior. Sometimes being with pain really does produce gain. Can you learn to sit with dignity in the midst of your life, even when the unthinkable—you've lost your best friend, an improvised explosive device has broken your back, you feel responsible for others deaths, or you'll never get to be a Marine again—has happened to you? Even if the waves of your life crash on you and are too big to ride, can you learn to keep your mind and heart above water, to not be completely downed by misfortune? Meditation will help you heal and it will give you the strength to tolerate the things that don't. Mindfulness is a dignified way of being. Meditation is a process that helps create that way of being. It infuses your journey with dignity. If you are reading this, then you are already halfway there, because your interest and participation are already on line. If you can notice your breathing—know exactly where you are on the in-breath and out-breath even while you read these instructions—then you have already begun. Find or create a quiet place where you can be. Listening into your inner world requires turning down the volume on your outer one. Find a quiet space and go through Exercise #3: Basic Meditation.

Exercise #3: Basic Meditation

1. Sitting with your back relaxed and upright in a straight back chair is a good position to take. There are many others but let's stick with this for now.
2. Move around a little bit.
3. Arch your back or bend forward.
4. Make the kind of motions you make when you yawn and get out of bed in the morning.

5. Really stretch yourself out as best you can. Stretch out your legs and point your toes. Reach you hands above your head or clasp them behind your back if you can. Feel all of your joints extend, maybe even crack a few times. Do whatever you do to help your body relax. You are going to be somewhat still for a while, so it's good to see if you can get some of the kinks out of your body.
6. Now, place your arms on your legs with either your palms down or you can have them nest in each other in your lap with palms up.
7. Bring your chin in toward your neck just a bit and line up your ears right over your shoulders. Keep your back erect but relaxed. Imagine your feet and the bottom of your spine rooted in the earth and the top of the spine and your head rising into the sky.
8. You can have eyes closed or half open. If open, keep your eyes soft focused in peripheral vision, but adjust your head so they are pointed at a spot about 4 or 5 feet in front of you on the floor.
9. Breathe through your nose if possible and enjoy watching your breath and the way it moves your whole upper body. You can even count each one if you want: **1** on the in breath, **2** on the out breath, **3** on the in breath, and so on up to 10 and then start over.
10. If you feel the need to move a bit, just do it, but do it as slowly as a snail moves. Don't worry too much about all this; just try to get comfortable. Not so comfortable that you fall asleep though, sleeping is not meditation.
11. Sit quietly in this position for as short or as long as you would like. You might use a timer and start with just 5 minutes. Keep enjoy your breathing. Any thoughts and emotions you have are just part of what you are observing. They are just inner weather. Any time you notice you are not paying attention to your breathing just come back to it. The moment you realize that you are dreaming you are awake. Just sit and appreciate how you feel.

After you have been sitting quietly for a moment or two with Exercise #3, check out how you feel now. Even though this was a simple activity, it's important that you get used to checking in with how you are feeling at the start and at the end of this and any of the exercises to come. That way, when you finish, you can see if they've made you feel any different. At first, you may not notice anything, but with time, and as the sessions dive deeper, we guarantee you'll begin to notice differences, real differences.

FOCUSED AWARENESS

Focused meditation is a resource that involves bringing all of your awareness to a single point. This single point can be literally anything: a candle flame, a favorite word repeated audibly, a common phrase in your head, a tree, the sound of a bell, traffic sounds, or whatever sound is around you at any given time. The clinking silverware and indistinguishable conversations of a popular nightspot can be a very interesting river of sound. Or, even the absence of sound, silence itself is especially good. Here, we'll be using your own breath as a focus. Breath is the most traditional object of awareness, because it is always with us, and it is the most essential element in our lives.

> *I was in Afghanistan for 2 tours and it was a rough, but sometimes just sitting still for 15 minutes can seem impossible. I'm way too antsy. I've never been a guy to sit still. It's like I relive everything I went through over there. When I remember to concentrate on my breathing even though all that stuff in my head is going on it really helps and I feel a lot better.*
> —Cpl Leon T. Church

Breath . . . is . . . life. It is the most important thing we do. Everything, *everything*, is dependent on this simple in and out movement. At birth we inhale, at death we exhale, and in between is our whole life. It is with us now as we write and it is with you now as you read. It is a constant companion. A warrior who really knows breath, who is consciously riding the sensation of this sustaining breath, is someone riding the blade of the moment. A warrior that knows breath is awake. Bringing attention to breath is bringing attention to life itself. What would it be like, if the simple act of breathing—something that is with you every moment of your life—was source of great pleasure to you?

In the next exercise, we use illume to explore *abdominal* breathing. Abdominal breathing brings your awareness to the point about 2 inches below your naval, deep into your belly. When it's slow and deeply felt, it generates a soothing and settling response in us. You might become aware of the fact that noticing your breath itself tends to slow it down. The trick is twofold,

- You have the *intention* to become aware of your breath and this spot in your belly, and
- You allow yourself to become *curious* about this breath and how it's moving you.

As you are going through this exercise, breathe in and breathe out. If any thought about anything shows up, that's okay. You are not trying to eliminate any thoughts. You are allowing your mind to become saturated with the sensation of breathing. You are continually remembering to enjoy riding the rising and falling waves of your own breath. This is subtle work, but with practice, time, and curiosity you will come to realize that, like snowflakes, no two breaths are alike. You may even get to experience it as something that is being done *to* you rather than something you are doing. Concentrate on any pleasure this breathing brings to you. Spend 5 minutes with Exercise #4: Power Spot Abdominal Breathing.

Exercise # 4: Power Spot Abdominal Breathing

1. Follow the instructions to Exercise #3.
2. Concentrate all your attention on a spot 2 inches below your naval.
3. Breathe through your nose and feel that spot move as the balloon of your lungs fills and empties with air. Think of the air traveling from the space just in front of your face all the way down to this spot below your naval.
4. Keep your attention on this single spot. Notice how it moves about for 5 minutes.
5. As before, if any thought about anything shows up, that's okay. You are not trying to eliminate any thoughts. You are just continually bringing your attention back to this single spot.
6. When you have done this for a while allow your attention to open and become interested in the whole body's sensation of breathing. Enjoy riding the rising and falling waves of your own breath. Concentrate on any pleasure your breathing brings to you.

None of these exercises will do anything for you if you do not give them enough time. To that end, we recommend that you get some kind of easy to use timer. You don't want to be checking the clock every minute. As much as possible you need to be able to let go of thoughts about how much time is passing. Feel free to use focused meditation as often as you'd like and in any setting that can. If you open your attention just a bit you can even use this breath practice when you're driving, operating a chainsaw, or listening to your girlfriend. Just remember,

- Find a quiet softly lit place.
- Stretch a bit to get some of the kinks out of your body.
- Sit upright in a chair with your hands on your legs or in your lap.
- Notice how you feel before you start.
- Have your eyes closed or soft-focused if open.
- Breathe through your nose.
- Focus on the movement of your breathing right at the area just below your naval.
- Ride the rising and falling waves of breath for 5 to 30 minutes.
- Let all thoughts come and go.

- Keep your senses open and notice any enjoyment that might arise.
- When you finish notice how you feel compared to before you began.

With time and practice, this breathing will wash over you and soothe you to your very core. Bringing focused attention to breath increases illume, relaxes us, and makes the world okay just as it is. Conscious breathing is a powerful ally. Focused awareness is how we first used our senses to explore and comprehend the world around us. Now, we are using it, along with breath, as a first step to understand our body and mind.

A Famous Zen Story

A Zen monk, after being instructed to watch his breath for long periods of time complained to his master, "Breathing is boring." The master promptly grasped him by the collar of his robe and thrust his head beneath the surface of the monastery pond. Shortly thereafter, with the young monk fighting and thrashing about trying to be released, the master pulled the young monk's head out of the water. As the student took a huge gasping breath and felt the relief that followed, the master asked, "Is it boring now?"

When you feel comfortable with focused awareness, consider including others around you. Invite your family to spend some time breathing with you. Teach them how to get started. Ask your other caregivers to become a part of it, even a health care provider or two. This work is appropriate for all of us. Not just for you, the service member this book addresses directly. Something profound happens when two or more people engage in this work together. The effects are greatly multiplied. We hope that you and the people important to you will create opportunities for conscious breathing within community. People that breathe together bond, heal, and wake up together.

ALTERNATING AWARENESS

Your hands are miracles. They are irreplaceable. It makes sense to learn to fully appreciate them. If you can, lift one hand right now and look at it as if it is something you have just discovered. If this is not possible or it's too hard, close your eyes and visualize your hand. Really look at your hand. Turn it over. Open the fingers wide. Make a light fist. Close your eyes and lightly rub your thumb and fingertips together. Move each finger separately. Really poke your mind down around inside your hand. Explore how many shapes you can make with it. You are not using it to accomplish anything. You are exploring. You are just marveling at it. You are expressing appreciation for it. When you bring your awareness into your hand, it wakes up the circuitry in your brain and wakes up the cells in your hand. Exploratory movement helps increases circulation and sensation, and further activates the brain and cells. Gentle, conscious movement feeds all the tissue and joints in your hand. Now, let your hand rest for a while, but continue to feel into it. Go back and forth between feeling it at rest and feeling it in movement. Take a lot of time. Spend sufficient time with your hand until it grows large in your awareness. We are introducing conscious movement of the hand as a way of increasing bodily awareness. You can do this for as long as you want or you can time it, but when you finish, bring your attention into your other hand. Do you feel a difference between the hand you just experimented with and the one that you did not?

Try this exercise: focus your attention on the same hand that you've just been moving and relaxing, while you also make yourself aware of the abdominal breathing we did earlier. Notice everything you can about how your hand feels. Maybe you're aware of some internal tingling, or a pulsing, or the warmth or coolness of air on your skin. Now notice your breath. How does it move you? Can you feel the air streaming into your nostrils past your sinuses, down your windpipe, into the lungs, and all the way into your expanding belly? Next, retrace that same air on your exhalation. Go back and forth between your hand and your breath a few times: focus on your hand, focus on your breath, hand, breath, hand, breath. Now, can you feel your hand and your breathing at the same time? Take some time and notice how easy it gets to alternate between these two types of sensation. Take some time and go through Exercise #5: Alternating Hand and Breath.

Exercise #5: Alternating Hand and Breath

1. If you can, lift one hand right now and look at it as if it is something you have just discovered. If this is not possible or it's too hard, close your eyes and visualize your hand.
2. Really look at your hand. Turn it over. Open the fingers wide. Make a light fist. Close your eyes and lightly rub your thumb and fingertips together. Move each finger separately. Really poke your mind down around inside your hand. Explore how many shapes you can make with it.
3. Now, let your hand rest for a while, but continue to feel into it. Go back and forth between feeling it at rest, and feeling it in movement. Take a lot of time.
4. Now, focus your attention on same hand that you've just been moving and relaxing, while you also make yourself aware of the abdominal breathing we did earlier in Exercise #1.

5. Notice everything you can about how your hand feels. Maybe you're aware of some internal tingling, or a pulsing, or the warmth or coolness of air on your skin.
6. Now, notice your breath. How does it move you? Can you feel the air streaming into your nostrils, past your sinuses, down your windpipe into the lungs, and all the way into your expanding belly? Then retrace that air as you exhale.
7. Go back and forth between your hand and your breath a few times: focus on your hand, focus on your breath, hand, breath, hand, breath. Now, can you feel your hand and your breathing at the same time? Take some time and notice how easy it gets to alternate between these two types of sensation.

You are beginning to consciously perform something that your mind has been doing since you were young, alternating attention. Becoming aware of two different things or processes at once. It's how you began to explore and then know the world. It was actually rather difficult for your mind at first, but then it got easier and you mastered it. You'll find the same is true with the exercise here. It's a part of the executive functioning that allows you to control the world you live in and to interact with that world and those who live in it. Once again, you're using breath, illume, and questions to enhance an understanding of yourself. You have started your mission and you are building the skills needed for it.

EXPANDING AWARENESS

In alternating awareness, you are opening the lens of your awareness to include both your hand and your breath. Although initially you focused on them separately, with practice you may find that you are holding both in the same space in the mind. So much so that you might start to feel that your hand is breathing. You can even move your hand in imitation of your lungs: fingers opening and closing right along with inhale and exhale. Almost like it's part of your lungs. Actually every cell in your hand receives the oxygen that comes in with breathing. Remember, inside of you, everything flows into everything else. You are using your imagination to help you perceive something real that is usually below our level of awareness. In this way, we will be expanding awareness to your entire body. We want to go through the same process with the rest of the body that we did with the breath and the hand. Adding a body part to the mix every time. Spend some time exploring this technique with Exercise #6: Full Body and Breath.

Exercise #6: Full Body and Breath

1. Bring your awareness into one of your feet. If moving your foot is too hard or not possible, simply think about doing it or visualize moving it.
2. Move your toes around. Press the foot on the floor. Coming up on your toes, roll around on the ball of your foot so your ankle moves from side to side. Let your foot become still. Then, barely move it. Experiment with different types of movement.
3. Notice everything you can about your foot. Rest and feel. Repeat.
4. Once you have put some time into the foot alone, introduce your hand into your awareness. Alternate between your foot and then your hand. Notice the differences between the movements and sensation. Notice how they are the same.
5. Begin to let your awareness blur between your foot and your hand. As you do this, add your breath to the mix. As in Exercise #2, take it slowly. Feel your breath flowing through your nose as you inhale. As you exhale, notice your hands moving in that same space as the exhaled air.
6. Get the idea? Breath, hand, foot. They are becoming one whole sensation. Take some time to become aware of all three of these elements: first one, then two, and then all three together. Keep adding parts of your body to your mind's awareness.
7. As you get more comfortable with these explorations, bring these parts of your body into the pleasant warmth of your mind's sunlight. This sunlight is expansive and includes the previous explorations that you've taken. Explore and then add the other foot and the other hand. Add your legs. Add your arms. Now you have: Breath, hands, feet, legs, arms.
8. Then, add shoulder, then spine, then neck. Bring in your upper chest, your face, ears, nose, lips and mouth, and whatever your internal scanning directs you to. One at a time, then add them to the mix. You are becoming aware of all of it simultaneously.

Do you see where this goes? You are cultivating a 360-degree awareness of your physical body. Your entire inner world of sensation is illuminated, and it's all breathing. You've been using this technique since childhood to take in the complexity of the world. You used it in school and basic training to learn and master all of the intricacies required. Now, we invite you to spend time using this amazing skill to fully scan yourself. To see how all parts of your body relate to one another and relate to your breathing. Even your symptoms can be brought into this. What is your pain in your neck like when you breathe? As you notice your hands and feet, what happens to your dizziness or your fatigue. What does awareness do for you? This is step three in awareness, an expanding awareness.

You are the knowing, not the conditions known.

—Ekhart Tolle

OPEN AWARENESS

Expanding awareness takes in all elements of you: your body, your breath, your symptoms, your feelings, and everything else that makes you up. It also begins to include everything around you, both for what it is and for how it affects you. With time and practice, this expansion will evolve into an openness. With open attention, your inner body becomes spacious and filled with illume. As you come to know this inner territory, you will see that its sensations are constantly evolving. You will start to become more aware of how the sensation of emotions and physicality plays through your inner world. What is within you becomes as interesting as what is outside of you. Open attention means that you let all feelings and thoughts come and go without judgment. Things that you like, pleasurable sensations and thoughts, come and go. Things you don't like, pains or anxieties, come and go. Coming to recognize that sooner or later all things come and go is a big deal. You recognize that they are just passing through and that you are bigger than all of them. This is executive function at its highest. This is a lifetime's worth of work and it is also where we start. The work to uncover this essential resource, this light within yourself, establishes the base for your healing mission.

We are well aware that some of you who are reading this may be in a great deal of pain. Don't worry, we will be addressing natural ways to dissolve pain later in the book. But there may be pain in your foot right now. Or, you may not have a foot. In these exercises it doesn't matter. Pick something else. Any part that you can bring your attention into is a doorway into your inner world. Find any body part that you can investigate with movement and consciousness, even if it's just your tongue. Please take these principles into your individual circumstances. You may also be feeling that reading this book is a pain. If you are feeling resistance and feel that you have had enough of this line of inquiry, we want to remind you that you are in boot camp, and *you* are your drill sergeant. Keep at it. Push through. You also have other options: try another part of the book—go drink some water—put all this down until it feels right for you to pick it up again. Or, if you absolutely have to, blow this book off entirely and get on with another process. You're the boss.

CONTINUUM MOVEMENT

We have spent some time understanding how we can use awareness to begin to explore our bodies, our minds, our thoughts, our behaviors, and our symptoms. In order to further use these skills, we need to better understand how our bodies work and how we can tap into our bodies as a resource. We have arrived at another resource that you should be aware of, the work of Continuum. Continuum is a body, mind, and spirit work that sees movement and the way we move as an extension of who we are and how we fit into the world around us. Learning about this movement therapy and applying it to our mission is a central part of your healing process. The visionary somatics pioneer Emilie Conrad, created the work and put forth the principles of Continuum in 1967. Continuum is a constantly evolving work but basically it's about movement—the type of movement that is already present in our biology and DNA. It is about what we are, and what is happening at the cellular and biological level within us, all the time. Continuum theory states that the key to healing and growth is learning how to identify this natural movement and to re-associate with it, to consciously become it. We recognize that these biological processes are what we most essentially are. A foundation of Continuum is the notion that we are fluid systems and anything we do to encourage and engage that fluid system will help us heal. With this fluidity, we become our most alive selves. It is a way of becoming a fluid warrior.

Learning Continuum movement is the next step. It combines with the work of awareness to help us see how our body and mind are relating to each other and the world. It encourages life force and increases our ability to feel sensation. An awareness of sensation, in particular, is a key part of restoring our internal movement. Now, we are going to experiment with movement and find out for ourselves what kind of movement enlivens and heals our system. You may be getting tired of hearing this, but we really want it to sink in. So we'll state it here again, with greater conviction. *The movement of water and the flow within your tissues is the key to your healing.*

It's important that you see the value and urgency in the exercises that follow. If you do not, the amount of time and energy you put into them may be insufficient. We're back to the notion of engagement. The choice is yours. You will feel a little better by simply doing some of the breathing and awareness exercises we've been through, or by trying out the ones that follow in this book. There's no harm in testing out the waters. But, just as half a dose of penicillin won't cure an infection or three-quarters of a tank of gas won't take your car to the end of a trip, you won't be able to get the most out of the healing process by just dabbling with Continuum. A deep dive into Continuum is the way to have it take full effect. It really is all or nothing. So, we have one last thing to do. Convince you that the upcoming exercises that come from this work of Continuum, when practiced with an open mind, conviction, creativity, and mindfulness on a daily basis will not only heal you, but will lead you into a life you may not even have imagined. Do you remember our discussion of expanding the sense of a warrior's identity from the beginning of the book? Well this is where the rubber meets the road. This is where the solid warrior learns to also become a fluid warrior. If you're ready to make that commitment, you'll find a series of movement explorations in the next several chapters. Before we get to these however, we'd first like to give you some insights into why Continuum works, how it can serve as a platform to build your recovery on, and what steps you should take to take full advantage of it.

> *Feeling important makes one heavy, clumsy and vain. To be a warrior one needs to be light and fluid.*
>
> —Carlos Castaneda

Water

Water is incredible. It is the source of all life. And yet, we have all almost completely forgotten about it. Sure, we may know we need it. We may believe it's the secret to losing weight or to exercising effectively. We know to drink some of it, because we get thirsty. They put it in smart packages or add some vitamins to it when we want to sell it to us. And when you were in Iraq or Afghanistan, you really knew it was important. Many days all you heard was "drink water and keep your rifle clean." But think about it, think how all important water really is. We drink it. Wash in it. Shit in it. Boat in it. Swim in it. Surf in it. Clean with it. We like to watch it flow in rivers and crash as waves on the beach. We fish our food out of it. We water our plants and sustain our animals with it. It is pumped down oil wells to bring up oil or forced through turbines to power generators. It is literally life-giving, one could even call it Life. BUT WE DO

NOT REALLY APPRECIATE IT. For millennia, human beings considered water magical and, regardless of whether we remember that, it is still magic. There are many places in the world where getting water is the main activity of each day. And why do you think every religion on earth has a thing about it? Because water is sacred stuff. Let us say it again, *Water is the source of life and life is not possible without it.* Have you ever been watching television and seen a *National Geographic* special on some desert, where the narrator opens with, "Most of the year, the desert is a barren waste land. Arid and windswept, the heat and sand make it completely inhospitable to life. And then – (the music swells) – the life giving rain begins to fall." THE LIFE GIVING RAIN, the guy says. The rest of the special discusses what arises from this rain—plants blooming, eggs hatching, micro-organisms reproducing, the water hole forming, which draws to it the birds and smaller animals, and then the larger ones who feed and them, and so on. A whole ecosystem springs up because of these rains. And then, the water dries up and the life goes away. The show discusses everything living that arises from this source, but it does not really discuss the source itself. It's too obvious. Like the nose you can't see, because it's right on your face.

But let's consider how quickly things would change if, say, the water that is constantly evaporating into the sky didn't come back to the earth as rain or snow. We'd die. We couldn't somehow figure something out or find some alternative source of life. We couldn't choose something else. Sooner or later, we'd just die. Actually, it would be sooner. Oh, for a while, you warriors would be in really high demand protecting the water that remains, but within a few years (or months), we'd all perish. All the people, all the animals, all the plants, everything would just disappear. Take a look at Mars (or the Sahara, if your telescope is broken). Nothing but sand and rock. Dry. Solid. Dead. No movement, no flow of tears, no nothing. We, and all the life on this planet, die. And then there's silence. Not the good kind of silence that religious people talk about or that you might find with mediation, because there is no presence in this silence. There is no presence because there is no one to perceive it. There is nothing of consequence. There is not even a single philosopher left to break wind over it. There aren't even echoes of doom.

So yeah, we think water is pretty cool, and we cannot think of anything more valuable, or deserving of our gratitude. What do you think? Can you really think of something better to appreciate?

These are not idle musings because water and the appreciation of it can affect every area of your life. Imagine, for example, if every time you drank water there was something of the parched desert traveler coming to the spring of an oasis. How do you think that would be? What if you slowed down and stopped and actually drank a glass of water with this attitude, with true gratitude? What would that feel like? Try Exercise #7: Water

Exercise #7: Water

Right now, put the book down, get up, go get a glass of water, come back, and sit back down. We'll wait.

Are you back? OK. Hold the glass up to the light, see how the light travels right through its transparency. Tilt it a little and watch how the water hugs gravity. Swirl it around and watch it slide around the glass. Really observe how it moves; how it's transparent. And then . . . take a sip. Swirl it slowly around in your mouth and then let it slide down your throat. Take another larger sip. Swallow and see if you feel it as it enters your stomach. Really . . .feel it. Take another sip.

Whatever else is going on in your life at this time should take a back seat to the front and center experience of drinking water, taking in life itself. What if you made it a practice to remember this every time you drank a glass of water? How would that be? Remember, gratitude is a type of energy.

But there is more.

Water is more astonishing than we can ever know, but it's not just the substance of water alone that is magic: It is the way water moves. The way it swirls and spirals, bubbles and pours, circulates and permeates, freezes, thaws, and turns to steam. It's the way it splashes, evaporates, and turns to clouds or mist. The way it ripples and waves. And it's the way water carries everything, either on it or in it, and rejects nothing.

Our Fluid Nature: Odo Story

We don't know whether you remember the character Odo on the science fiction series *Deep Space Nine* or not, but his story is instructive. He was what they call a *shape shifter*. His natural state was a liquid form. In order to be a Star Fleet officer, he had to take the form of one. He had to physically shape himself into a human body in order to perform his duties and not freak everybody out. Every few days, however, Odo had to go off and be by himself in order to return to his natural fluid state to rejuvenate himself. He would have to let go of his form, his pattern if you will. Otherwise he would start to break down and become ill. He would die.

We are actually all like that. There are some definite patterns to the way we live and function. The way we take care of ourselves, or don't. Sleep is a way of returning to a fluid state. We have to stop running mental circuits and patterns and just kind of float. We break down pretty quick if we don't sleep regularly. Our minds and bodies need to let go and shut down. But, we are even more like Odo than that. The human body must keep moving and shifting in order to maintain health. Even when we are awake, if we maintain the same form too long, we too will start to break down. This same form could be as straight forward, as in lying in bed or on the couch. Or, it could be doing the same type of physical activity or life routine over and over. For instance, using the same repetitive gym machine over and over, or exercise routine. Just as running or walking on the same treadmill or swimming in the same lane every day gets boring. It isn't the actual exercise or activity that is bad for our system, but the lack of fluidity. Like Odo, we need movement variety. We need to return to a fluid state on a regular basis in order to restore and maintain our health.

The exercises we show you in Chapter 7 are about de-patterning. They are about letting go of rigid patterns in the body and the mind, so that the natural intelligence of your healing system can do what it needs to do. Thinking, moving, and being the same way all the time leads to illness and injury. Repetitive or cumulative trauma is the most common injury to the body in sports, work, or the military. Doing the same task over and over again is not healthy for the body or mind. Illness or trauma can create a rigid and highly repetitive state in our system. So it works both ways. Repetition and over-patterning can create illness and trauma or illness can create repetition and over-patterning. Either way, dissolving our form, learning to come into flow brings us out of the realm of illness and into the realm of health. If we want to re-form we first have to un-form, just like Odo.

Resetting Your System

In order to hear what the body is telling us, we must figure out some way to get the noise out of our system. It drowns out our listening and fragments our attention. If we want to get the noise out of our system, we have to begin with getting the noise out of our environment. The emails, the Internet, the TV, the movies, the traffic, the constant talking, all of it is a source of noise. When this outer noise begins to abate, the inner noise of our thinking begins to become apparent. We discover we can turn down the TV, but we find it impossible to turn down our thinking. That's where all these practices come in. In battle, it's not a problem. The inner noise, the unnecessary thinking, is turned down automatically. When a warrior is in battle, there is adrenalin and riveted attention. A life-threatening situation puts one completely in the moment. There is no room for anything other than the situation at hand. Your body and mind are constantly speaking to you and sending you signals, and from all the information coming into your system you select what is most important for your survival. It some ways it's simple.

> *War is a lot of things and it's useless to pretend that exciting isn't one of them . . . . War is supposed to feel bad because undeniably bad things happen in it, but for a nineteen-year-old at the working end of a .50 cal during a firefight that everyone comes out of OK, war is life magnified by some number that no one has ever heard of. In some ways, 20 minutes of combat is more life than you could scrape together in a lifetime of doing something else.*
> —Sebastian Junger, from *War*

This condition of being fully present, being completely in the moment, is something all people, whether they know it or not, long for. It is the feeling of being alive. It's something that as a soldier you have experienced in spades. It's why coming home and the rest of your life can seem so boring.

> *After I got back from Nam, the rest of my life just felt like boring gravy. I knew I'd never feel that alive again. Even rock climbing didn't do for me what battle did. I read somewhere it's one reason there is so much war. The decision to go to war is mostly made by men who haven't been there, but a lot of the fighting is done by guys who really dig it.*
> —Veteran of the Vietnam War

Over time, these exercises will take the noise out of your system and reveal the rich inner, and outer world in which you live. They will help you become completely present to your life. They will make you aware of, and exhilarated about, what is alive within you.

Attitudes

You must continually ask yourself how you can cultivate interest and enjoyment in this process. In battle, these and many other emotions were coursing through your system. Now sometimes boredom, sadness, anger, anxiety, frustration, or any of a host of other negative emotions can obscure these fundamental attitudes of being interested in something and enjoying the process of learning about it. Working to create that and working to create appreciation and gratefulness is important. They are energies that lift us. There is more of a choice here than people realize. Learning to create and keep and optimistic attitude can be difficult, but you don't have the luxury of choosing not to have one. You need all the juice that you can muster to get through this. It's imperative that you discover what you are grateful for and what you are curious about. Here's that question from before: *What is alive in me right now, and how can I join with it?*

> *Sometimes your joy can bring you a smile; but sometimes your smile can bring you joy.*
>
> —Thich Naht Hanh

The gist of this book is that awareness and movement, particularly creative movement that is enjoyable and that imitates our biological nature, cultivates the life force within us. In other words, listening, feeling, and understanding our mind and body, and allowing them to work the way they've been pre-programmed to work is a key to returning to health. It's the marriage of consciousness with movement that listens into internal sensation. Even if you don't fully buy in completely, give it all a shot. Begin to layer these initial exercises over the treatments you've already started or have used in the past. Medicines that didn't seem to work in the past will now have a better effect. Getting back on a program of exercise or a more healthy diet will bring added benefits to you when you are using breath, illume, questions, awareness, and movement to open your body's channels. Give it some time and give it your full effort. Make that decision.

> *Yeah, I did some of the breathing stuff. It made me feel totally weird and it's totally boring. I'm breathing all the time anyway. There's nothing anybody can do for me.*
>
> —PFC Lori Stefano

We are asking you to dedicate a portion of your time to increasing illume through meditation and learning to listen to the wisdom that lives within you. We are asking you to become as soft and fluid as water, so that you reshape yourself and become healed. This can be difficult because it runs counter to some of the ideas of the solid warrior. Some of your military training has is been in opposition to this. But it's time to move on. It's time to expand. Can you become adept enough to become either the solid warrior or the fluid warrior depending on the circumstances?

A military force has no constant formation, water has no shape. The ability to gain victory by changing and adapting according to the opponent is called genius.

—Sun Tzu, from *The Art of War*

The Ahh Factor

One final thought about the goals of this mission. The body lets us know what it likes by giving us enjoyable sensations. When we come to understand something and we see it clearly, we say, "Ahh, I get it". That's an expression of mental pleasure. When we let out a sigh of relief we also say "Ahh." If we are really thirsty after playing ball and drink a cold one we say "Ahh." If we are quenched by cool spring water at the end of a long hike, we definitely say "Ahh." When we get a massage, or move in a way that causes flow, we also say "Ahh." We call this the *Ahh factor*. It's a sign of physical and mental enjoyment. It's our body's language for "Yeah, that's what I'm talkin' about." It usually means something's been nourished or that something has let go. There has been a change for the better. It means there is more flow and it's a sign of health and recovery. We are talking about the natural organic expression of our bodies, like the sheer pleasure we can get from sex. Sex is one example of an authentic Ahh factor. Although authentic enjoyment is a sign of recovery, there are other types of enjoyment that are not and we must be able to recognize them. Authentic enjoyment lifts and heals us. It connects us to what is alive in us. But, there is a type of enjoyment that means we have dissociated or escaped from our body's preferences. We've numbed our selves. It's not true enjoyment and it can leave misery in its wake. This misery can take the form of a hangover, indigestion, or the side effect of a medicine. Although there's nothing wrong with some alcohol, good food or the right medicine, we need to understand how to approach these things with the correct lens in place. We have to find the balance. We have to be careful here to make sure that our enjoyment is wholesome. Fluidity tends to be pleasurable, but pleasure is a byproduct of living the right way, not the goal. If we think that achieving pleasure is our life's goal, we'll go crazy searching for it. People do it all the time. The maximum pleasure of achieving a meaningful life or achieving healing means we have to submit to disciplines that are sometimes not instantly pleasurable. You know that from being in the military. Although we may have to postpone immediate pleasure, that doesn't mean we have to ignore it or push it away when it shows up naturally. For the body, and especially in regard to healing, authentic pleasure is a natural signpost that we are heading in the right direction.

In this chapter, we discuss a few basic methods for increasing mindfulness and bodily awareness. We watch and experiment with breath to see if we can increase the way it nourishes us. We identify and recommend experimenting with a few states of attention—focused, alternating, expanding, and open. We look at the principles underlying the type of movements that the body finds most natural and, therefore, most healing. We began to see how water and fluidity are something to more fully appreciate. And we see that the body lets us know when we are on the right path, by expressing authentic enjoyment. In the next chapter, we put all this to work. We take these principles and skills we are learning and put them in service to healing. This mission is just starting to get off the ground. Lock and load.

7

Applying Healing Principles

The body responds to love, not tyranny.

—Emilie Conrad

It's now time to begin putting many of the basic resources we've discussed into action. The main emphasis will be on using movement therapy to bring your body back into working for you, awaken your mind and senses, and establish a connectedness between your body and your mind. We'll also re-explore the keys to restful sleep, introduce important principles of nutrition, and highlight the value of aerobic and body strengthening exercises for you. Each of these steps will be valuable to you in and of themselves. You will feel better just from following the individual measures in this chapter. Make sure you take the time to appreciate the sense of improvement and well-being you feel. This appreciation is another key to your recovery. Once you've identified which elements feel good and are beginning to help you, you'll need to begin to incorporate them into your everyday routine, to make them part of who you are. Then you'll not only get the pleasure that they bring, but you'll also be constructing a foundation for true wellness.

The Continuum movement exercises and principles that follow will bring your healing resources on line. They are *moving medicine* that will generate health. The instructions are initially given in some detail. Read them through once or twice and then try them. You might even read them into a tape recorder and then play them back so you concentrate on just doing them. Keep an open mind, learn the exercises, and, more importantly, the principles and incorporate them into your daily schedule. Coming to breath is always a great way to begin, so try and begin any exercise session with one of the breathing exercises.

Exercise #8: Full Body Breathing: Joining with the Movement of Breath

1. Place one hand flat on the center of your upper chest and one hand flat on you belly at your naval and breathe through your nose.
2. Spend a minute or two feeling the natural rise and fall of your breathing.
3. Bring your hands slightly in front of your body and have them imitate the movement of your lungs: moving away from the body on your in breath and toward the body on out breath. You're acting as if your hands and arms are part of your lungs.
4. On the in breath, loosen and tilt your head and shoulders back to create more space in the lungs. On the out breath, bring the chin and shoulders closer to the chest to help squeeze a bit more air out of the lungs.
5. Feel your hands, arms, head, neck, shoulders, belly, back, and sides all beginning to ride and enjoy the movement of breathing.
6. Do this for about 5 minutes.
7. Take your hands and arms down and rest them in your lap. Notice any changes. Feel your own heart beat.
8. Return to normal breathing and rest in open awareness.

Our nervous system changes in response to the way we breathe. Our state of mind is tied to the breath that carries it. The breath of battle differs from the breath of the mess hall. The breath of confrontation is different from the breath of communion. The breath of exertion is different from the breath of relaxation. This is true not only because of the need for varying amounts of energy but also because of varying states of mind. The breath of a panic attack, for example, is vigorous and agitated out of all proportion to the body's actual need for oxygen and the breath of a skilled martial artist can be fluid and controlled even in the midst of battle. If you want some choice about the state of mind you have, it's important to investigate how your breath reflects and influences it. Entering breath with curiosity is part of the warrior's path of awakening. Unconscious mouth breathing puts our nervous system in the territory of the "fight or flight response." Slow, easy, conscientious breathing through the nose stimulates the "soothe and settle response."

Exercise #9: Luna Breath: Quiets Nervous System

- Breathe easily through your nose and bring your attention to the back of the tongue and throat. Feel where your tongue is fastened at the back of the throat.
- Gently pull the tongue back and up to the roof of the mouth and slightly close off the opening in the back of the throat.
- Shape the back of your throat and mouth as if you are going to make a humming sound.
- Breathe out of your nose.
- Lengthen your exhale. The slight extra pressure generated by the smaller opening at the back of the nasal passages produces a quiet hissing sound. Listen and see if you can make it audible. Lengthen this breath and follow it with all of your attention until its completion. The image and sound of a space-suited astronaut walking on the moon might be helpful.

THE HEALING ENVIRONMENT

The first 9 months of your life were spent floating in the inner ocean of your mother's womb. For almost all of us, that was a very warm, secure, and peaceful place. There was no stress, nowhere to go, nothing to defend against, only floating and growing. There was a lot going on developmentally, but there was absolute safety. There was no separation between your mother and you. That time represents a state of complete rest, of complete nourishment, and there is something about it that is still with you.

These exercises can bring back an unconscious memory of that time. They can elicit the same stress-free nervous system you had then. There is something fundamentally healing about the rest that comes when you curl up in that place, the time before all the stimulation of this world came upon you. Nothing is more healing then that state of security, that state of peace. What can you do to recreate the feeling of this state within you?

Setting up a Space

You can create a special place where you can practice all of this. A quiet space with low light and a floor with some kind of cushioning—soft carpeting, thick yoga mats, blankets, pillows—is ideal. It need not be large. Relaxing music that you like can be very helpful as well. This is a time and place for

- Breathing
- Doing Continuum movement
- Pausing to notice sensation
- Unwinding, decompressing
- Resting
- Connecting to your inner resource
- Breathing some more, feeling some more, moving some more
- Napping
- Listening to music
- All of this can be done in bed if it's that time and you're ready to get a good night's sleep

The Community Field

This practice becomes more powerful if you can do it with someone with whom you feel comfortable. It becomes nuclear if you can do it in a larger community. There is something extremely positive about the energy generated when a group of people explores movement together. We think that energy is the most powerful healing energy on earth. It would be ideal if you can practice this with at least one person who you are close to and feel safe around. There is strength in camaraderie. This way of being is in stark contrast to what you went through in war. That is why it is so difficult and why it is so important. It may be only thing that can balance your life. What goes up must come down, what has been traumatized must be soothed. Nothing will soothe you faster than being with a group of people to whom you feel connected. We are moving away from the solid warrior here, but we are right smack dab in the home of the fluid warrior. If you want to move forward in your life you must be both.

Slowness, Depatterning, and Creativity

In war, speed is of the utmost importance. Your life depends on it. In healing, slowness is of the utmost importance. Your life depends on it because it stimulates healing. Slow movement increases the relaxation response in your body. That reduces stress, promotes your immune system, and alleviates inflammation. Slowness means that you can feel everything that's going on within you. Think of driving down the highway at 70 miles an hour. The details are a blur. Now think about strolling leisurely through the same landscape. You notice the birds, the texture and color of the bark on the trees, the varied vegetation, and even the insects around you. Your inner landscape is like that as well. When you direct your attention to what you are really feeling in your body, you are unifying your body and your mind. Focusing on what you feel, even and especially pain, mobilizes all of your body's healing resources. Your cells wake up when they know you give a damn. That's why we push this slowness thing so hard.

Patterning is great. You cannot function without it. It means you can walk without thinking about it, or learn to play golf, or master the guitar. But in movement designed to encourage healing, patterning can become habit. That means there is a loss of awareness. Awareness is a key component of your success. When we are on autopilot we lose the mind body connection. It's hard to fully participate with, or appreciate, our bodies. That's why we are not recommending mechanical exercise machines.

You'll notice that these exercise forms are fairly open. That's because they are about discovering what your personal body needs. If you take them seriously there is not really a wrong way to do them. Allow plenty of time and just do your best to get in to them. Follow the instructions as best you can and then make them your own. They are much more potent if you are creative with them. We are encouraging you to slowly shift your body into as many different shapes as you can come up with: a leg slowly moving over here, an arm over there, and a head twisting in the opposite direction of the spine. Imagine a slow spiraling flowing along the whole length of your body from head to foot. It's very important that your whole brain becomes interested in what's going on. This type of creative movement activates your brain in novel ways. It creates new neural pathways. Mechanical movement does not. Mechanical movement sooner or later bores the brain. The brain quickly figures out what's going on and awareness is no longer needed. We check out. We start to think about something else. It's why people watch TV or read magazines while on exercise bikes and treadmills. That's not what we are doing here. We want to notice every little detail about the movement and what we are feeling. We want to innovate both our body and our brain and we are doing everything we can to avoid mental or physical ruts. Acting like a machine is not nearly as cool as the experience of say, taking your dragon spine flying. We want to use your imagination and all of your senses, not just your body. That's a whole other level of engagement. It's why we emphasize making these exercises yours. Time spent investigating these Continuum movements is called a Continuum dive.

General Principles of a Continuum Dive

1. Take the position of whatever exercise you are going to explore.
2. Practice mindfulness and maintain awareness of your breath.
3. Continually scan, head to toe, the sensations of your inner body.
4. Begin the exercise, moving extremely slowly.
5. Play with movements that
   - Curve
   - Arc
   - Spiral
   - Wave
   - Twist
   - Flow
   - And that are complex
6. Avoid movement that is
   - Mechanical
   - Repetitive
   - Patterned
   - Fast
   - Linear
   - Right angled
7. Explore moving and shaping your body in unusual ways.
8. Play with gravity orientation.
9. Notice any aches and pains in your body and also stay alert for the Ahhh factor.
10. Go back and forth between feeling inside yourself while moving, and feeling inside yourself while still.
11. Be creative. Give yourself permission to come up with your own movements.
12. Rest in open awareness and notice what's still moving inside of you.
13. Remember how you were before your Continuum dive.
14. Repeat the exercise or sequence of exercises three times with creative variations.
15. Enjoy your life.

Once you get the gist of how to approach these exercises, you can think of them as launching pads to personal discovery. *How* you do them is the skill you are learning. A long period of slow creative mindful fluid movement that is saturated with sensation, curiosity, and enjoyment is your way home. Trust us. It may even be to a home you never had.

Appreciation

The principles and exercises in this book can lead to gratitude, even wonder, for the body and life that you do have. If we don't take them for granted, if we can come to appreciate our breath, our spine, our feet, for the miracles that they are. Even if damaged, we will recognize how much they serve us and they will become a source of strength—physically, emotionally, and spiritually. Just for a moment, stoke your appreciation for your spine. Imagine what it would be like to have a broken back, to be paralyzed, to have a spine that didn't work. Sit with that for a moment. Then approach these exercises in that light. How do you think you would feel if you couldn't move or feel at all for a time and then were miraculously healed? How would that be?

Paralysis

We are well aware that many of you may indeed have some form of paralysis. Please know that we are with you. There is much this healing movement can do for you as well. The principles and quality of the movement is the same, how you proceed just has to be adapted. You start where you are. All of the principles in this book are still applicable. Remember, we are interested in what you can do, not what you can't. If all you can move is your neck and above, that's where you begin.

RESTORING THE BODY'S NATURAL RHYTHM

Trauma disrupts the body's natural rhythm. These exercises restore that natural rhythm. They are the means for us to come to know and appreciate ourselves for what we fundamentally are: fluid beings. The spine that can flow like a wave, or like sea kelp or a dragon, is a spine that is remembering its fluid nature. It is completely alive. Doing what we can to move like fluid reminds our bodies of this healthy and youthful natural rhythm. Moving like fluid enlivens our fluid system. We know when we are on to something when the movement starts to feel good. The truth is that it's very difficult to get the feel of these exercises from a book and it's the feel that we want to emphasize. It's what distinguishes them from other types of exercise. But it's not difficult to know, to feel, when your body starts to relax, when there's more flow. If you really listen within, you will find it is not difficult at all to tell when your natural rhythm is returning. We are confident that if you give Continuum movement a fair shake, it will begin to open, and heal you. Exercises #10 and #11 are simple everyday exercises that are an extension of what we and animals do naturally when we wake up. Spend some time testing out the waters of movement therapy with these exercises.

Exercise #10: Unwinding the Animal Body

- Sitting, standing, or laying on the floor, breathe, and stretch out in any position that feels good to you. Think about how a dog or cat stretches when they awake.
- Twist and turn in such a way that it feels like you are wrapping your muscles around your own bones. Make unusual shapes with your body. Play at the edge of your range of motion. Don't try to push through. Use breathing to help you open and elongate. No forcing.

Exercise # 11: Swaying Shoulders

- Lean against a tabletop, a chair back, a wall, or the corner of a room. Bring your head and chest forward like you are going to do a pushup.
- Gently push away with only one arm at a time. This will cause your back and neck to shift over one arm or the other.

- Slowly alternate back and forth until you create an easy swaying motion as your head travels from one arm to the other. Pause. Repeat. Vary your rhythm.
- See how many different shapes you can make. Do this until you can feel some movement and warmth coming into your upper spine, shoulders, and neck. Keep noticing your breathing. This is not a strengthening exercise. It is a movement awareness and tissue lubricating exercise.

The Spine

Very few things will enhance your life as much as paying attention to, and caring for, your spine. It is the literal center of your being—your personal super highway. When it flows, you flow. When it feels good, you feel good.

Just like breath, your spine, and the amazing way it can move, is always with you. You can experiment with it when standing, lying in bed, sitting in front of a computer, taking a walk, waiting for a bus, or even subtly in the grocery store check out line. One of the things we are trying to do is to get you to see that the way you pay attention, and what you pay attention to, determines the quality of your whole life. Whether it's children, animals, gardening, the creation of a career, or in this case the healing and optimization of your spine's health, we have to come to understand that attention and care are what bring life into things. If exploring your spine, the way it moves, and all the intricacies it's capable of, becomes something really interesting to you, you will never be bored. You will always have something to do. All you have to do is make awareness of it a part of your life. The idea is simple, but remembering it requires daily practice. This is especially true if there's pain in your spine or if it has become numb as a result of contracting against pain for a while. We are going to learn to feel deeply into the spine and to introduce fluid movement that nourishes it. Where there is constriction, or things are frozen, let us see if we can thaw them out. Where there is inflammation, let us see if we can cool things down. Where there is rigidity let's see if we can create flow. The trick, as always, is to experiment with moving in a mindful, gentle, and appreciative way. Because the spine can move in such a snakelike fashion, capable of bending and twisting and even undulating, it can be fun to think of it as a sea serpent or a dragon. These spine exercises are great to try with some gently rhythmic music. After introducing breath into your system, spend some time with Exercises #12 to 15.

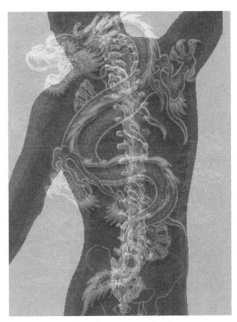

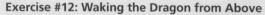

Exercise #12: Waking the Dragon from Above

1. Sitting upright with your back away from the back of a chair, notice your breathing and come into open attention. Let your awareness surf the waves of your breath.

2. When you feel settled let your head move gently and freely in any direction. Tilt the right ear toward the right shoulder, or the left to the left. Slowly nod your head in a yes motion, or swivel it from side to side in a "no" motion. Let it roll slowly around.

3. Poke your chin out and think of it as the tip of an imaginary pencil and write your name in the space in front of your face. Or write the sentence: "This is weird"; making sure to cross the t's and dot the i's. Or, how about writing: "I wonder if any body can see me?" Make sure you write in cursive and maintain a slow easy flow in all your movements.

4. "Feel into" the area in the center of your head about 2 inches in on either side of the lower part of your ears. That's a remarkable joint called the atlas. It's the place where your skull rests on your spinal column and it's responsible for the way your head moves and swivels all around. Get to know it from within.

5. Keep noticing your breath and feel free to move in anyway that feels good to you. Remember the Ahhh factor. Rest in open attention.

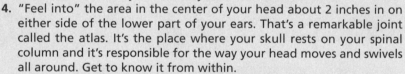

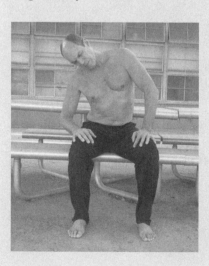

Exercise #13: Feeding the Dragon

1. Let the movement of the head start to create movement in the upper spine. Now you are aware of movement in the spine itself.
2. Curling forward, arching back, twisting one way or the other—you are moving and bringing fluid and nourishment into all the joints of the upper spine. Roll your shoulders to add more movement.
3. In your imagination, your mind's eye, see and feel the dragon waking up. You are the snake charmer of your own spine. Keep noticing your breathing. You might also see your spine as kelp moving and flowing in the current of the ocean floor.
4. If you start to feel weird, use solid warrior and executive function to push through any resistance you might have to this exercise. Use fluid warrior to really feel and be aware of everything that's happening in your dragon spine. You know you are on to something when it starts to feel good.
5. Rest in open attention and repeat.

Exercise #14: Waking the Dragon from Below

1. Staying seated and upright in your chair, bring your attention to your seat. Notice breath as always.
2. Think of yourself as sitting on a compass: north to the front of you, south to the back, west to your left, and east to your right. If you drop your chin, slump forward, and curve your back you will roll your pelvic bowl, your bottom, toward the south of the compass. If you throw back your shoulders, thrust your chest forward, and arch your back you will roll your pelvic floor to the north.
3. With awareness and breath, slowly, and easily rock back and forth between north and south. Get it? To accomplish this you have to flex your spine both forward and back. Roll over one half of your butt to the east or west. Notice the way the spine moves to accomplish this. Roll all over the compass: north to south, east to west, northeast to southwest, around the whole compass from north to northeast to east to southeast to south to southwest, you get the idea.
4. Roll around on this compass in anyway that fells good to you. Keep breathing. You are freeing up the lower spine. Feel the dragon waking up from the below.

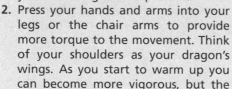

Exercise #15: The Dragon is Awake

1. As your dragon wakes up from below, add waking the dragon from above. Your entire spine starts to become fluid. Don't force anything. Stay within your comfort range. This gentle flexing, curving, rolling, twisting, even spiraling movement is feeding all the joints, muscles, ligaments, and connective tissue around your entire spine. It is also causing movement in the spinal fluid that your spinal cord is bathed in. Keep noticing your breathing and keep with it.

2. Press your hands and arms into your legs or the chair arms to provide more torque to the movement. Think of your shoulders as your dragon's wings. As you start to warm up you can become more vigorous, but the emphasis for now is on moving awareness not on physical fitness exercise. Later it can be, but not right now.

3. Be creative and keep an eye out for the Ahh factor. Fall in to a state of enjoyment. There's nowhere to go and nothing to do but this. You are discovering the dragon that lives and moves within you.

4. Bring in our earlier full bodied breathing exercise and you have a full-blown fire-breathing dragon. If you practice this enough, you will come to feel that you are not moving the dragon but that the dragon is moving you. If you put on some relaxing music you like and do this for 30 minutes a day for 1 week you'll feel like a million dollars.

5. Always remember to rest in open attention at the end of your exercise. That's the time where you can soak in the nourishment that this kind of exercise gives you.

I never thought of my spine in this way. I actually never thought of it at all until after I got rolled and I was in constant pain. I didn't lose consciousness but my back got messed up. The x-rays don't show anything and the MRI just said there was some scaring around T2. I couldn't even take a decent breath because of the pain. Nothing was any fun. This is making a difference.

—Cpl Tim Owen

Space, Gravity, and Balance

We are relaxing, unwinding and decompressing your entire spine. We are creating space in all of its muscles and joints and discs. Creating space in the body is one of our primary goals. That's why we are so intent on creating fluid muscles that are not too dense. There is more space for the fluid to flow within. Fuller flow means faster healing.

We can create even more space and decompression by putting our bodies in different and sometimes unusual positions. Experimenting with how we are in gravity aids this process tremendously. It makes us more flexible. It pushes and pulls us all around. It creates traction. Without even trying to make it happen, stuff lets go. That creates space.

Changes in gravity orientation also affect all the fluids in the body. Your blood is being pumped through your body by your heart. That's why exercise that causes blood flow is so great. But blood, and all the fluid in your body, like everything else, is subject to the laws of gravity. Fluid always seeks the lowest point. Remember how water always hugs the bottom of the glass. It does that in your body too. Some fluid like lymph has no pump at all and is dependent on movement and gravity to flow. When you experiment with movement in a variety of positions you hydrate muscle, ligaments, tendons, nerves, viscera, connective tissue, and even brain tissue. Blood flows everywhere. Playing with how you are in gravity is a really healthy thing to do.

Gravitational play also engages your sense of balance. It activates and maintains the balancing mechanisms of the inner ear. That's important for all of us, but it's crucial if you have experienced trauma and feel disoriented in gravity. It's a natural skill we take for granted until it's gone. But it's a skill that can be relearned and developed. Let's explore all this in the next couple of exercises. Exercises #16 and #17 are variations on the dragon exercises. In all of these spinal exercises you may notice pops and cracks in your spine. With practice you will become your own highly skilled spinal manipulator. These are very nourishing exercises and will relieve a tremendous amount of tension and pressure in your back, shoulders, and neck in particular. These are great to do if you spend a lot of time on a computer and they are extremely helpful if you are having difficulty with sleep. Exercise #18 is a slightly more challenging spinal movement exercise.

Exercise #16: The Dragon Takes Flight

- Come onto all fours on a soft padded rug or some kind of matt or even pillows.
- Start with hands right under your shoulders and your knees apart about the same width.

- Your spine is horizontal, parallel to the ground. Enjoy breathing. This position helps your spine elongate. Letting your head hang down will immediately take pressure off of your neck and create more space in the discs in the upper spine.
- Wake up the dragon. Initiate the movements of the previous dragon exercises in this position. Remember the moving head and the compass seat. The hands and knees position allows your spine a much greater range of motion.

- Twist your spine by bringing one shoulder, and then the other toward the ground. Arch your back toward the sky and toward the ground. Play with the idea of getting the spine to ripple, or wave. It's one long flexible creature. Put your forearms on the floor so that your bottom is raised and try this spinal movement in that position. Keep breathing and be creative.

Exercise #17: Flipping the Dragon

- Lay on your back with your knees bent and slightly apart. Place your arms to your side or just above your head, whichever feels more comfortable. Press your feet into the floor to lift your bottom and lower spine off the floor. Raising and lowering yourself from the floor from just an inch to as much as a foot is part of the movement you are exploring. Gently curve and twist and play with all the dragon movements from the previous exercises.

Exercise #18: Moving Cobra

- Lay on your stomach with your legs together.
- Place your arms close to your chest, elbows bent with your hands flat on the floor directly beneath your shoulders.
- Start with your forehead flat on the floor or even bed. Press down with your hands, slowly tilt your head back and roll your neck back and then gradually up your spine until you are curving backward up from the waist. Do not strain. Do not hold. There is no effort here. Do not worry about "doing it right."

- Play with pressing or releasing into the floor, curving, moving, and relaxing your spine. Alternate pressing with one hand and then the other, as in the swaying shoulders Exercise #11. Enjoy your breathing.

- In yoga this is called the cobra pose. Our cobra moves like one. This will relax all the muscles in the back of the neck and shoulders. It's a particularly great exercise to help you relax at bedtime.

Your Feet

Healing means you have to tend every part of yourself. The condition of your feet determines how your entire musculature responds to the demands of gravity. Our feet are how we meet the earth. They are miracles of design, strength, and flexibility. They carry us around all day long, but we rarely acknowledge them. We hardly care about them unless they are damaged and are unable to be our pack animals. Then we're just mad. What about throwing them a bone every now and then? What about offering them a little care? If they're messed up, you're messed up. If they're tight, your whole body's tight—or will be very soon. The way they meet the earth is the way your whole being meets the earth. It's all connected. If you could walk barefoot over fertile earth and grass, and occasionally wade in streams over rounded river rocks for a week or two, your entire nervous system would light up. We know that your feet, and you, would feel more alive. When possible, walk on the earth barefoot. Exercise #19 is a simple introductory exercise with your feet.

Exercise #19: Happy Feet

- When standing barefoot, experiment with moving all the areas of the feet (toes, balls of feet, heels, side edge) with creativity. Organize your balance over one foot to allow more freedom of movement in the other one. Flex, point, and spread your toes. See if you can grab the floor with your toes the way a cat kneads its' claws into your leg. Lightly twist and rotate your feet from the ankles. Work your calf muscles.
- Shift your stance so that you can roll around on all the different areas of the bottom of your foot where it comes into contact with the floor—sides of the foot, heel, ball of the foot, flat toes,
- Use your imagination to "breathe" into your feet. Cultivate an attitude of appreciation. If there is pain or tightness go extra slowly and move/play at the edge of where the pain becomes apparent. Damaged feet require even more care and attention than healthy feet.
- Try this same exercise while lying down with your feet raised off the floor.

Headaches

Headaches are the most common symptom of post-deployment syndrome (PDS) and all of the common diagnoses that accompany it. Here's an opportunity to use the principles of mindfulness and movement as self care in a specific situation. As breath and mindfulness practice become a regular part of your day, you will become more finely tuned to the first stirrings of a headache. As soon as you notice a headache starting to stir, try Exercise #20.

Exercise #20: Making Head Room

- Slow down. Turn off any lights and any extraneous sound (TV, radio, etc.).
- Take an ibuprofen tablet (200 mg) or an acetaminophen tablet (500 mg).
- Sit or lie down. Breathe. Come into open awareness. Scan the whole body.
- Relax. That is, see how many muscles you can let go of. You might flex or contract them first, and then let go, to remind you of what letting go feels like. Give all of yourself to gravity.
- Next, bring your full awareness into your head and neck. Very gently tighten, release, and move the muscles in the head (scalp), neck, jaw, and face.
- Play with shaping your facial muscles in a variety of ways: smiling, frowning, opening the mouth wide, or squinching the whole face into a point around the nose and lips. (Playing with the muscles in your face is extremely important. More of the brains movement areas are dedicated to the face than any other body part. It's so important we might put out a whole book on it.)
- Close your eyes and gently roll them in their sockets.
- GENTLY. This is about increasing sensation and internal flow. You are trying to get to know and relax *into* this headache. *You are not trying to power the headache away.* You are creating the space in your mind and your head so that the headache can move.
- Remember to keep noticing your breathing.

Self-massage

What do most of us do automatically if we have a headache? We put our hands to our heads, or we might bring our face to our hands and rest it there. We might rub our forehead. We don't even think about it, it's just our bodies natural way of offering itself care. Let's take this a step further: let's do it on purpose. Bring your fingers to your forehead and temples and rub in a circular motion. Use all your fingers and lightly begin massaging the jaw and sinuses. Let your fingers travel over the top of your head. If you have hair, you can give it a little tug. You are trying to bring as much awareness as you can to the whole head. Press into, and explore the muscles running up the back of your neck, not too light and not too deep. Press lightly into the dent at the top of the neck and the base of your skull. Let your head move slowly around and be creative about how you move your hands around and gently into all the nooks and crannies of your neck, head, jaw, and face. Continue with this creative exploration of movement and self-massage. Keep noticing your breath as well. The bottom line is that you are offering care into your own system. It is not vigor, but the quality of your noticing, and the refinement of your touch that matters most.

Over time, and with practice, you will learn to enter into and diffuse (make them go away) and defuse (prevent them from starting) your headaches. You will be able to do it even in less than ideal circumstances and, eventually and ideally, you will be able to head them off at the pass. They will become less frequent and finally, a memory. Please don't give up if this doesn't work right away. It takes a long time, or something major has to happen, for the body to get this far out of whack, or flow, and it may take a while for healthy flow to return. Remember, this pain is the body's way of asking for your attention.

Please learn and practice this when you don't have a headache. It is an ideal preventative measure and is a part of our larger goal of self-knowledge. There is no reason in the world why you cannot use your own hands to care for, explore, open, and encourage physical flow in your own body. There is not a more direct or fuller expression of self-love than this. Learning self-care is really the crux of this entire book. Can you put real energy and thoughtfulness into caring for yourself? Do you think this is silly? Can you use a warrior's strength to push through any internal resistance you have to this idea? If you were ever to use your executive function, your ability to buck up, to see, understand, and not be sidetracked by inhibition or resistance, this would be the time. If *you* can't offer yourself this kind of care, who can?

Inhibition, Vulnerability, and Kindness

We want to talk about something that is essential in this work, something that can stop this process of awakening our organic healing ability dead in its tracks. We know. We see it all the time. It's the main reason we've spent so much time explaining why we do all of this. As far as we are concerned, joining the military, going to war, and going through what you've been through, means that your courage and toughness have been proven beyond a doubt. You are a bona fide badass and we salute you. But inhibition is a different type of animal, requiring a different type of courage. Inhibition and embarrassment can paralyze a warrior and keep them from exploring something new, something as simple as moving in a different way, or trying out a drum circle with others. If you have never considered creative movement or if you have not played any kind of music before, you might suck at it. Big deal. It's not like you're being shot at. And yet trying new things does take courage: the courage to allow yourself to feel and look like a fool, the courage to let your guard down. In short it is the courage to feel vulnerable.

Vulnerability means a lot of things. It can be the relief that comes with letting out a full exhale and releasing contracted muscles at the end of a firefight. It can mean telling someone you are attracted to them even if you don't know how they'll respond. It can mean deciding to give something new a try even if you feel silly and are not sure what you are doing. Coming to vulnerability can be like putting down a weight. It might be another name for freedom.

It might mean: just . . . letting . . . go.

Letting go of muscles. Letting go of the past. Letting go of ideas about the way we think things *should* be. Letting go of even our ideas about who we are. This letting go can allow us to encounter this moment just as it is. Sometimes, when we are overprotecting, we cannot even feel what's happening inside us. Remember, all the clues about how we personally work with healing are revealed within our internal sensation. If you are overly guarded, you cannot even feel.

One of the most difficult things that any of us can come to understand is that *there is great strength in vulnerability*. Why is that? Because, like cellular walls that open, vulnerability allows for change, exchange, nourishment, and growth. It is exhausting to maintain constant defense. Nothing can get in, or out. A defended body/mind uses a tremendous amount of energy and sooner or later wears slam out. Rejuvenation requires rest. Sleeping itself is a kind of vulnerability. It's ironic, is it not, that your survival, your healing, and the quality of your life may now depend on the courage it takes to be vulnerable, rather than the courage it takes to be invulnerable?

For some it means to let down your guard. It can mean something as simple as realizing you are not under attack. No one is asking you to become vulnerable in battle. But can you learn to let your body truly relax while at home? Or walking around your neighborhood? Or going to the store? There is work involved. We want you to know that now your survival is dependent upon dropping your guard.

Learning to be kind to one's self is one of life's steepest challenges. Even defining what it means, is difficult. On one level it is what this entire book is about. Please take the time to ask yourself the following questions. Really. Ask each question and sit with it a while. Breathe. Let the question float within you and see what comes up.

> What does the word kindness mean to me?
> How do I feel inside when I hear the word kindness?
> What does it mean to me to be kind to myself?
> Does kindness have anything to do with opening the flow of healing energy?
> Is it possible to think of yourself as the source of your own nourishment?

These are questions only you can answer. The answers are all over the map. For some of us these are really tough questions. Some of us have not experienced much kindness in our lives. But do these questions interest you? Are you curious about them? Can you stay open enough to look at them? Here's one more:

How can I express this kindness to myself and in my life?

How do the solid warrior and fluid warrior answer this question?

Rest

Rest is a major part of your mission. You must make it a priority and dedicate some part of your waking hours to the pursuit of it. It is not a luxury. If you are suffering from problems associated with PDS, it is a requirement. Rest is not simply "doing nothing." It is not having a few drinks. It is not watching TV. It is not vegging out. It is a creative, active, restorative process. It is an art form and a state of being that can actually be very difficult to come by. What's more, our culture does not really respect it and, in the military, the need for it can even sometimes be thought of as weakness, not bucking up. In battle doing without rest may be advisable, but in healing it is totally misguided. You cannot simply exercise yourself to health. Do not buy into this. Your whole being, indeed, our whole world, is hungry for rest. Rest is the time when we turn over all our problems to our innate biological intelligence.

Continuum movement unwinds the tightly wound body of a war torn soldier. It helps you let go and increases your ability to rest. When you practice Continuum movements and then bask, even doze, in the soothing state they create, you are doing a great deal to bring about healing. Going back and forth from moving to resting deepens that process. Again, please do your best to dedicate some time each day to this process. If you have a work schedule that won't allow you to do this, then we suggest a weekend time, say a Saturday or a Sunday morning. We encourage you to take the time—a couple of hours—to put aside everything else in your life and just rest.

Sleep

Balm of hurt mind, great nature's second course, chief nourisher in life's feast.
—William Shakespeare, *Macbeth*

> *I woke up this morning and my girlfriend asked me, "Did I sleep good?"*
> *I said, "No, I made a few mistakes."*
>
> —Stephen Wright

Sleeping well is a big part of your new mission. It is essential to your life and healing. It may be the single *most* essential part of your healing, for both your body and your mind.

There are some fairly obvious things that you may be doing now that are working against your body's need for adequate restorative sleep. They are a part of so many folks lives that you may not even know you're doing them. Here's a short list of some of the *worst* things you can do to prepare your body and mind for sleep:

- Drink at least 2 or 3 cups of coffee, or at least a few energy drinks (Red Bull is a favorite of ours), before retiring for bed each evening.
- If you don't have any tequila to take the edge off, then a few beers or a couple of glasses of wine can be quite helpful.
- Smoking is important, too. Nothing like some stimulating nicotine to relax the brain.
- Make sure you spend at least 3 hours on the Internet, playing video games, or watching TV. Really, any screen will do. As sleep connoisseurs we prefer watching the news and red-faced political commentators: either left or right wing is fine, as long as they're angry.
- Make sure your stomach is full, preferably with a pile of real chili cheese fries, extra jalapenos. Andy Capps Hot Fries are a good choice as well, but chips and dip are an adequate substitute in a pinch. Just make sure you're really full.

All kidding aside, most recommendations for sleep are common sense, but if you don't do them you are unlikely to consistently sleep. Even if you do succeed in getting and staying asleep, there's a much better chance that you will get the appropriate balance between nonrapid eye movement restorative sleep and rapid eye movement sleep:

- Establish a sleep rhythm. Whenever possible go to bed and get up at the same time every day. If a short afternoon nap becomes part of that rhythm, that's okay too.
- Make your bedroom feel as peaceful and restful as possible, like a sanctuary. No televisions, computers, video games, or text messaging. A book or magazine on your bedside table can be a friend if sleep eludes you.
- Sustained vigorous exercise or manual labor is the most direct path to a good nights sleep. Do some. Real cardiovascular stuff,

yoga, the movements we are recommending, gardening, physical labor, or something as simple as a leisurely walk after dinner can make all the difference.

- Cut out, or keep to a bare minimum, all stimulants (coffee, soda, tobacco, sugar, chocolate, alcohol, drugs, etc.), especially in the last 2 hours before bedtime.
- Slow down your pace and mental activity. Chill as the time for sleep approaches.
- If you really can't sleep, and are getting frustrated, get up and take a nap from sleeping. Drink some water, and do some of the breathing exercises in this book.
- Prescription drugs may help in the short run, but they can lead to a whole new set of problems. Use them only as a last resort, using with extreme caution, and for a brief period of time (1 to 2 weeks). Your new mission blows right past them.

Sleep can be a kind of heaven, or a kind of hell. For those in physical pain, with chaotic and disoriented thoughts, or whose nightmares are filled with the graffiti of war, real, blessed sleep can seem an unattainable goal. There is a reason sleep deprivation is considered torture. The tension and anxiety that won't let sleep come on, or the nightmares that knife through it can make nighttime feel like the devil.

I'd go for days in Iraq with just a couple hours of sleep: totally amped on energy drinks and adrenalin. I was always exhausted but I didn't even realize how much until after I got home. And as much as I wanted to I couldn't get more than a few hours at a time. Sometimes I'd come home and just drop. I'd fall asleep on the couch and 10 minutes later I'd be having some nightmare about being buried in bodies. I was drinking till I'd pass out just to get to sleep. The drugs they gave me knocked me out and left me totally useless. And I still didn't feel like I was getting any sleep.
—PFC Lori Stefano

As always, we recommend mindfulness, breath, body awareness, and movement as the primary means to accessing healing and, in this case, sleep. Here are some more specific recommendations that can help you fall asleep, stay asleep, or get back to sleep if you do wake up. Having a strategy, something to do, can make all the difference. Don't even worry about worrying. Try light versions of the previous practices.

- A few minutes of light, slow, *Unwinding the Animal Body* (Exercise #10) with breathing before bed is extremely helpful. This can be done on the floor right next to the bed or on the bed itself. This is really just doing consciously what we do automatically when we yawn and get ready for bed.

- Try 5 or 10 minutes of the *Luna Breath* (Exercise #9) to quiet your nervous system.
- *Moving Cobra* (Exercise #18): Even a minute or two of this can make a big difference. You can even do it in bed under the covers. Don't work at it so that your heart rate becomes elevated. Just think of it as a way to loosen and become aware of your upper back and neck. A little bit can go a long way
- *Breathing into sleep*: Heavenly sleep comes with a heavenly breath. One doorway to sleep is the fully experienced pleasure of breathing. We recommend always breathing through your nose and sleeping on your side. The left side is preferable because your heart doesn't press on your lungs and they can expand and relax more easily. If you snore, you probably breathe through your mouth, or experience sleep apnea; we encourage you to place a small piece of light cloth medical tape over your mouth from just under the nose to just below the bottom lip. Stick and unstick the tape to your hand a few times to lessen the adhesive so that it will be easy to remove in the morning. As weird as this might sound, if you can get comfortable with it, it will keep you breathing through your nose all night long. You will wake considerably more refreshed. *Again, remember, breathing through your mouth is fight or flight; breathing through your nose is soothe and settle.* The practice here is to see if you can consciously follow your breathing all the way into sleep. Any time you find yourself thinking of anything else just return to your breath. If you come to know breath, you will come to know sleep. It is the universe's way of rocking you.

Half of the problem with following these suggestions is just remembering to do them. They have to become available to you; something you turn to automatically. To that end we suggest placing an index card with a few notes by your bed stand. Something like: "Unwinding, luna breath, moving cobra, breathing into sleep." You have nothing to lose so come on, give it a shot. Don't give up if it takes a little time to see results. We think you will come to treasure this time in sleep preparation.

Rules of Sleep Engagement

1. Establish a waking and sleeping rhythm.
2. Get some exercise.
3. Don't put funky things in your body.
4. Chill before bedtime.
5. Engage in the sleep practices.
6. Sleep.

TIME TO ENGAGE

We are going to go out on a limb here and tell you exactly what we think is happening here. These exercises—learning to rest, learning how to sleep again—are essentially a way to express empathy and care for your own self. This is the kind of care to which your cells most respond. They are an act of self-love. This is not rocket science, but it does take the guts to buy in to it all. Things like this have been working for people for thousands of years and they are working everyday for warriors like you. Coming to the physical experience of pleasure can run counter to solid warrior training. We think of it as self-indulgent, not hard, or tough enough. Indeed, it's about softening and, with some exceptions, runs counter to our whole cultural orientation. Yes, it's underground, but somewhere along the way the pursuit of authentic physical pleasure became taboo. We are certainly not advocating that you drop everything and run to your nearest house of pleasure, but would it really kill you to get a professional massage every now and then? Or to spend some time with these exercises cultivating the Ahh factor?

Nutrition

When you are in the service you hardly ever have to think about food. You eat what they give you. You rarely have a choice. It ain't great, and if you have spent time in the hospital, well, that's some fine dining, but even the institutional stuff tends to be better than the average western diet. The truth is, if you don't already have them, healthy eating habits take time, forethought, and a little discipline to form. Mindless habits are easily formed, but not so easily broken. But now that you are home, do we really have to tell you not to eat crap, or not to smoke? Really? Do you really think chips and sugar and sodas and energy drinks and burgers and fries and funnel cakes and all the stuff in convenience stores is really food? Look, you can eat anything every once in a while, but if that stuff is your main source of fuel, you're going down, with or without PDS. That stuff screws up your body and what's more it screws up your mind. If you want to slow or even halt the healing process, or deepen depression, just keep pouring that stuff in.

Becoming really conscious about the food you eat and the way that it makes you feel is a huge part of your healing mission. You might even try a mini-fast occasionally. Make the decision to only drink water, or only drink water and eat fruit for a meal or two, or even for a whole day. You will find that you become more aware of how food functions in your life outside of its role as nourishment. Some people find that a missed meal or a short fast every now and then sharpens their mental abilities. Don't just eat stuff, experiment.

Whether you've adopted the lifestyle of a warrior, a patient, a worker, or just an average American, it's likely that what foods you put into your body may be affecting your recovery. Although highly active service members or athletes may be able to get away with taking in thousands of calories every day from a variety of healthy and not so healthy sources, it is not a recipe for success for you. Despite what your mother, great aunt, or last girlfriend may have told you, it really is better to be on the skinny side to feel well and live a long, active life. More than 60% of all Americans and 70% of Veterans are considered overweight by standard measurements. Although there are many ways to measure this, body mass index (BMI) is the most common and having a BMI of 25 or higher is considered overweight. Other factors that are looked at to determine your overall body health include your waist circumference and disease risk factors. Although these are valuable measures of health, even if you are within the normal or safe level for these, it is still important to carefully consider what your overall nutrition is doing. Because there are hundreds of diet and nutrition books in the stores and on the Web already, we'll just steer you to the mainstream healthy approach for good nutrition:

- Balance and moderation are the key principles to success.
- Aim for a target of 2,000 total calories or less in 3 to 5 meals a day.
- No more than 30% of calories should come from fats.
- Avoid as many canned, prepared, and preseasoned foods as you can.
- Use olive oil for all of your oil needs.
- Drink no soda, instead use water (6 to 10 glasses a day).
- Feel free to eat as many raw or steamed vegetables as you wish.
- Feel free to eat as many legumes (peas, beans, lentils, peanuts) as you wish.
- Use whole grain, unrefined cereals for your starch needs (wheat, oat, rye, barley, triticale, sorghum).
- Use fresh or frozen fish for your meat dish for 4 to 5 days per week.
- Use poultry, pork, lamb, or beef as your meat dish no more than 2 days per week.
- Eat low fat dairy products (yogurt, cottage cheese, sour cream) 4 to 5 days per week.
- Eat fruits for all of your desserts.

A diet of this type (sometimes called a Mediterranean diet), along with aerobic exercise and the movement therapy outlined, will not only help to get your weight where it needs to be, but will also begin the process of healing you from within. You'll notice that you have more energy, sleep better, move your bowels better, and simply feel more alive and alert.

Body Mass Index (BMI) Calculator

1. Take your weight in pounds and multiply it by 703.
2. Take your height in inches and multiple it by itself.
3. Divide #1 by #2 and you have your BMI.

A BMI of 18.5 to 24.9 is considered normal.
A BMI of 25 or more is considered overweight.
A BMI of 30 or more is considered obese.

Waist Circumference Measure

1. Stand up and place a tape measure around your waist.
2. Your waist is the region just above your hipbones.
3. Measure your waist just after breathing out.

A waist size greater than 35 inches in a woman is considered a risk factor for heart disease and diabetes.
A waist size greater than 40 inches in a man is considered a risk factor for heart disease and diabetes mellitus.

Weight-Related Disease Risk Factors

- High blood pressure (greater than 140/90)
- High LDL cholesterol (greater than 160)
- Low HDL cholesterol (less than 40 for men or 50 for women)
- High triglycerides (greater than 200)
- High blood sugar (greater than 125)
- Family history of early heart disease (before age 50)
- Physical inactivity (less than 180 minutes a week)
- Cigarette smoking

Along with being overweight, these factors increase your risk for heart disease, diabetes mellitus and related diseases.

Aerobic Exercise

Regular exercise that significantly increases your heart rate at least three times a week has been shown to do all of the following:

- Improve your heart's conditioning and reduce cardiac disease
- Reduce high blood pressure

- Reduce your weight
- Improve your strength
- Improve your balance
- Improve your sleep
- Improve your bowel movements
- Improve your sex drive and performance
- Improve your mood
- Improve your thinking and memory
- Reduce your pain

Aerobic exercise can take many forms, including walking, jogging, sports, martial arts, swimming, bicycling, or any other activity you enjoy, and it's actually best to alternate activities (cross train) to help condition your whole body. You should always begin slowly to build up your body's ability to safely perform the activity and you should only begin after getting a clearance from your doctor. We don't recommend using specific machines for exercise (like stair climbers or elliptical trainers), as patterned movement is not particularly healing; however, something is better than nothing. Remember, as with everything in this book, there is no rush with how often or how much you exercise. Just know that the more of any aerobic exercise you do and the more frequently you do it, the more beneficial it will be. The most reliable exercisers are those who find pleasure in what they are doing and who see the benefits of their efforts. So, use the techniques of mindful awareness and breathing to make sure you are monitoring how you are doing before during and after exercise and to get even more out of the natural pleasures of using your body.

Reaching the Aerobic Threshold

1. Subtract your age from the number 220; this is your maximum heart rate.
2. Multiply your maximal heart rate by 0.6; this is your target heart rate for aerobic conditioning.
3. Maintain your heart rate at this 60% of maximal (but no more than 85% of maximal) for at least 30 minutes, three times a week, to begin the process of aerobic conditioning.
4. Performing aerobic exercise for 180 minutes (3 hours) a week, over no less than 3 days per week is your goal.

There are some medications called beta blockers that prevent your heart rate from elevating. If you're taking one of these, ask your doctor about exercise parameters.

Exercise and Strengthening

Traditional exercise—calisthenics, running, weight lifting—is great. If you like it, you should do it. It gets the heart and lungs pumping and increases blood flow to the brain, elevates your mood, and helps you sleep. It's why they call the places that specialize in it *health clubs*. But consider this: from your body's perspective, it's a like being sent to obedience school. It denies that our bodies might have some say in determining what's good for them. Repetitive, mechanical, patterned movement shortens muscle. This makes it dense and less fluid. Our range of motion becomes limited. Ever seen a body builder who can't tie their shoes? Because this type of exercise is so repetitive, so patterned, and so mechanical, it bores us and our brains sometimes check out. We're just doing our routines each week. The way we use our bodies is a big part of the way we use our brains. Overly patterned movement in the body creates overly patterned movement in the brain. If your sole exercise is to move like a machine, you will tend to think like one. Because the movements in the body are wired into the brain, mechanical movement tends to make for mechanical thinking. It makes our thinking dense, less flexible. Although we aren't in any position to offend anyone, when you see one of those body builders on the cover of some "pump it up" magazine, you rarely think: highly integrated mind at work here. We applaud the discipline and dedication that takes to be thickly muscles and to have washboard abs, but wonder if it might be misplaced. When you see a basketball player move down the court, using slight of hand dribbling, float in the air to the basket, and tap the ball on the backboard to sink it in the basket, you know you are seeing a body and mind work together in flow. *That* is *intelligent* movement.

We are interested in movements, and in bodies, that heal. This should be your goal. But, we also realize that there is value in also building a body that has strength. The fluid warrior is strong, but this strength is fully integrated into all aspects of the mind. There is a continuous flow between the two that encourages healing and a return to health. Once you start to get better, start experiencing more flow, we want you to add strength training. This mostly involves doing some of the same exploratory movement exercises we have done before, but adding moving contraction, or what Continuum people call *harnessing*. *Harnessing* is learning to move or flow in a state of contraction. It's almost like the fluid in your body has gone from the light transparent quality of water to the thick quality of wet clay, or even the quality of lava. Make your fingers and hands feel like claws. Keep your feet taut. Flex your chest muscles and abdominals while you move. Slowly shift shape while maintaining conscious tension in your muscles is an astonishing tonic for the body.

Add some light weights to your movement routines and activities. Wrist or ankle weights are ideal, but light dumbbells will work as well.

Remember to use Continuum principles when exercising. Stay in touch with your breathing throughout the exercise period. Slow way down, so that you can really feel how the weights work your muscles. Twist, turn, and curve your body to use your muscles in unusual ways. Think of the way an octopus moves. Stay in a continuous state of unfolding movement; there is no beginning or end, just flow. Avoid repetition and strive to find ways of lifting and moving that are novel to you. Seek constant innovation in the shapes in which you put your body. Explore movement from a variety of positions: standing, sitting, laying on the floor, sitting or draped over an exercise ball, or using a foam roller to open your joints and help create space in your body. Work at the edge of your range. Stop and come into open awareness if you encounter pain. An excellent way to capture all of the benefits of Continuum movement, while incorporating strengthening contractions, is to use water as the medium through which you are moving. Try doing a few of your weekly sessions partially submerged (to your lower chest, for example). Use water dumbbells (or air-filled milk containers) while doing your movements. Vary the level of water you exercise in. Try walking, hopping, or running while moving your arms. Go backward, sideways, and frontward. You'll find that no two movements are exactly the same and that all parts of your body will come into play.

Using an Exercise Ball

The large inflatable exercise ball is incredible. Do not think of it as just exercise equipment. It invites movement exploration. It activates your inner gyroscope—the balance system of your joints, muscles, inner ear, and brain. It lights up brain circuitry in a novel way. Conscientiously rolling around on a ball brings fluid lubrication to all the joints of the body. It

engages all your musculature and connective tissue in an ongoing, constantly moving relationship to gravity. If you are old, it makes you young again. If you are young, it makes you younger still. It will loosen your spine, your shoulders, your hips, and even your butt. The more you use it, the better you'll feel. It's the bomb.

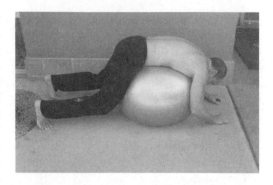

You can try all of the breathing practices we have done while you are sitting on it. Try the dragon spine movements we covered while sitting on it. The simple act of watching television while sitting on a ball can bring fluid movement to the entire body. Any size exercise ball can be useful and the more sizes you

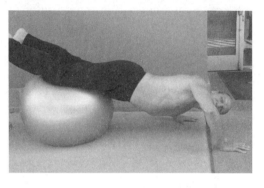

can get and use the better. If you can only get one, get one that's just above the height of your knees as you stand next to it. Blow it up till it's firm, but with some give. Don't make it too hard. Do not inflate it to within an inch of its life. Once that's done look at it. Give it a name—big boy, roundy guy, Heinrich, killer—whatever. Its presence will do more for you than you realize. Even if you just watch television on a ball, instead of a chair or the couch, and you just roll a bit on it whenever you think of it, you will start to feed all the joints and muscles in the knees, upper legs, hips, and lower back. You will increase the amount of synovial fluid lubricating your joints.

APPLYING THE HEALING PRINCIPLES

Restful sleep, healthy nutrition, aerobic conditioning, and movement therapy are four pillars of recovery. Linked together with enhanced understanding, breath, questions, illume, and mindful awareness, you have the beginnings of a foundation of wellness. The simple pleasures and Ahh factor that all of these activities can bring certainly makes it an easy decision. But, in order to fully leverage all of these elements, you need to have a full engagement with this mission. For many, it is this "leap of faith" that separates them from success. It's more than just trying some things or giving something a chance. It requires *full engagement* to be a successful warrior. Let's advance and use all of these resources to help us see and understand how our emotions and our thinking create the very quality of our lives. In the next chapter we'll be looking at cognitive-behavioral therapy and few of the therapies used in treating PDS. What is the nature of depression, of anger, of irritability, of guilt, and grief? What's happening in the body and mind when they are present and how can we learn to deal with, and hopefully dissolve them? We'll also be examining the nature of the therapeutic relationship and what you can do to foster a good one. Feel into your warrior's heart. You are another step closer to your recovery.

8

Re-establishing Normalcy

I think they have the letters all wrong. It shouldn't be PTSD,
Post-Traumatic Stress Disorder, it should be PTGP, Post-Traumatic
Growth Potential.

—Anthony Robbins, paraphrased

UNDERSTANDING EMOTIONS

In the last two chapters, we have established that mindfulness and continuum movement practices are important healing resources for you. They help you participate with and encourage nature's restorative forces and prepare you for the healing powers of both traditional and nontraditional health care. When we become more skilled in the art of seeing and encouraging flow, our minds and bodies become healthier and our emotions become lubricated and move through us more easily. This is a good thing. It means we are more alive and are becoming more fully integrated. In some cases, emotions we didn't even know we had may float to the surface of our consciousness. In other cases, the true nature of the things that are affecting us becomes clearer. That's what you want to happen. You want to learn what your emotions have to teach you, to figure out how to process these feelings, and then to move on. The final goal is to have everything that happens to us and everything we feel about it to be appropriate to the present moment we are in and to flow through us in that moment. Your feelings, thoughts, and sensations should be seen as moving through you and should be recognized as temporary. This understanding can give us better control over how we react to these feelings, how we behave when we experience them, and how we can act in a way that creates the life we want. On the other hand, if we allow our feelings to become more than simply transient occurrences, then those feelings will be too strong and they will just push us around. Even if you happen to have the strength to try and resist or ignore these feelings, then they will only be pushed down deeper into our system, ready to resurface again and again. They will weigh us down from within, just as too much weight can weigh us down from the outside, no matter how fancy a set of clothing we wear. All of these feelings can make us seem out of control or, just as bad, if we repress them, they can make us incapable of feeling anything at all. That's hard on you and the people around you.

Being in war means you have been exposed to extreme situations that bring up correspondingly extreme emotions. There is a good probability that you have experienced many things that were too difficult, too painful, or too inappropriate to experience fully at that moment. If you lose a buddy in the middle of a battle or see some horrific things, you may not be able to fully deal with the rage and grief you feel at the time. If you had dealt with it, it would probably have put you on hold, or even paralyzed you to the point where you might not be around to be reading this now. So, you had to suck it up and drive on, just as you had to keep moving and staying on mission if you had a physical injury. Even if something didn't happen directly to you or your friends, living with the anxiety and fear that something might happen at any minute, which is a common feeling when you're in a battle zone, can be just as overwhelming. Actually, being in war also means that these strong emotions, like anger, hate, and rage, have been purposely ignited and even cultivated to get the job done. Although it may not be hard to stir up these feelings when the heat of battle is upon you, it is hard on your mind and body to continually be at this fever pitch and also hard to eventually rid itself of these extreme feelings. None of these emotions are easily shed when the job is over. So how can you begin this process?

The next step in your healing mission, getting a better handle on emotions, requires you to learn another set of skills. Unlike most of the exercises we've shown you up to this point, this one can only be done right with the help of experts. People who can partner with you to get this process started. Just like no matter how handy you may be around your car or your home, there are some things that just need to be kicked up to the specialists, so you don't end up with a bigger problem than you started (or a bigger bill)—just think about the last time you messed with your plumbing or your transmission. You need to work with an expert to understand what makes you tick inside your head. That's the work of psychotherapy and, to be done right, it should be done with a licensed psychologist.

You've already begun the process of preparing yourself for the next part of the mission. Two of the things we've already learned about, meditation and continuum movement, serve as a foundation for the work of psychotherapy. Learning how to better question yourself and look inward for answers, giving your body and mind the needed rest by improving sleep, putting healthy nutrition into your tank, exploring the healing power of movement, adding regular exercise to your routine, making sure you had the right clinicians helping you, and giving the right kinds of medicines a chance to work have all been necessary steps in recovery that *you* could be responsible for. All of these self-care tools have been necessary to pre-pare you for this next, harder step. Even if you've tried before and failed, armed with the tools and resources you've reviewed in the past several chapters, you can now more fully engage and benefit from therapy. Now it's time to take advantage of all of the tools you have been equipped with so far and to partner with a professional to take you even further along the path. Even if your problems feel mostly or all physical—like pain, diz-ziness, or poor coordination—therapy is a vital step in recovery. As we said before, the body and the mind are so interwoven that it's really quite impossible to separate them.

There are *very real changes* that occur to the brain from post-deployment syndrome (PDS) that directly affect the way your mind and body works. In order to give yourself the best chance for returning to normal, it is cru-cial to get your brain working better. To do this, the two approaches are to either reverse the changes in your brain brought on by PDS or rev up other parts of your brain to make do for these injured areas. You've already be-gun that process with the advice and exercises within this book, using the body's neuroplasticity (brain and nervous system's ability to regrow and to rewire) and adaptation (the brain and body's ability to adjust itself). A psychologist can further bring out these brain improvements. In this chapter we'll show you how and why this works and give you some ideas about how to best work with your psychologist. Let's first look at how the how the brain works, what it's doing when it's healthy, and what's hap-pening when it's not.

THE BRAIN: HOW DOES PDS AFFECT IT?

The brain is the most complex structure in the body and more complex than any computer or machine ever developed. It makes the most sophis-ticated computers used by governments and militaries look like children's toys. Like all complex machines, it can easily get off kilter or broken and needs frequent readjustment. Because the brain is so complex and has so many interconnections across the body and even within itself, it's really not accurate to just blame one part of the brain for difficulties you're hav-ing. It's also not accurate to assume that each person's brain is built or wired in the same way. So we'll talk about the way the brain works in a general sense and try to give you an idea of what may happen with PDS and related diagnoses.

There are definite changes that happen to your brain when you develop PDS. These are changes that we can see with special x-rays (functional magnetic resonance imaging, diffusion tension imaging), elec-trical (or neurophysiologic) testing, computerized evaluations, and even simple pen and paper tests. In some cases this may be obvious, such as if you've had a mild brain injury or concussion, where the blast waves from improvised explosive devices and rocket-propelled grenades can cause some really horrific damage to the brain. But, even when the difficulties you're having deal with purely emotional issues or involve pain in a part of your body far away from the brain, there are changes in the way your brain functions, talks to the body and itself, and even the way it looks on tests. We'll give you a basic framework of how to understand your brain's structure and function, so that you will have at least some understanding of what you and your psychologist will be working on.

The simplest way to picture the brain is as an onion folded over like a fist, with millions of two-way connections going in all directions and between all of the layers. The brain can be thought of as having three major parts: the neocortex (new brain), the limbic system, and the paleocortex (old or original brain). The outer layer (neocortex) allows us to consciously integrate with the world, the middle layer (limbic system) allows us to process how our body and brain perceive and respond to the world, and the deep layer (original brain) manages the internal workings of the body.

The neo- or cerebral cortex (also called your gray matter or cell bodies of the brain), plays a key role in memory, attention, perceptual awareness, thought, language, and consciousness. It's what makes us the advanced functioning human beings we claim to be. High-level thinking or executive functions occur in the front part of this neocortex, movement and touch occur just behind this, perception and spatial orientation behind that, and hearing and seeing closer to the back. High-level memory and communication functions are located on either side of this cortex, around the level of the ears. For our discussions, the front-most portion of the neocortex, called the prefrontal cortex, is particularly important in helping to integrate what we perceive all around us with what we know, remember, and feel, so that we can function and interact with the world. This prefrontal cortex and its linkages to the midbrain limbic system are one of the first regions injured with mild brain injury and are commonly found to be abnormal with stress disorders.

The region of the brain just beneath the neocortex is often referred to by the collective term limbic system (a part of your brain's white matter or connecting wires) and has a number of structures that help to integrate the outside world and the inner body. The components of the limbic system have multiple roles, many of which are affected or are malfunctioning with PDS. One role of the limbic system is to help to integrate sensory and motor signals between the body and the brain, so that we can be aware of and use our bodies effectively. Oftentimes, after being in combat or when exposed to trauma, people may complain of problems with coordination, balance, or just general moving around. You may feel slower to react than before or a step or two off your game. That's your middle brain layer not integrating well with the rest of your body and deeper brain structures.

This middle section of the brain also plays an important role in regulating sleep and maintaining an appropriate level of arousal. Altered levels of arousal can be seen with post-traumatic stress disorder (too much), anxiety (too much), pain syndromes (too little), and brain injury (too little). The limbic system also helps to control the numerous brain hormones that affect the body's responses and emotions. These hormones represent one of the direct linkages between your brain and the rest of your body. Probably the most important role of the limbic system for folks with PDS is its responsibility in emotions and long-term memories.

Two key structures of the limbic system, the amygdala and hippocampus, are particularly important in dealing with significant events and stressors and in putting down long-term memories of these events. The limbic system is directly linked by nerves and brain chemicals to all of the organs and parts of the body that may be involved in these emotions. These linkages, particularly the vagus nerve, result in all of the bodily responses (sweating, rapid breathing, fast heart rate, tightening of the gut, bowels, and bladder) to fear and other emotions. Fear response and conditioning (such as with PTSD, anxiety, or pain) are two common emotional issues that the limbic system regulates. The amygdala is the center of emotional memory, emotional learning, behavior, alcohol overuse, and long-term memory development. The other key structure, the hippocampus, plays key roles in long-term memory and spatial navigation. Although the amygdala may house the primary emotional responses to stress or trauma, it requires integration of the stress or trauma experience by the hippocampus to truly recall, be able to process, and clearly remember the specifics of the exposure. Otherwise, you may recall how you felt during your periods of stress (anxious, uneasy, palpitations, short of breath) without actually be able to objectively recall the specific events that initially made you feel that way. This disconnect between how you feel about an event, what you remember about that event, and what you think may be causing those feelings is a common factor limiting recovery. Injury to or disease of the hippocampus, such as with PTSD or Alzheimer's disease, results in memory problems and disorientation as the first symptoms.

The original or paleocortex (also part of your white matter brain or connecting wires) joins all elements of the body, from the nerves receptors of the skin, joints, and the internal organs to the action nerves of the muscles and heart, to the higher centers of the brain, including the limbic system and neocortex. In addition to providing the pathway for all of this sensory data to be transmitted to the higher brain, signals from the brainstem are essential to maintaining the minute-to-minute life functions of the body. The main cells of the vagus nerve are located in the brainstem and any injury or other problem to this nerve can cause issues with regulation of heart, breathing, stomach and intestinal motility, and bladder

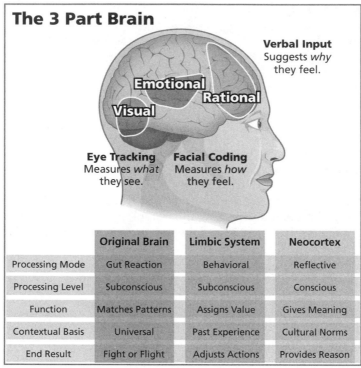

The 3 Part Brain

Verbal Input
Suggests *why* they feel.

Emotional
Rational
Visual

Eye Tracking
Measures *what* they see.

Facial Coding
Measures *how* they feel.

	Original Brain	Limbic System	Neocortex
Processing Mode	Gut Reaction	Behavioral	Reflective
Processing Level	Subconscious	Subconscious	Conscious
Function	Matches Patterns	Assigns Value	Gives Meaning
Contextual Basis	Universal	Past Experience	Cultural Norms
End Result	Fight or Flight	Adjusts Actions	Provides Reason

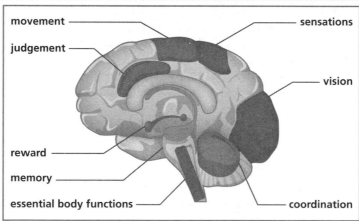

movement

judgement

reward

memory

essential body functions

sensations

vision

coordination

Major components of the brain

functioning. The vagus nerves connect your brain to the largest collection of nerves outside of the brain, the huge celiac plexus, which goes all through your stomach and intestines.

Emotions

It's important for you to have some understanding of how your emotions work. Emotions are chemicals and nerve impulses that wash through the brain and the body. They create the way you feel, put color in your world, and motivate you to act. Without them, we just wouldn't give a damn one way or the other. If they disappeared, then we wouldn't even get up. Apathy would overwhelm us. We wouldn't even feel too depressed to get up. We just wouldn't feel anything. Our emotions are affected and stimulated by things that happen outside of us—a funny joke, an attractive person, a gorgeous sunset, a firefight, a painful accident, an idiot on TV, an obnoxious salesperson, the birth of a child, music that touches us, watching our favorite sporting event. And they are affected and stimulated by things that happen inside of us—the things we eat, drugs or alcohol, body illness, and, most importantly, our thoughts, beliefs, and memories. All these things stimulate our emotions, but we also need to remember *that all our emotions stimulate us*. They stimulate us to think and act in certain ways. It's all part of the way our bodies and brains work. The emotions that we had as infants and children actually determined the way our brains are initially wired. These also determine how our brains are wired now. They determine what we like and don't like, how hard we work or don't work, and how we relate to others. We don't always have to do what they say, but they prod us never the less.

Sometimes these emotional chemicals and impulses are just way too intense. They can burn us. They can blind us. Anger, fear, distress, grief, and guilt can become the only thing we are aware of. Or, they can control us from beneath our awareness. Sometimes they get stuck in a holding pattern, recorded in our amygdala but not processed by our hippocampus or prefrontal neocortex. Long-term moods that won't go away, like depression, can be thought of as a stagnant internal chemical environment or an electrical short circuit. When they become stuck in us or live beneath our awareness, we can become our own worst enemies. We can try to avoid them or just seek relief from them, but that's not the same as understanding what they are trying to tell us or trying to change them. As all of us know, sometimes these emotions are much stronger than anything that's actually happening to us at that moment should warrant. We are walking around mad, sad, or in some other emotional state for no clear reason. They are conditions within us. They are coming from our thoughts, our attitudes, our belief systems, our chemicals, and our internal wiring.

There may be no relationship between what's going on inside and what's actually occurring outside of us in the present.

When we take the time to examine the emotions, the sensations, and the thoughts we are having, we become freer. We have more choice. If we are aware that "emotions are chemicals and impulses" and that they are tied up with our thoughts, we may come to some new perspectives. Our executive function can say: "Whoa, this is some interesting and wild stuff I'm seeing going on in my body and mind. I better take the time here to make sure I'm seeing this situation clearly so I don't do something stupid." Or we might be like one of those logical characters or robots from science fiction and say to ourselves, "Fascinating, there is sadness moving through this biological system that my awareness occupies," rather than saying, "I am sad." Or we might say, "Wow, this thing they call anger is like a burning fluid that streams through the veins of this body I live in. It's very uncomfortable, but it's also very interesting and a wild thing to watch. Maybe I should take a few of those breaths I learned and let it die down a might before I do anything." It's a weird little mental Jujitsu trick that can make all the difference, but it's not necessarily something that comes easy or naturally to us. It's all about freedom and it's one of the healing results of following the steps in this book, especially the ones we are coming to.

BIG PROBLEM

You might have already guessed that there is a big problem here. We want to examine and feel what's happening in the chemicals, impulses, and emotions of our bodies. We want to examine them so that we can understand what they are telling us, allow them to move through us, let them do what they need to do. But, if emotions are chemicals and sensations, which can be deeply painful, and by bringing awareness into your body you will be reactivating these emotions, why in the world would you want to do it? Frequently, a body and mind that's been through hell won't stop feeling like hell. It's hard to live in a body that has been wracked by trauma. Who wants to live in hell? All of those internal chemicals and electrical discharges are still burning. It means your own body does not feel safe to live in. No wonder the oblivion of drugs or alcohol is so attractive. At least they temporarily deaden the pain and emotions. So, we resist feeling things and, in turn, drive them deeper into our body and subconscious. But, remember that these chemicals and impulses we call emotions have, or had, a function. We need emotions to live and prosper. With PDS, they've just gotten channeled into a blind alley or loop. They have overstayed their welcome and we have to show them to the door. But you must first recall and understand where they are coming from, acknowledge them, and learn to live productively with (or sometimes, despite) them. Although all the work of mindfulness and movement will create a body that can really feel, the big problem is that *war creates a body that does not want to feel anymore* or only wants to feel certain things. It is very difficult to enter a body you don't want to be in. But, the good (or bad) news is that you really have no choice; you already live in there. What we need to do is to find ways of being in the body that feel safe, to find little pockets of security, and then expand them. It's a bit like establishing a beachhead in enemy territory from which to launch your next mission.

It is extremely common for warriors with PDS to become sleepy, disinterested, freeze, shut down, or agitated (fight or flight) when starting mindfulness or sensation increasing movement exercises. These are defense mechanisms. You may have already experienced this when trying to do the simple exercises in the previous chapters. This is also common with psychotherapy. We've talked about the body and mind connection, the way the brain works, the nature of emotions, how the violence of war can produce such extreme emotion, and why it so difficult for many returning warriors to deal with the illness of war. Before we show you some of the types and choices of psychotherapy, let's first talk about what role medications may have in your recovery because they are so commonly used after PDS and can often further prepare your body and mind for the healing powers of therapy.

MEDICATIONS

There are hundreds of medication used to treat PDS and the common diagnoses that are part of it. If you've had PDS for any period of time, then you probably are already very aware of this. So, if you are suffering from depression, anxiety, pain, headaches, insomnia, stress, or any other of a host of psychological and physical ailments associated with PDS, there are a host of old and new medications that can help you. Although most of you reading this may not have had the best of success with some of these medications, there are many, many people who respond well to their effects. Even without all of the annoying commercials, medications are big sellers because they help a lot of people. In many cases, they can fairly quickly alleviate suffering with little to no side effects and, when used with care, can be an important part of your recovery process. You may not need them at all or not for a very long time, but if you do need them they are meant to be a stepping stone from illness to wellness. They are not the whole answer, but rather a temporary solution that can help you get your feet on the ground so that you can begin to walk the path of healing. Once you can *keep* your feet on the ground, you may not need them anymore.

Although medications alone will never be the entire solution for PDS, for many of you it could be a way to bring some cooling waters to your emotions or pain or a way to put a little more gas in your tank. The only way to know exactly which medications may be best for you is to find the right doctor for your difficulties, work with them to identify the symptoms you're having, and to see if a specific medication or medications can get you moving in the right direction. The specific types of physicians to seek out and the types of medications that are usually most effective for each of the common symptoms of PDS are listed in Chapter 5. The Internet, e-mail, your neighbor, or even this book is not a substitute for good medical care. It's important to realize that medications are not miraculous; they need to be administered for the right diagnosis, by the right person, in the right way, and for the right period of time. If you are about to begin a medication or are currently taking some, you should make sure you follow the following recommendations;

- Be sure you understand why you are taking a medication and what are potential effects or side effects to watch out for, so you can keep track of how things are working or not working.
- Keep a written or digital log of what your target symptoms are like before beginning the medication and how they are doing each day. Also, record any other affects you notice. Share this log with your clinician.
- Take the exact dose (number of pills, how often, what times) that your doctor and nurse told you—make sure they write it down for you. Make sure you understand how to use the medications before you leave the clinic, hospital, or pharmacy. Taking a higher dose because they are only partially effective may not always be the right thing to do and can even be dangerous, so don't do it.
- Most medications for PDS symptoms will take a minimum of 2 weeks to begin to work and won't have maximal effect until 4 to 6 weeks after starting them, so be patient. If medications are working, do not stop taking them until your doctor tells you to. Some problems of PDS, like depression, must be treated for a full year to prevent relapses. Giving up on medications too early is the most common reason for medication failure and for medication and doctor shopping.
- Figure out in advance when you will run out of medications and make sure you get refills way in advance. Medications don't work at all when you don't take them.
- Most medications that work on the brain will make you feel a bit odd (dizzy, sleepy, disconnected) for the first several days, but this should improve by the fifth day or so. If it doesn't, call your doctor or clinic.

- If the medications don't work well enough for you to want to continue, discuss this with your doctor. Don't just stop them on your own or change the dosing. It can be just as dangerous to suddenly stop a medication, as it is to take the wrong dosage.
- Don't take anyone else's medications or share yours with anyone. It's not only illegal, it's also pretty dumb. If you and your clinician agree that a medication is not for you, then properly dispose of the extra pills (give them to your doctor or ask them how to get rid of them).

I went to this one Doctor at the VA and he kept telling me I was depressed. I was like: Duh! All he did was give me anti-depressants. Then all he did was try to find different combinations that would make me better. But none of them did anything for me. I couldn't feel anything. Well, I guess they kept me from killing myself.

—PFC Lori Stefano

Bodywork

As a way to help jumpstart your body *and* mind's recovery, you may wish to treat yourself to a new experience through *bodywork*, which is likely to both help begin your actual physical mobilization and help prepare you for the benefits of psychotherapy. Bodywork is a term used to describe any therapeutic, healing, or personal development technique that involves working with the human body using manipulative therapy, breath work, or energy medicine. In addition to making you feel great, bodywork techniques also aim to improve posture, promote awareness of the mind–body connection, manipulate the energy field surrounding the body, and improve your overall health. It would be ideal to establish an ongoing relationship with a skilled body-worker or alternative medicine practitioner. They will help you in ways that no one else can. The array of possible styles and philosophies is astonishing, from traditional physical therapy to massage therapy to energy work therapy. You might try acupuncture, Reiki, Tragerwork, or any of the varied styles of massage. Some of these "alternative therapies" are so effective that they are less and less being called alternative and more mainstream medicine. Some of these practitioners are even covered by insurance; however, most are not. Do not let that stop you. Make it a priority. Find the money. Nothing comes close to being as important as your health. Instead of having your truck detailed or eating out at a fast food restaurant, treat your body right. The important thing is to find someone with whom you feel comfortable and see them with some regularity. Just like with psychotherapists, the methods or even credentials can be inconsequential, compared to the presence and sensitivity of the person treating you. Bodywork can be challenging for warriors who are in the defensive mode, particularly when you have PDS. Allowing someone to touch you means that you have to drop any defensive postures. But you need to know that, when you feel ready, it is an extremely important resource for you.

WHAT COMES FIRST: THE BODY OR THE MIND?

With emotions, it's very difficult to figure out which comes first: the chemicals and electrical impulses, or the thoughts and beliefs that accompany them. Sometimes thoughts and emotions mirror each other and, at other times, they don't seem to be connected at all. It's certainly true that if you change the chemicals in the body your emotions and thoughts will change. Exercise alone can do that. It's also true that seeing where your thoughts and beliefs are distorted, and changing them, can change your emotions. Changing either thoughts or actions can change chemicals and changing chemicals can change thoughts. Are exhilarating or depressing thoughts the result of exhilarating or depressing chemicals, or are exhilarating or depressing chemicals the result of exhilarating or depressing thoughts? It's not always clear. We don't know. We do know you can work both angles and should. One of the key principles of this book is that your recovery doesn't require you to choose either a traditional or a nontraditional approach. This blending of approaches will help to lead you to a more complete healing.

Excellent therapists have the ability to shift approaches dependent on what you need in the moment. We are going to talk about a few therapy methods you should be aware of, but let us state the key to success with using therapy in the mission to recover from PDS: If you have been diagnosed with or suspect that you have PDS, **you must find a therapist that you trust and feel comfortable with**.

Although you should choose a therapist based on how well you connect to them and the logistics of getting to actually see them, we have identified four broad psychotherapeutic approaches that would be helpful for you to know about.

1. Cognitive behavioral therapy (or CBT)
2. Byron Katie's approach, known as *The Work*
3. *Somatic Experiencing* and Peter Levine's trauma-oriented therapy
4. Daniel Siegel's interpersonal neurobiology

> **The Two Basic Types of Psychotherapy**
>
> **1. Mind centered, or top down**
>   These approaches use the language and logic of the upper brain, executive function, to correct distorted thoughts and beliefs in order to bring harmonious flow into life.
> **2. Body centered, or bottom up**
>   These approaches work directly with the physical body. They work with sensations and energies in the body to help induce healing. Their focus is on listening into the body for clues to what needs to happen in order to jumpstart the body's natural capacity for self-regulation. Sometimes this can be as simple as getting a massage.

THE STIGMA OF THERAPY

In the past there has been stigma against admitting the need for, and seeking, psychological help. There are still some in the military who think that a soldier who admits that he or she has mental or emotional difficulties, even as a result of war, is weak, perhaps even morally inferior. They think you are supposed to just get over it. We do not mean to be unkind, but that is ignorance of the highest order. Who would dream of not going to the hospital if you had a heart attack? Or, who would not seek out the emergency room in the event of a broken leg? Fortunately, this stigma about seeking help is rapidly dissolving. Knowing you need help and seeking out a therapist is really the sign of a *healthy* mind. If you get drunk all the time, have bouts of volatile rage, get fired from a job, are in the middle of a divorce, can't get your bills in order, and generally feel like your life's a bummer and you don't think you need help, well, that's the sign of another kind of mind. Of course you wouldn't even be reading this book if that was the case, but you get the picture.

Don't get us wrong, we are absolutely for sucking it up and toughing it out. That's what standing up to what's bothering you is. We are actually asking you to tough it out to read this book, to apply its principles, and to maintain the forward march. Like a true warrior, we are asking you to keep going with this mission, even if the idea of something like therapy feels weird to you, even if there are those around you who don't understand, even if you feel like you can handle it, or even if you feel like you want to give up. How you think can determine the quality of your whole life. There is a profound mental component to many of the problems relating to PDS. Suffering itself has a huge mental component. It is how we respond to it that can make all the difference. While working with professionals, as well as in more informal support groups, your response to your PDS and your recovery process is extremely important to your overall recovery. We are guessing that if you are reading this book, your thinking is bugging you as much as your physical ills. The trick to healing is in getting a little distance from your problems by using your mind to look at them. In addition to the psychotherapy we'll be describing, journal writing is an excellent way to do this. Write a thought down. Then ask yourself, is that true? We'll talk more about keeping a journal in the next chapter.

> *You might as well stand and fight because if you run, you will only die tired.*
>
> —Vern Jocque, Sei Shin Kan student

The Therapist's Presence

Therapy is human beings helping other human beings get through suffering. Although there are numerous philosophies and methods, basically, when it comes to human beings it takes one to know one. That's where the healing power is: in actual face-to-face flesh and blood meeting. Our brains are wired and healed in relationship. The simplest form of therapy is just sharing your thoughts and feelings with an understanding friend. That's why talking to a buddy can be so helpful. This book can't do that. It's not a human being. What it can do is give you some insights into how therapy works and why you need to make it an integral part of your healing mission. A good therapist is worth their weight in gold. They have made therapy their life's work because they are interested in what makes us tick and how to help people end suffering. They will help you. It's their job. We want you to consider the idea that seeing a therapist is like going to a dentist, a doctor, a chiropractor, or a podiatrist. It's not a big deal. It's just something you do on a regular basis. You may do it for a long time, maybe your whole life. You may find it's one of the most important things you'll ever do. It's just like having a coach. Remember, even Michael Jordan, Tiger Woods, and Peyton Manning all had coaches.

One more thing about these psychotherapeutic methods: like meditation, they are not fluff. The way you think, and what you believe, and how you use your mind and body change the circuitry and the chemicals in your brain. Remember, that's called neuroplasticity. Actually, the brain is one of the most changeable parts of the body. Over time, even people with profound difficulties from massive brain trauma learn to rewire their brains and learn to have happy functioning lives. Do not give up. Effort over time will yield results. The primary component of all therapy is listening. The most important tools you and your therapist have are presence and empathy. When you begin therapy hold these questions in your mind: "How present am I in this time with my therapist? How present is my therapist with me? How empathetic am I to this therapist, and how empathetic is this therapist to me. Do I feel like I have an ally here?"

What follows can get a little heady. If you don't feel like messing with it right now just check out the guidelines for therapy at the end of this chapter and then skip to the next chapter. We think eventually you'll find this information extremely helpful.

Cognitive Behavioral Therapy

If you have been pondering the questions that we have been posing throughout this book, then you have already been engaging in a type of top-down psychotherapy, called cognitive behavioral therapy, or CBT. Questions, especially if not answered too quickly, throw open the windows of the mind. They help make us open to other possibilities of thinking and being. They help us look beneath the surface of things. Many psychotherapeutic methods use questioning as a primary tool. Questioning reveals the nature of our thinking. Questioning is a primary tool of CBT. Restructuring your conscious thinking and learning to alter your behavior are primary ways of getting through the thicket of PDS. These are direct ways to get your higher brain to tell your lower brain to chill out and stop pushing you around. Seeing clearly that your thinking is distorted or that your behavior may be out of control is extremely important. CBT is the most commonly used psychotherapeutic method for PDS. It is useful in the treatment of traumatic brain injury, PTSD, generalized anxiety disorder, any combination of these diagnoses, and an array of other problems. CBT is like going to school, to study yourself. It is analyzing your own thinking and behavior. It is a training that gives you the skills to think and behave in a rational manner. It helps you see where your thinking is dysfunctional and how to change it. It helps you accept stuff you can't change and do something smart about the stuff you can. It emphasizes that, by changing your behavior, you can change your thinking and feeling. It is an empowering process.

One of CBT's great strengths is that it is interested in the present moment, rather than the past. It is particularly good at addressing specific fears and phobias and learning how to deal with stressful situations like fear of crowds, standing in lines, driving, or in being in situations one can't control. One of its main behavioral tools is something called exposure therapy, where you are gradually exposed to the source of your anxiety. If going to the mall is too much for you to handle, for example, you just drive by it and feel what that feels like first. Then, you park in the parking lot and experience what that feels like. Then, you hang just outside the door of the mall for several sessions. Then, you enter the mall in a series of steps. Each step is done gradually to limit any elevation of your anxieties or fears. You learn to deal with your uncomfortable feelings and eventually they dissipate.

CBT teaches some very useful skills. It particularly suits people with a military background because it is a highly structured and easily measurable method. It is a process of asking lots of questions and making evaluations about how you feel about things. It helps you determine what's bugging you and how severe those bugs are. It is a highly organized plan for examining your emotions, thoughts, beliefs, and actions and how they might be screwing up your life. It is a making sure that what you feel, what you think, and how you act are grounded in reality now, not fantasy, or in something that happened before. With the guidance of a therapist, CBT is a fine tool for healing.

Epictetus: The Ultimate Warrior

You should know the Greek Stoic philosopher Epictetus. He is a favorite of many in the military. He said that what happens to you is a kind of fate you can't do anything about, but how you respond and think about what happens to you is within your control. Therein lies freedom and happiness. Epictetus said that you can decide how you think and how you behave, that you are the master of your interior life. This is a central viewpoint of CBT. Like Epictetus, CBT says you can determine how you feel and behave if you can examine your thinking and behavior rationally. It is a noble proposition. If your therapist is a practitioner of CBT you will go through an entire program designed to help you do just that.

Exercise #21: Taking Inventory

CBT and complete healing definitely means looking at what we think and what we believe. To that end, we recommend taking a thorough inventory of your own thought processes. Ask yourself,

- What are the thoughts in my mind?
- What is my attitude?
- What is the nature of the thoughts in my mind?
- Do I assume the worst?
- Do I blame myself for some of the things that happened in theater?
- Do I blame others?

- How do I feel when things don't work out the way I think they should?
- Is my thinking repetitive? Do I keep thinking the same thoughts over and over again?
- Do I feel that I am not able to control my behavior or that I am stuck in repetitive behaviors?
- Do I have thoughts that just won't go away?
- How do my thoughts make me feel?

Byron Katie's Approach

I discovered that when I believed my thoughts, I suffered, but that when I didn't believe them, I didn't suffer, and that this is true for every human being. Freedom is as simple as that. I found that suffering is optional. I found a joy within me that has never disappeared, not for a single moment.

—Byron Katie

Your healing will also require that you examine your own thinking and belief systems. Just as we don't think as we did when we were 6 years old, we must examine our own beliefs and see where allowing for some change might be helpful. Byron Katie's *The Work* is a very simple but very profound tool that can reveal where your belief system is causing you anguish. Although, again, we stress the importance of a professional therapist to help you engage in this, once you've worked with your therapist, you will find that Katie's approach is simple enough to practice on your own. Katie's approach is another top-down one that consists of four questions, which you can use to challenge the nature of any thought that takes away your sense of peace. It's one of those tools that's easy to acquire, but can take a lifetime to become skilled with. But, with an open attitude, it can be pretty helpful very quickly. These questions are particularly helpful if you can train yourself to ask them whenever you feel unsettled with negative emotions. So here are the questions to ask yourself:

1. Is it true?
2. Can you absolutely know it's true?
3. How do you react when you believe that thought?
4. Who would you be without the thought?

Exercise #22: Byron Katie Questions

First, sit down in your chair or in the quiet place you've set up, do some mindful breathing, and really feel into your body. Take a thought or emotion that may be running through your mind, such as

- I'm alone; no one knows what it was like over there.
- This culture sucks. Everything happening in the U.S. is trivial and stupid.
- I got screwed for nothing. Life is not fair.
- I'm never safe.
- Now that I'm home, nothing matters.
- I'm a failure. It's my fault. I could have done something. I should have (*write in your perceived failure here*).
- Or, any other thought that makes you feel bad.

Now, ask yourself Katie's questions. Really reach down deep and inquire. Is it true? Can you absolutely know it's true? Don't answer right away. Really sit with it. No one is telling you what to do. It's completely up to you how you answer these questions. Ask yourself the next question. How do I react when I believe that thought? What do you feel like inside when that thought shows up? Really sit with it. Now, answer the fourth question and really ask yourself, who would you be without the thought? Consider what your life would be like if the thought that is bothering you just weren't in your mind. Who would you be? There is just the tip of this process. Please refer to Byron Katie's book *Loving What Is*, or check out her website www.TheWork.com for more information.

Subjecting your emotions or thoughts to Byron Katie's questions may seem silly at first, but, her point is, when you are in emotional pain, *the thought is the problem*. As her last question indicates, without that thought, whatever you were feeling in that moment would be very different. The beauty of this work is no one is asking you to do anything except think about it. No one is telling you to change your thinking or to drop the thought, but instead you're being asked to consider what it might be like if you did. What tends to happen if you apply this approach to things is that you begin to realize that your thoughts are creating your life. They are how you see the world. Without them, you'd just be paying attention to what's happening around you right now. You'd be free to just take it all in and enjoy the show. Sure, you could apply your thoughts or emotions to situations when you want to (like when you're amazingly happy to be somewhere), but you'd only have to do that when you wanted to and when it created something positive for you. With time one becomes more able to let go of the thoughts and the feelings that accompany them. You could be taking fear and anxiety out of the system. Then you can just be. Change your thoughts; change your world.

Somatic Experiencing and Peter Levine's Trauma Resolution Therapy

> *Trauma is a fact of life. It does not, however, have to be a life sentence. Not only can trauma be healed, but also with appropriate guidance and support, it can be transformative. Trauma has the potential to be one of the most significant forces for psychological, social, and spiritual awakening and evolution.*
>
> —Peter Levine

Somatic experiencing is a form of therapy, developed by Peter Levine, PhD, aimed at relieving and resolving the symptoms of PTSD and other mental and physical trauma-related health problems by focusing on the client's perceived body sensations (or somatic experiences). It is a bottom-up approach that he based originally on his observations of animals in the wild and how they dealt with and recover from life-threatening situations. By understanding some of the reasons that wild animals can deal fluidly with almost daily life threatening experiences, you can also effectively deal with the traumatization that accompanies PDS. The procedure is done in face-to-face sessions and involves a client tracking his or her own felt-sense experience. Somatic experiencing attempts to promote awareness and release of physical tension that is felt to remain in the body in the aftermath of trauma or stress. These tensions have been aroused in the nervous system, but are not fully discharged after the traumatic situation has passed. Relieving these tensions restores your inborn capacity to self-regulate. There are a number of techniques used to dissipate the physical tensions, including tracking, titration, and pendulation.

Tracking

Tracking involves using awareness to note and monitor the sensations moving through the body in the present moment as well as in relation to past memories. It's labeling the quality of a sensation. It's becoming more deeply aware of all the nuances of sensation occurring within you. Most of the time, when someone asks us how we are, we just say something like okay, fine, or not so good. But, what is the bodily sensation of those statements. What does "okay" really feel like? Does it mean you feel light, energized, calm, or something else? Does it mean your hands feel warm or your mouth is moist? In tracking, you may begin feeling the tip of a finger after you gently push into it. You may next note how the tip contrasts with the rest of the finger. Then, how does your entire hand feel compared to that, and so on. It is only in entering into these sensations in the present moment using mindfulness and then similarly noting the sensations that accompany emotions that we can join with the body and mind in its natural healing process.

Titration and Pendulation

Titration basically means changing little by little. Titration involves initially focusing on barely perceptible changes in the body, such as creating a slight loosening of tension in the muscles of the upper arm and then very gradually building this release to larger and larger areas. It means establishing locations or resources of safety such as familiar, normal sensations, so that you can comfortably visit the memory and, more importantly, the sensation of the traumatic event gradually. This little-by-little swinging between two extremes of feeling, from regulation (the sense of safety and security) to dysregulation (the sense of fear or danger) is called pendulation. This is a place where the earlier breath work you have done can be extremely helpful. It helps create a sense of ease and security. This movement process is done repeatedly and the body learns to discharge the energies that fear or horror can leave in the body. The more the therapist and client do this together, the more the body corrects itself. This work is best done with a professional therapist, but if you can understand why this tracking is important, and learn how to do it, you will become a much more powerful ally in this battle against PDS.

Exercise #23: Tracking

Although the process of tracking sensations or feelings in your body may bring up stored or repressed emotions, it is really about noticing what you feel in your body right now. A little bit of understanding about this process can go a long way. Here's a short example of a possible tracking session between a therapist and our friend Lori Stefano,

Therapist: What are you feeling right now?
Lori: I don't feel anything. I'm tired. This is stupid.
Therapist: What does the sensation of tired feel like?
Lori: Well, I feel kind of heavy, dull maybe. I'm sleepy.
Therapist: What do you notice in your body?
Lori: I don't know. It's just kind of there. (*Pause*) Actually, now that I think about it, my back aches a little bit.
Therapist: What does that ache feel like?
Lori: It's like a brick. It's knotted up. It's really hard. I've been a little numb to it, but it makes it a little hard to breath.
Therapist: Can you say more? What else do you notice?

Lori: Nothing.
Long pause
Therapist: What does nothing feel like?
Long pause
Lori: I guess it feels cold.
Therapist: Where do you feel cold?
Long pause
Lori: I guess in my heart.

This process goes on for a long time, with the therapist being with Lori as she explores her own sensations and the memories and thoughts that arise along with them. There is no agenda. They are just looking together and trusting that what needs to happen will happen. The therapist is helping her look into her inner world. The therapist is also continually monitoring her own feelings. It's hard for Lori because she is numb and, like a lot of us, she has difficulty finding language for all this. Most of us just don't have the vocabulary for sensation besides words like: hot, cold, heavy, light, good, bad. For much of what we are feeling there are no words at all. But if we keep coming back to this tracking we start to hear what the body is telling us. Movement occurs. Things start to shift. We learn and grow. Eventually Lori starts to notice more about what she's feeling and remember more details about what she has experienced. She becomes more comfortable with her therapist and the process and notices that she usually feels different after a session. Sometimes sadder but most of the time more relaxed as if some pressure within her is released. She is gradually feeling more flow in her emotional system and noticing that the therapist is not telling her what to think. She's just curious about what's happening with Lori. She's an ally. They are tracking the movement in Lori together. The hope is that over time Lori's biological and psychological system will become fluid enough to self-regulate.

This approach of feeling into your body shouldn't be new to you. It's similar to many of the practices we have already explored. Our mindfulness practices focused on breath and witnessing internal sensation. Our movement practices helped to loosen, creating space and flow in the body, and thereby increasing sensation. You can use the light of illume to track exactly what you're feeling. So much of the time what we are feeling and what we think we are feeling are not in line with each other. In the terms of somatic experiencing, in PDS all of the charged energy that we used to deal with the life-threatening situation was not discharged. It's still stuck in the body and the brain is continuing to secrete chemicals and electrical signals into your system to deal with a crisis that is not even happening anymore. The upper brain, the prefrontal neocortex where your executive function is located, loses the ability to calm the system down. The three parts of the PDS brain are no longer in communication. As you do these somatizing exercises along with the work of tracking how you feel, you will become much more aware and interested in what you are feeling. As we watch how these feelings move, as we become interested in what is going on with them, a new emotion emerges, a sense of wonder about the whole process emerges. This means that there are always two levels of emotions within us. The one that is traveling through us as a result of history or unresolved trauma and the one that arises from taking an interest in these feelings that are traveling through. There is the emotion, the sensation we *are* watching and then there is the emotion, the sensation, that we get *from* watching. This may seem like a subtle distinction, but it's not. It makes all the difference. That second emotion has the taste of freedom. That interest is pleasurable in and of itself and, whether we remember it or not, it is always an option for us. The emotion that interest creates, in this case a sense of wonder, begins to mix with and transform the original negative emotion. That is empowering and liberating and, more than anything, it increases our tolerance for the negative emotion we are feeling. In that way we are retraining the mind and that's changing the chemicals in the body. By using mindfulness and movement, we can help to discharge the system, take notice of the feelings that arise from this, and create a restored system and positive feelings at the same time. If you think about it, this is probably the most important skill a human being can acquire. Because everything else depends on the way you think.

Interpersonal Neurobiology: Dr. Daniel Siegel's Approach

> *When we feel presence in others we feel the spaciousness of our being received by them. And when we reside in presence in ourselves, others and indeed the whole world are welcome into our being.*
>
> —Daniel Siegel

A complete system of healing must take into account both the top-down and the bottom-up methods. It takes sensation, thinking, seeing, moving, emotions, and how we are in interpersonal relationships into account and learns to bring them together in the way that the brain and body are meant to work. It's the way that highly functioning humans work. Putting all this together makes common sense. It's a lot to understand, but basically, once again, it's about flow. Things aren't working right when there is rigidity (when we are over controlled and can't stop doing the same behavior) or when there is chaos (when we are out of control). Flow feels good. Rigidity and chaos feel bad. The work of therapist Dan Siegel, MD, and his interpersonal neurobiology approach to psychotherapy focuses on creating flow. Siegel's approach moves an individual towards connection, or *integration*, within him or herself and with others. The therapist works with his or her own presence, listening ability, and empathy for the client to help the client understand and create harmonious flow. This lack of flow, this chaos, this rigidity is symptomatic in conditions like those seen with PDS. Siegel's work identifies nine different domains of integration that the therapy and concepts of interpersonal neurobiology can help bring about, which can give you a guide as to ways to look at the your healing brain.

The Nine Domains of Integration

1. Conscious integration: You learn to see what's in your own mind and you learn to direct your attention, to choose what you are conscious of. This is what mindfulness practice does.
2. Vertical integration: You integrate the sensations occurring in your body into your awareness. You are aware of your physical being, from your head to your toes.
3. Bilateral integration: You are aware of and have access to the way both the left and right side of your brain see and organize your world. The left side is great at logic and language. It likes counting, labeling things, and putting things in order. The right side is great at seeing things whole, like a whole picture all at once. It's also the part of the brain where the story of your self is located. It's thought of as the place where creative ideas just show up. We need both sides to work well and to work together smoothly.
4. Integration of memory: You are able to recall in consciousness everything that's happened to you. Memories, particularly traumatic ones, are not buried in your subconscious mind and don't push your buttons every time there is a reminder of them. This is critical since you cannot deal with something that you cannot remember.
5. Narrative integration: You have a sense of who you are, you understand how you have developed over time, and you have the ability to tell the story of your own life in a way that makes sense. You are also aware that you are writing the story of your life as you live it. You are aware of the patterns of your life and how you might be able to change them to create a future you envision.
6. State integration: You become aware of the different states (peaceful, agitated, angry, fearful, relaxed) that move through you in the moment and are particularly aware of those states in which you become unraveled or out of control. You are able to monitor your own state of being and through mindfulness practice and things

like breath awareness are able to have some control over those states. In this way you learn to have control over your actions.

7. Interpersonal integration: You are aware of how you are connected to and affected by other people in your life. You can see how those around you literally change the way energy and information flows in your body. Empathy—the ability to feel and understand the way another person feels—is a big part of this. You have the ability to open yourself and join with others so that there is flow between you. You can fully link to another person.

8. Temporal (time) integration: This is the ability to connect past, present, and future in your own mind and to consider the problem of how temporary life is. It's the ability to see your own self as a changing process through time and that (whatever your beliefs about an after life) this life will one day end. It's also about coming to grips with that.

9. Transpirational integration: You start to feel that all of these other forms of integration are all connected with each other. Your story, your sensations, your awareness of death, the different ways the two sides of your brain work, your shifting inner state, and your relations with others are all breathing together. You also become aware of the infinite ways you are connected to everything else, even things not in your physical locality. You see that your being is composed of emotions (chemicals and impulses), water from a river, tomatoes from California, your grandfather's DNA, old TV commercials, or memories of a dead child or friend in war. You become aware that your warrior's heart and warrior's mind are connected to everything. You are a part of the larger flow of the universe.

We think these nine domains of integration are really important and you should do your best to understand them. Even knowing about them can lift you into another state. If you learn about them, they can help you evaluate where you are in your own psychological healing, and help you cultivate it.

NEXT STEPS

Siegel's work clearly emphasizes how vital it is to integrate all aspects of yourself as well as yourself into the world around you. But all of these approaches, and the many others we haven't discussed, can help you. There isn't really a right or wrong therapy approach or place to start. Remember, it's the actual relationship with your therapist that is most crucial. But your first step has to be to spend time and feel how your emotions play through the body and mind. Sit still and watch. How do your belief systems fit in with all of this? How does the way you move fit into all this? How can you coax the intelligence of the body and the mind to work together for you?

All of these thought and talking activities will lubricate the way emotions move within you. You will feel a whole lot more. Overall, that's a really good thing, but as you've learned it's also a bit of a problem. When what you experience is too much for your system, you will have the urge to either run away or shut down. As much as you might want to tackle these problems head on, your body, your nervous system, and your emotional being may have other ideas. It still wants to protect you even when the threat is just a residual memory. So that's why you have a professional there to help you through this. And that's why it may take some time, maybe even your whole life. We think of therapy as adult continuing education. You're in the process of getting smarter on your way to getting better. You're also getting healthier by doing this, a whole lot healthier. Here are a few guidelines to help with your therapy.

Guidelines for Therapy

1. Go—Do not skip sessions
2. Prepare for your sessions. Practice any exercises you're given. If you have homework, do it.
3. Plan what you will talk about but stay open to what's on your mind at the moment.
4. Before any session you have, practice mindful breathing and go into open attention.
5. Ask you therapist to spend a few moments in mindful breathing with you before you start.
6. Listen carefully to both what your therapist is saying and what *you* are saying. Learn to pause and let what you say echo in your mind.

These psychotherapeutic methods, like meditation, are not fluff. They really work. The way you think, and what you believe, and how you use your mind and body change your brain. Remember, that's called neuroplasticity. Actually, the brain is one of the most changeable parts of the body. Over time, even people with profound difficulties like severe brain trauma or devastating PTSD can rewire their brains and learn to have happy functioning lives. Do not give up. Effort over time will yield results. We guarantee it.

> *It does not matter how fast you go as long as you do not stop.*
>
> —Confucius

All of this is a lot to learn. But, don't worry, if it seems a little overwhelming, you don't have to get it all. All *you* have to do is take one step at a time. You just have to understand that you are in a process of using your own mind, no matter how challenged, to bring yourself together. Move at your own pace. You are becoming a fluid warrior. You *will* get stronger. You *can* change your inner world. You *can* heal. You can do it with mindfulness, you can do it with movement, you can do it with medication, you can do it with questions, you can do it by putting yourself in different environments, you can do it with both traditional and nontraditional methods, you can do it by engaging with others, and you can do it with the help of a professional ally, the therapist. You will know you are getting better when you sense the connection to those around you deepening. Eventually, if you are not already, it will be *you* that is reaching out to help others heal. It's amazing, isn't it, what conscious living beings can do?

9

Creativity: Integrating Health into Your Life

We have looked at mindfulness practice: ways to increase illume, executive function, and awareness in your life. We have talked about Continuum movement: the power of *fluid movement* to bring about both physical and mental healing and to increase your ability to feel sensation. We've stressed the importance of rest, sleep, nutrition, and exercise. In the last chapter we explored the nature of emotion and looked at the way the brain works. We discussed a few approaches to therapy and the importance of engaging an ally, a therapist and/or a group, in your quest to get a handle on your emotions, order your thinking and beliefs, and to learn to discharge any unwanted residual effects of war from your body and mind. All of these things, to various degrees, need to be incorporated into your life. But all of these things do not have to *become* your life. Wellness is the road you are back on and although it's sometimes tough to navigate the road perfectly, it's important that you spend your time enjoying the scenery all around that road. That scenery is what makes your recovery fun and worthwhile.

The scenery of life may not be the final destination for your recovery, but it's some of the reasons why you'll want to stay on that road. What are some of the things that healthy, productive, happy people do with their time that expresses and creates that happiness? For most people, creativity and wellness are synonymous. In addition to being fun and fulfilling, these creative activities can actually also help you to recover. Let's look at creativity, how bringing new things to life—*in your life*—can have a healing impact. Below is a list of creative and life-affirming activities. A complete list of these things would be infinite, from playing poker to cliff diving to astronomy, so we've just listed a few that are easy to engage in and highly therapeutic. If you have a passion, be it golf, locking and popping, yoga, chess, or whatever, and you are able, do it. The activities listed are far better than many of the things many Americans do regularly—like watching TV, surfing the Internet, or video gaming—and all of them will keep your mission moving forward.

- Writing your story
- Sound and music
- Working with your hands (crafts, engine repair, sculpting)

- Humor
- Sex and sexuality
- Sports
- Outdoorsman (nature, camping, gardening)
- Spirituality

PLEASURE

Part of your mission has been to identify things that are pleasurable in your life. You are particularly encouraged to focus on those creative pleasures that won't get you hurt or killed. Although returning to war, fighting in bars, and challenging the world's highest peaks may be a true source of joy for some, most of us would do best to find pleasures in life's simpler (and safer) things. What are the parts your life that bring you the most pleasure? Aside from all this transformative therapy crap you've been reading about here, what are the signs of a healthy, creative, wholesome life? If you want to feel better, a good place to start is by doing creative things that people who feel good are doing. When you do, you will feel best to your core. This chapter concentrates on exploring that creativity.

CREATIVITY AND MEANING

He who has a "Why" to live for can bear almost any "How."

—Nietzsche

Creativity is work and it is play. It's trudging along and it's riding effortlessly. Creativity is natural. It's so natural that every cell in your body is doing it all the time. At each moment some thing is being created. When you are consciously in service to a creation, everything you do has meaning. When you are in service to creating your life, your whole life has meaning. Coming to creativity makes a person feel whole and useful, challenged, charged, and eventually, blessed. It is channeling life force. It is an investment into your present, and therefore, your future. Being in service to something—a team, the squad you were in, your country, your kids, fixing a motorcycle, painting a painting, creating a journal, playing music with others, tying a fishing fly, setting up a space, or sculpting something in clay—makes you a part of something larger than yourself. When we are not always front and center in our lives—when we are concentrated on the task or creation rather than ourselves—we tend to feel more alive, less constricted, and freer. This is one of the things that is so pronounced in war. As hard as war is, you were part of something much, much larger than yourself. That's a hard thing to lose. But it's really not as hard as you might think to get back. It's just that it's not just thrust upon you like most other things in your teenage life or the military; it's a decision you have to make and it's directed from within. Creativity, either alone or with a group, is an immediate way to be of service to something outside your self. It provides an immediate sense of purpose.

One of the fundamental challenges from post-deployment syndrome (PDS) is loss of meaning or purpose. Purpose motivates us. You have to have a reason, and it has to be a good one, to stay with your mission. Without it, depression and despair can win out. The nights seem longer, the pain greater. You are living in the moment or, worse, you are living in the past. You have to see a future for yourself. You have to see yourself going somewhere. You have to know that you can get there, if you apply yourself. You have to know that you matter. You have to be in service to something. It's one of the things the military does for so many, giving deep meaning to life. The purpose and meaning that comes with dedication to the mission, staying alive, and protecting your friends is rarely duplicated in life. Creative activity is a way of generating that level of meaning again.

But creative activity is more than just a way of giving you a distraction or even a purpose—it's also one of the best ways of actually helping yourself to improve. If you have been diagnosed with a traumatic brain injury (TBI) you will find coming to creativity is a highly effective brain developer. It requires that you use your entire brain, including parts of it that you seldom use. In this way, you can not only keep yourself busy, but you are also helping your brain to rewire. The same is true if you have chronic pain. By actually using your body again and identifying a positive reward by doing something you like or have an interest in, you will be helping to rewire the parts of your brain that have associated movement with a bad feeling into a good one. This way your own brain will dampen the pain signals it has been sending to your joints or muscles and instead will even block some of the negative feelings. Accomplishing tasks by creating something positive will help all facets of PDS, from the physical to the cognitive to the emotional. And remember, creativity is not about competition, it's about discovery. It's about making something out of the tools at hand. In the process, we make something of ourselves. We are definitely not interested in your just coping with your difficulties. We want you move past them to become a true fluid warrior. That's not dependent on your skills or on whether you have disabilities. It really only connected to your warrior's heart. Although all of these creative activities are a way to heal, they are so much more than that. They are a way to live. When these activities and practices become a part of your day to day routine, when creative expression is a regular thing, when you are involved in being in and lifting a community, then you have reached the true level of service that befits a warrior. Offering yourself to the world is a way to heal and a way to live.

> **How Creative Am I?**
>
> One of the things you might ask your self is: "Do I spend my free time consuming things—food, alcohol, videos, Internet, cigarettes—or do I spend it creating things?" Consuming things like food or water may be necessary for maintaining your body's health, but beyond that you'll not get much return from it. It's hard to believe that you truly "want" these extra things. You cannot ever get enough of what you really don't want. Creating things on the other hand will give you something that everyone wants—energy, inspiration, and a sense of connection.

I'd go back if I could but I'm just too broken down. I was a damn good Green Beret and I really loved training the younger guys, but I'm getting used to the idea that I need to make the rest of my life work and stop worrying about being a soldier. I was always a pretty good mechanic. I want to open a Harley Davidson repair shop. I just wanna get my act together enough so I can make a living doing something I like. The only time I really feel connected is when I'm working on my Harley.

—Cpl Leon T. Church

TELLING YOUR STORY: KEEPING A JOURNAL

Telling your story and understanding your own life experience is one of the most important things you can do. It begins with telling it to yourself. Keeping a journal is one of the most effective ways to do that. It elevates your perspective. It helps you see things from a high place. It increases illume. Trying to see clearly what has happened to you in the past, what happened to you today, or what is happening in your mind right now is an excellent way of waking up and participating with your own healing. It exercises and integrates your whole brain. Putting your thoughts on paper or dictating them into a tape recorder is like doing mental pushups. It's also a discovery process that will give you more energy than it takes. In psychotherapy, a big part of your healing will come from sharing your story, your thoughts, your inner most self, with someone you trust. But first, you have to share them with yourself. You have to make the attempt to see and really understand what's happened to you and what you think about it all. In the case of something like guilt, you might have to admit things to yourself before you can admit them to anybody else. Journal writing transforms us. If you write about your anger, it is anger "seen." If you write about your grief, it is grief "seen." That changes things.

That's why we are recommending you keep a journal. It's for telling your own story to yourself and for giving you a way to track your own ideas about what happened and about what's happening right now. Journal writing brings the unconscious to the surface. Just like conscious breathing practices bring together the mind and the body, journal writing brings together the conscious and the subconscious. With time, it clarifies our thinking. It integrates the conscious with the unconscious. You'll want to write exactly what's in your mind at the moment you are writing it. If you think it's a stupid idea and a waste of time then write, "I think this is a stupid idea and a total waste of time." It's a fine place to start and, hopefully, will break the ice so you can put down more . . . much more.

You may not consider yourself a writer. You may or may not be comfortable with written expression at all. You may have liked or hated school. Your spelling, grammar, and word choices may not be perfect. We don't care. That doesn't matter. That's not what this is about. No one need ever see it. It's just for you. Just write. This is a process called free writing, where you just right or talk into a tape recorder almost as fast as you can. No censoring and trying to make sense. One way to do this is to see if you can make it so your pen never leaves the paper. This is about looking deeper into your own being. It's about really seeing what's happened to you from a larger perspective. It's even about seeing how your brain does or doesn't work. You may come to see even more clearly that you are not who you were. That may generate more heartbreak for you. But, if you write, if you build your journal, you will also build yourself. As you build your journal, it will build you. It's about becoming aware of what and how you think. It's about leaving your mark.

As you know, sharing your story with buddies who were there with you is a good place to start. In some cases, it can be too horrible to revisit your experiences or there might be profound guilt. You might think they could never understand. This can be really hard and it may take a while for you to be ready to do that. But when you feel like you want to try, put it done on paper or on a recorder, so that you can have a record of what it is that you think you went through. If you have been going to doctors or therapists in the military or the VA, you may feel like you have already told your story several hundred times or so. You may have even developed a tape recording in your head that you play for them. You might even consider it a nuisance. *But have you really told your story to yourself?* Have you written it down or recorded it in some way so that then *you* can look at it? Have you done this in a way so you can see if what you think happened or what you think about what happened is true?

Keeping a journal will help you. It will help you even if you are the only one to ever see it. It will help you if you see a therapist. A therapist may even assign journal writing to you. It will also help you tremendously if you become involved in a support group that relates their stories to each other. Remember though that your journal is yours. What you write in it is for nobody's eyes but yours and it will help you if you only keep it to yourself. It will lift your consciousness. Only share it if and when you want to. When you put down on paper a few thoughts about what happened to you, what you are going through, or what you are thinking about at that exact moment, then you are creating a record of your own mind. You can then sit back and read it over. You can ask

- Is what I wrote true?
- What do I think about what I wrote?
- Is there another perspective I could come to about this subject?

It is a crucial aid when it comes to expanding the mind. If you are incapacitated physically, you might find it will become your ticket to a whole new world. There have been many great writers or thinkers that have been incapacitated. It's very interesting exercise in and of itself. Just the act of writing, regardless of what you actually write, can be helpful. But, it's also something that over time may begin to help you even more by revealing things about yourself and your experiences that you didn't know or couldn't previously remember. It's something that may happen to you right away or in a few days, or it may take weeks, or months, even years to fully discover. Eventually, if you get into it, you will find yourself writing down things you didn't remember before. You will discover thoughts and opinions you didn't even know you had. If you start to develop a real interest in writing, you certainly have something to write about. A lot of young people's main experiences are going to the mall or getting high. You'd be surprised how many writers joined the military for the sole reason of getting life experiences to write about. You've already had that experience. Here's another thing to think about. You may decide to go back to school. This is a part of deciding to do that. Actually, the fact that you have gotten this far in this book means that you are ready for that challenge. Journal writing starts to grease the wheels of that process. What about being in a group of warrior writers? How would that be? The degree to which you become involved in all these processes is a measure of just how far you emerge from the rubble. There is nobility in the choosing.

SOUND AND MUSIC

As is well known, sound has great power over inorganic matter. By means of sound it is possible to cause geometric figures to be formed on sand and also to cause objects to be shattered. How much more powerful, then, must be the impact of this force on the vibrating, living substance of our sensitive bodies.

—Roberto Assagioli, MD

In the middle of everything that has happened to you, we're betting there is one thing that has never let you down: music. Whether it's rap, hip hop, country, jazz, rock, alternative, Emo, classical, or the music of nature all around us, we are guessing that it has stood by you. Even if you were unconscious or really out of it for a time, it waited for you. Even if your nerves were jittery and loud sounds were intolerable for you, music sat next to you. It has been waiting for you to return to it. Returning to it is more than just pleasurable, it is also extremely therapeutic. Music can be a healing fluid. It is healing when you immerse yourself in the music that other people create. It is even more healing when you create your own music. It is a friend and it is a way to make friends. When you are in pain, music can soothe you. When you are depressed, music can lift you. When you are recovering your ability to concentrate, music can instruct you. Music is a type of food or nutrition. It replenishes your spirit. It moves you and rejuvenates your body. It brings you into a relationship with yourself and with others. It can carry you off to distant places and, at the same time, it can bring you fully to the place you occupy at this very instant. Never underestimate music's ability to transform you.

Music is rhythmic sound, which is formed when vibrating air molecules move the ear drum, which vibrates the small bones of the inner ear. Those vibrations are converted into electrical impulses that are transmitted through the vestibulocochlear nerve to multiple layers of the brain. These impulses are eventually conveyed as other impulses and chemicals that wash through the brain and affect everything that is going on within you. Music does not just *color* your world; it *is* your world. Even on an unconscious level music affects us, it can change our heart rate or breathing patterns just by its rhythms. But, when we pay attention and join in with the sounds and rhythms driving the ear, all the cells in our body start to work in consort.

With just a little help from your executive functions in your prefrontal neocortex to make a conscious decision to focus completely on and to participate fully with music, it can involve your whole body and your whole mind. Remember, bringing your entire being on line to move in harmonious flow is one way to unscramble the body and mind that has been fragmented by war and trauma. It is this loss of flow, this loss of our normal *rhythm*, and this loss of a connection to the moment, that is so disorienting, so isolating, and so painful. Music has the power to unify us again. It unifies the body with the mind and it does so by pulling in our heart. It unifies people. Think about it, from gospel churches to rock concerts to halftime shows to African villages and Irish pubs, music creates community. In the long run, healing and wellness are not just about alleviating pain, they are about experiencing a sense of belonging. We hear again and again that the sense of camaraderie and belonging is one of the best things about military service. If you're looking for yet another way to bring that to your life outside of the service, look no further than music. In this regard, music leads the way to that reconnection.

The strength of music is not fully effective, however, unless you actively participate in its production. Although listening or tapping your feet to it is enjoyable, and dancing to it can be both inspiring and physically rewarding, it is the actual production of the sounds and harmonies that holds the full power of music. Unfortunately, in this country we live in a culture of musical haves and have nots. Some people play and other people only listen to music. We think that's sucks, it's just not the way it needs to be. Everyone has a heart that beats in rhythm, lungs that expand and contract to the beat of your life, hands or feet that can clap or stomp, and a mouth and vocal cords that can make sounds. If you are conscious, you can participate in music in some way. If you have already played music in your life, you can recapture its joy. Don't be concerned if you feel that you have lost some or all of your musical ability. It doesn't always have to be concert hall or CD quality music to be a healing force. Music doesn't care. Just start where you are. Starting where you are is the same advice we give those who are new to musical creation. You are fortunate to have a lifetime of learning and discovery ahead of you.

Exercise #24: Basic Music

You can bring creativity into your life right now, in this very instant. Try this little exercise to take simple counting and turn it into a true rhythm.

- Count 1-2-3-4, 1-2-3-4, 1-2-3-4, 1-2-3-4 . . .
- Now try and come to rhythm, by putting emphasis on the first number ("1") of each foursome.
- Count **1**-2-3-4, **1**-2-3-4, **1**-2-3-4, **1**-2-3-4 . . ., until it gets steady.
- Okay, now keep doing this but try adding a tap from your foot or hand each time you say the "1," **1**-2-3-4, **1**-2-3-4, **1**-2-3-4, **1**-2-3-4 . . .
- Now, move your head forward with each "1" as well, **1**-2-3-4, **1**-2-3-4, **1**-2-3-4, **1**-2-3-4 . . .
- As simple as that, you're starting to make music.
- Make sure your entire spine is involved (remember the dragon exercises).
- Listen and move to music every chance you get. Live or recorded. Really get into it. Do not sit there like a bump on a log. Move your whole body.

This leads us to thinking about what type of music you can use, how to become a part of it, and how to use it to personally reengage your healing systems. Let's look at three types of music:

1. Music you listen to.
2. Music as an environment to be and move in.
3. Music you participate in.

Music, like all art, covers the entire range of human expression, from love to hate and everything in between. Some music excites us and some music soothes us. If you are a back from war, it is more than likely that soothing music is what will help you most. If you are suffering from the effects of post-traumatic stress disorder (PTSD) or anxiety where your brain and body can't get out of overdrive, we are certain that soothing music is what you need. On the other hand, more activating rhythms may be more appropriate if you are in need of stimulation or motivations, such as after a brain injury or if you have bodily pain and can't get moving. Simple rhythms with light themes may be easiest to appreciate and relate to at first. As you progress, more complex pieces with deeper themes imbedded within them may help you to not just get inspired, but actually to grow your brain's and body's complexity.

Exercise #25: Vocalization: Sounding

Here's another really simple exercise to use your voice and breath to make sound and then music. If you are with others, or even if you're alone, this may make you feel embarrassed or even silly. Even worse, you may think you sound horrible. Get over it. Push through it and give it a real try. Do you really want a vibrant life? Weren't you that solid 21st-century warrior who could do anything? Have you become a wuss? All we're talking about here is making some simple sounds, not singing karaoke. Just give it a try and get it going on.

- Enjoy a few easy breaths, in an out. Feel your body and mind ease.
- Now, lengthen your out breath and make a breathy "haaaa" sound. Haaaaaaaaaaaa.
- Just keep breathing in and out, letting this sound come with each out breath. Haaaaaaaaaaaa.
- Haaaaaaaaaaaa (breathe in), Haaaaaaaaaaaa (breathe in), Haaaaaaaaaaaa . . .
- Now, enlist your vocal cords to actually start to sing Haaaaaaaaaaaa each time or every other time. Try singing all the different vowel sounds: A, E, I, O, U. Sing one long easy tone on each out breath. Try to make the sound as smooth as possible. Feel the vibrations coming from your vocal chords as they spread through the tissue that surrounds them. Over time, you will strengthen your breathing and the vibrations will become pleasant and feel like a light massage. You will discover that you will become more and more resonant.
- Play with it a bit and have some fun. It may even start to sound pretty good (or not). Don't worry, Simon Cowell ain't listening

Rules of musical engagement:

1. Make listening to music, especially soothing music, a part of your day.
2. Use soft soothing music as a backdrop to your mindfulness and movement activities.
3. Sing easy long notes for a few minutes every day. Any vowel sound will do: A, E, I, O, U (and sometimes Y). If this is new, remember you will get better. Be curious.
4. Please find and join some type of music group. Drum circles, garage bands, choir, singing rounds with your kids.
5. Do not be intimidated by your lack of musical experience.

Have you ever seen sound vibrations in a glass of water sitting on a loudspeaker? Sound vibrates the fluid in our bodies as well. Vibration is a very refined type of movement that decompresses tissue and increases flow. It travels through water, tissue, and bone. Sound is the most delicate surgery there is.

Humming: Getting Your Brain in the Act

One of the main difficulties in PDS is that there is disconnection or lack of integration between the world and your brain, your brain and your body, and even the different layers of the brain. The workings of the lower or paleocortex have become separated from the middle limbic system and the upper neocortex. Real brain, body, and environment integration has either never occurred or has become undone by the psychological and physical traumas and stressors you've been through. The different regions of the brain cannot communicate with each other and with the outside world. One reason is that the brain's chemicals, signals, and even its source of nutrition and oxygen, the cerebral spinal fluid, are not able to flow where it is needed. Flow and connection are not working properly. Because communication has been disrupted, the lower brain is frozen or stuck in a gear, and it's usually stuck in fifth gear. It can't stop releasing the hormones needed in fight or flight and the upper brain can't signal it to knock it off. Although this causes some of you to be always amped up, hypervigilant, and ready for action, in others of you there has been a near total shut down despite the firing patterns, like the emergency brake is on and the wheels are smoking. Your brain's clutch is jammed, your transmission is busted, or your emergency brake is locked on. That's one reason why we advised you against trying to fix some of your car's problems alone in the last chapter. It's time to repair this flow and link the processes occurring inside you.

You may also recall from our earlier discussion on how sound acts upon the body, that sound vibrates fluid, and in doing so permeates and relaxes tissue. In doing so, sound can create more space and encourages greater flow both literally and figuratively. Especially when that sound can originate close to the source of the problem, when making the sound involves conscious intention and when that sound is homemade, organic, and basic. These types of soundings and the sensation of vibrations they create can also bring attention into the area that is vibrating. Humming is one way to make basic sounds and music that can be felt through the skull (the jaw bones is actually one of the brain's major ways of picking up sounds) and heard through the ears simultaneously. It not only is easy to do and feels good, it may also provide some direct stimulation to the deep structures of the brain (called the brainstem), while at the same time being recorded through the ears into the neocortex. It may be a way to flush out your transmission, unstick that clutch, and release the parking break all at once. Give Exercise #26 a try and see how it feels.

Exercise #26: Humming

- With your mouth closed, begin humming one sound in an easy and relaxed manner. You are going to be doing this for a while, so try and feel comfortable doing it. Mmmmmmm, Mmmmmmm, Mmmmmmm.
- Feel how your lips and face vibrate. If you can't feel the vibrations right away, that's ok. Just keep at it. Keep humming. Mmmmmmm, Mmmmmmm, Mmmmmmm.
- While continuing to hum, gradually press your tongue into the roof of your mouth. Slowly let your tongue slide back along the roof of your mouth until it's as far back as you can get it, without straining the muscles at the base of the tongue.
- How does it feel to you? If your tongue cramps up, bring it forward a bit until it's more comfortable. Can you feel the vibrations going through your jaw?
- Mmmmmmm, Mmmmmmm, Mmmmmmm. Keep doing this for as long as it feels comfortable.

The tongue channels the vibration from your vocal cords directly into the base of the skull to the deep paleocortex and brainstem. At the same time, the humming sound your neocortex is sensing through your ears is soothing. This has a much more powerful effect than you think it would. The trick is to suspend your judgment about it, get into it, and really put some time into it. It's a type of meditation, too. As well as perhaps activating the brains fluid system, you are also becoming acquainted with the sensations inside your own head.

Without a doubt this tongue-humming thing was the goofiest thing we did. All the guys were laughing like crazy and nobody was taking it seriously. At least it was funny. One guy just got up and left. He was kind of an A-hole any way. The second day was the same. But the third day I had gotten used to it and I decided to really give it a try. When we finished I really felt different. I don't know exactly what happened but I felt better. After that the whole group got into it. It was like being in a river of sound. It was really interesting the effect it had on everybody.

—Cpl Tim Owen

Drumming

Sound and music is a part of your human inheritance. In some other cultures, the idea that some of us would not be part of the musical celebration would be considered a societal sickness. In Tibet there is a saying: *He who does not sing every day is dead.* Sing or play one note, then another. You are making something up. Whistle or hum a tune. Become interested. If we've said it once, we've said it one hundred times: coming into healing is coming into flow. A primary way of coming into flow is to come into rhythm. Coming into rhythm in community brings in our whole nervous system and brings us to integration. It gets us in rhythm, even if we don't think we can get in rhythm.

Drums are a traditional, but forgotten, part of a warrior's path. Tribal cultures like the Native Americans used drums and rhythm to take warriors into and out of battle. Drums have the power to fire us up and to cool us down. In some parts of the world, warrior culture is synonymous with rhythmic culture. Drum corps have traditionally established the cadence of the fighting warrior, even in our modern American forces. Although many aspects of the modern world and modern warfare may be different, the human body is not. It is still powerfully moved and healed by rhythm. If you have not experienced the power of a drum circle in full flight, then you are in for a profound and profoundly healing experience. Nothing lifts the spirit, integrates our body and mind, or fosters community in quite the same way. There is great passion and power in a drum circle.

A drum circle is not about being a professional musician. Mickey Hart, famed Grateful Dead drummer and internationally renowned drum circle advocate, calls them community rhythm parties. Research has shown that drumming in community has powerful therapeutic benefits. Here's what music therapists know about drumming:

- It reduces tension, anxiety, and stress
- It helps alleviate pain

- It releases endorphins, the body's pain blockers
- It boosts the immune system
- It helps to release feelings of all types
- It can soothe emotional trauma
- It creates a sense of connectedness with self and others
- It gives us a sense of ease by allowing us to ride natural rhythms of life
- It creates flow in the body

Coordinating both hands on a drum coordinates both halves of the brain. Bilateral integration is a crucial component in overcoming PDS. Do not worry if at first you feel inhibited or don't feel like you are very good at it. Just do it as often as you can. You will start to notice subtle and then profound changes in your state of mind, your ability to concentrate, and your balance. You will flat out feel more alive. There are very few things that will obliterate a sense of isolation faster than being a part of a drum circle. Drumming is a blast. Drumming with a bunch of Vets is pure warrior joy.

Give yourself an introduction to drumming with Exercise #27.

Exercise #27: Drumming

- Get a drum. Get a conga, djembe, dumbeck, frame drum, or some such beast. It can be as simple at first as a coffee can. Eventually you'll want to get a drum that you easily hold and feel comfortable wit. One that allows you to feel its vibrations on your body, such as an Irish drum or bodhrán, is ideal.
- Sit down and find a comfortable way to hold the drum.
- Breathe and rub your hands along the head of the drum. Really check it out. Don't sound the drum just yet.
- Move your arms and roll your shoulders. Hold the palm down and pretend to dribble a basketball. Feel the whole arm move and feel a light whip-like motion in your wrist as you dribble the imaginary basketball. The trick is to enjoy a flowing motion with the whole arm. Your wrist and elbow should move freely.
- Begin sounding the drum. Try one hand and then the other. Strive to get a full resonant tone by bouncing your hand off the middle of the drum head. Really get into the sound of it. Don't worry about rhythm just yet. Just enjoy being with the drum and the sound that it makes.
- When you feel comfortable try this rhythm. Count out loud 1-2-3, 1-2-3, 1-2-3, 1-2-3, slowly and evenly, emphasizing the "1."
- Then play on the "1" and the "3" with your dominant hand and the "2" with the other hand.

- Now start playing with the "3" beat. The "1" stays accented. Assuming your right hand is your dominant one, the rhythm should go like this. Right-**Right**-Left-Right-**Right**-Left-Right, 3-**1**-2-3-**1**-2-3. The sound is Ba **Boom** Du, Ba **Boom** Du, Ba **Boom** Du, 3-**1**-2-3-**1**-2-3. This rhythm imitates the sound of your heart beat.
- Put your left hand on your chest and see if you can feel your heart beat. Keeping your left hand over your heart, keep playing on **3** and **1** with your right hand and mimic the sound and rate of your heat beat. Feel and play. Do this until you feel you are in a simple comfortable groove. It's a good place to start.
- You might also just put on some of your favorite music and see if you can drum along. That's always fun and will allow you time to practice.

Check out YouTube for hand drumming videos and lessons. Play along. We really want you to find a drum circle, but this is a start.

HUMOR: IT IS A LAUGHING MATTER

- Is laughing fun?
- Is laughing one of the reasons life is so cool?
- Do you think laughing might be good for your biology?
- Do you think we are dorks for asking you these obvious questions?
- Does the Pope wear a funny hat?
- Does a bear shit in the woods?
- Does the bear shit in the Pope's hat in the woods?

Author and doctor Norman Cousins claims to have cured himself of cancer in the 1960s by only watching funny movies, mostly *Three Stooges* movies, actually. Recent research has shown that genuine mirthful laughter affects your body's hormone levels. It has a direct affect on your body's cortisol levels. Cortisol is a hormone that we produce in tremendous amounts when we are in acute stress to prepare our bodies for impending or just occurred calamity. It's part of the fight or flight response we've talked about. It's also elevated when we've been under stress for long periods, such as with PDS. Although your body absolutely needs it during an acute trauma or crisis, it's actually disadvantageous when elevated for long periods of time. It's like that stuck transmission or clutch we spoke of earlier. Lowering cortisol levels by lowering perceived stress has also been shown to be associated with a boost in your body's immune system, which lets you then better handle diseases and infections. So humor is the way to go. Even the physical act of laughter causes tremendous movement and breath. It's possible that the medicine of the future may consider humor one of its primary tools. Ask Dr. Patch Adams of the Gesundhite Institute, he's got a prescription pad full of jokes. The entire institute is based on using humor as a source of healing.

We don't really need any research to tell us that laughter makes us feel better, because we can feel its effects instantly. We know you know this about laughter, everybody gets the concept. We are just reminding you that it's not only okay to smile and laugh, it's really good for you, and your doctor has ordered it! We are encouraging you to make it a goal, a daily activity. We tend to think of laughter as a spontaneous unplanned occurrence, but humor, laughter, and lightness of spirit, like every other human condition, is cultivatable. Consider the comedy writer who makes the funny bone his or her primary concern, the comedian who actively tries to elicit laughter, or the comedy club junkie who is actually a connoisieur of laughing.

Please watch funny movies, standup comics on the Internet, and upon waking each morning think of something funny and laugh out loud. Or better yet, tape a note to your bathroom mirror that says: "What's so funny, Bozo?" Keep that question in your mind until you discover something that is. No, you're not allowed to talk back to the sticky note, "Nothing's funny you idiot, I'm totally screwed by war." If you can honestly find an answer to that question, can give yourself permission to do so, and realize that there really is always something funny, then you will feel better. Get a tattoo that says, "I laughed my ass off and all I got was this stupid tattoo." You might want to make it a temporary tattoo, at least at first. But this should be ingrained into your routine. There is even a movement in Yoga called Laughter Yoga, complete with a laughing guru. In *Laughter Yoga* people get together and basically fake laugh until it becomes so funny that real laughter comes upon them. The proponents of this practice unanimously claim that it has improved their lives. Think about it, all that energy, all that blood flow, all that internal movement, all that fullness of involvement, and all that shared community over something as simple and easy as laughter. You know doggone well that it was one of the best things about being with your buddies.

It may be that the ability to laugh and particularly the ability to laugh at one's self are two of humor's most freeing and healing powers. People can get really good at laughing. It's infectious. Take a moment and think of some of the funniest things that have happened to you at least twice a day. Feel free to really laugh out loud. Better yet, try and describe it to a friend or family member. See if you can get through the telling without totally cracking yourself up each time. If you need to, supplement that with a truly funny book passage or video clip. Don't save humor of laughter up for a special occasion or day of the week. Every day is good humor day.

I am thankful for laughter, except when milk comes out of my nose.
—Woody Allen

SEXUALITY

Sexuality and its accompanying physical sensation is one of the most direct experiences of life force we can have. It is the sap rising up within us. When we see a beautiful woman or a handsome guy (or both, whatever works for you) and experience the internal pull, we are feeling elemental forces of the universe at their most urgent and enjoyable. From a biological perspective, there is a lot going on. Your blood vessels are dilating, your pupils are widening, your lungs are bringing in more oxygen, your intestines tightening up, your heart is pumping more blood, and that's just the beginning. Not the least of all, your brain is focusing maximal attention on the moment. You are engaged, hopefully fully. Very few things in life hold us, and our bodies, in more rapt attention.

When we are freshly in love, our immune systems are at their peak. The body is awash in *oxytocin*, the love hormone. The urge to promote new growth is a concentrated life force. The experience of sexuality and sensuality is our own biology telling us that whatever *we* might think we actually want, *it absolutely* wants this. It's also usually what *we* want. For a moment, let's set aside all the moral implications, all the right and wrongs of sex, and just look at the biology and psychology of sex. Birds, bees, urges, and life begetting life.

- Is there something that sexuality has to teach us about healing?
- Is sexuality something that manifests because we are at the top of our health game, like 19-year-old college students on spring break?
- Is it possible that physical intimacy can create, as well as express, health?
- Can it be possible that making a decision to move toward the expression of sexuality in one's life is another resource; another means of jump-starting life force?
- What if sexuality, breathing, and illume were all brought together in a conscious unfolding?
- What do the feelings, sensations, and accompanying movements of *sexuality* have to teach us about healing?
- What do the feelings, sensations, and movements of *love* have to teach us about healing?
- Which comes first, the health that allows us to feel, experience pleasure and express physical love, or is it that choosing to express physical love for someone (even when it is difficult) might be priming the pump to the well of healing?

Don't get us wrong, sex is not, outside of the intention to procreate, a utilitarian act. We can run into trouble when we think of it that way. But, the obvious connection between sexuality, the physical acts of sex, and the road to wellness should ignite your curiosity. Young, healthy, vibrant beings are teeming with the substances, urges, and thoughts of sex. Why should they have all the fun? Enjoying sex is a whole body, whole brain, and whole being experience.

But, make no mistake, this is a tough subject. Intimate human relations involving sexuality can be a minefield even for those who are healthy and fully functioning. It's like playing with fire. Sex can warm you inside and make you feel special, or it can burn you to the core and make you feel like dirt. It's an area where shame, a sense of rejection, or the inability to connect with others can be quite painful. We know that if you have been wounded, suffer from TBI, have been diagnosed with PTSD, are in pain, or are depressed or anxious, then there may be a loss of desire, and sex might be the last thing on your mind, or even the source of tremendous heartbreak. Your sexuality and sex may be something with which you have a troublesome relationship. There are numerous reasons why it might not be an avenue open to you. That's okay for now. One of the goals of this program for PDS is to make you want to return to it. We bring it up because it is one of life's most profound experiences and, as one possible component of your healing practices, it is a great way to express yourself physically. If not now, perhaps in the future. Touch and human intimacy are both sources of healing and sources of heartbreak. But, even inquiring into the implications of sexuality may bring you wisdom about what constitutes a healing, or a healed, life. We are not pushing this; we are just putting it out there as a possibility. If sexuality is an option for you, we'd like you to consider what role it might have for you in bringing about healing. What would it be like to bathe in this healing elixir with some regularity? Sexuality has the most potential to bring about healing when we are the most conscious. So if this is an avenue for you, we encourage you to do some breathing, mindfulness, and movement practices with your partner before, during, and after your time together.

SPIRITUALITY

This is a big one, as big as they get. It's also a tricky one and one that can often offend more than help. It's so big and so tricky, we're not even gonna try and cover it directly, although in one sense it's what this whole book is all about. It's also what the world's scores of religions are trying to come to grips with. So, if you're a part of one, take full advantage of all it has to offer. Use this book to supplement the positive messages you get from your faith and spirituality. If you're not part of any organized religion or don't feel particularly drawn to the notion of spirituality, use this book in any way that seems to fit who you are. Returning your body and mind to its natural state of flow and fluidity may be all you truly want. It may be all you need. That may be a type of spirituality unto itself.

Creativity on the Internet

Unless you are doing school, paid or volunteer work, you are using your computer to create something or you are spending scheduled time each day time having a huge laugh, then time spent on the Internet is not time well spent. Time spent there is time spent outside of living flesh and blood community. As part of your new recovery mission's schedule in Chapter 10, you will not find time for surfing the Web or gaming.

SPORTS AND OUTDOORSMAN

There's nothing that is better for body and mind than to actually use it in a challenging and interesting way. Although it's important to always be monitoring your body for its ability to safely withstand and prosper from physical or competitive activity, pushing yourself a bit and returning yourself to exercise, sports and outdoor pursuits will help your body to return to normal functioning and allow you to figure out just what your limits and abilities are. It is also a key component of fully reintegrating your body and mind, the various components of your brain, and your brain to the outside world. And, it's a great way for you to re-engage in community, whether it is a community of other team players, a community of hunters or fishermen, or the community of nature itself. If possible, include key members of your family and support system in some, if not all, of these activities. And, also try to be mindful of a common habit of using these activities to hide from your problems or your family. Sports and outdoor activities must be part of a fully integrated program of recovery, not the sole answer. Use all of the elements of wellness that are outlined in this book to incorporate the skills of question, breathing, and movement into your pre-athletic ritual. While you're enjoying the outdoors, use your illume to see how you're feeling, use some of the psychotherapy techniques you've learned with your counselor while you're outdoors enjoying a warm afternoon fishing on the lake. What better time to integrate all of these resources than when you're enjoying a creative expression of sports, the outdoors, music, writing, or just having a good laugh with your friends?

Similar areas of creative activity that entail interacting with nature and, at times, the outdoors include gardening, horticulture, animal husbandry, and keeping pets. Each of them involves using your body and mind in a highly constructive way while focusing on something outside of you and your needs. Raising and caring for plants—whether for the purposes of producing food, growing flowers, or just maintaining vegetation, shrubs, and trees—is an ideal way to productively and creatively remain active. Although each of these types of horticulture require dedication and time, the pressures of doing so are minimal and the rewards are often tangible and attainable. It is also an activity that may be done on a small scale or even indoors, but as your interest and skills grow, the activity can also grow. A good place to begin might be volunteering to be a part of a formal or informal cooperative of gardeners that allows you to provide your services for a few days a month, or perhaps to take a course in one aspect of horticulture and provide some volunteer services at a local park or even in your neighborhood. With time and experience, your skills or interest may increase to the point where formal employment or money making opportunities may arise. Similarly, breeding, training, or just keeping animals can be extremely rewarding, relatively low pressure, and highly variable in the intensity of time and effort. Considerable research has shown that caring for or simple being near domesticated animals provides both physical and psychologic benefits. As with horticulture, the amount of time, physical and cognitive abilities, and the commitment needed to care for animals can be varied to what you can offer and increased or decreased over time. A number of volunteer opportunities exist in the care of animals, too. These include volunteering weekly at a local animal shelter or veterinarian's office. The most important aspects of the areas of both animal and plant care is the range of opportunities, the flexibility of the hours and commitment, and the intrinsic integration that occurs during these activities.

BE CREATIVE

There's no right, wrong, or better way to return to pleasure through creativity. As a way to move from the turmoil and struggles within you to the activities of the world around you is, little can beat the joys of creative arts and activities. On another layer, the positive physical, intellectual, and emotional stimulation that is brought to your mind and body by these activities helps to create flow that enhances the fluidity and connectedness that are the signs of a healthy functioning human being. So use these activities to not just improve your life but to actually *become your life.*

10

Resuming the Productive Mission: Basic Training

Action is the foundational key to all success.

—Pablo Picasso

If you've come this far, we think you're pretty serious about taking on this mission and are getting some idea about how to go about this healing business. But it's just an idea; you haven't taken the training. It's not part of you yet, not in your bones or soul. It's more like a catchy jingle that's running through your head, like you've seen the "Be all you can be" or the "Army Strong" ads on TV, and it's gotten you all pumped up. You are standing at the recruiter's door, but you don't really know what's in store for you. You don't really know squat about healing, but you're interested in the concept. If you're buying what we're selling, or even if you're still not sure, now is the time to take the leap, to put action before words or thoughts. What follows is a 12-week basic training program to become a fluid warrior who is marching down that recovery road. Now it's about commitment and discipline. It begins with a question and an act of will. What are you made of and what do you want?

The achievement of your goal is assured the moment you commit yourself to it.

—Mack R. Douglas

PERSONAL MISSION STATEMENT

Your first challenge and assignment is the creation of your personal mission statement. A mission statement is a short written declaration of your intention, your goals, and the principles you want to live by. It is a primary act of your executive function and will help guide you to the life you want. A mission statement's power to energize arises when you ponder it, create it, and refer to it on a regular basis. Creating and having a mission statement is like waking up in the morning and saying to yourself:

> Given the reality of my life circumstances, what is important to me, what are the principles I want to live by, and where do I want to go? What do I want to do with this new day?

Time spent in forethought, figuring this out, will help you to make a commitment and put all of your energies into your mission, which saves you time later on and demonstrates decisiveness. Mission statements create clarity, and clarity is a sword that cuts right through the world's and your own bullshit. They establish guidelines and destinations. Without a destination, there is nothing to steer toward. It's like you're just being blown by the wind without a rudder. Hell, even if you had a rudder, it still wouldn't matter, since you don't know where you're going. We have suggested that your *new* mission is to heal, to become a fluid warrior. That needs to be where your energy is placed first. But, it has to be something you want, not something we want. It has to come from within you. You must put it in your own words. Creating a mission statement that summarizes your plan and then implementing that plan, means that you, and nobody else, are in command of your life.

How do you write a personal mission statement? Start by writing down what's important to you.

- What are your values?
- What are your dreams?
- What *were* they?
- Are they different now?
- What do you believe in, or not believe in?
- What kind of life do you want?
- What are your goals?

The first few pages of your journal are a great place for this. Don't worry about anybody seeing it or about making it look good, just slop it all down the best you can. It doesn't even have to be whole sentences. You can always tear it up or maybe decide to frame it later. That doesn't matter right now. The point is to get started. Write a few sentences to activate your prefrontal cortex and then rest and think. Then, write some more. If you have had a traumatic brain injury (TBI) or have been diagnosed with post-traumatic stress disorder (PTSD), this may be difficult for you. But, if you have difficulty concentrating hard, generating clear thoughts, or even writing things down easily, then this step of developing your own mission statement is even more essential. If you need help doing it, find a friend or loved one to help you. Go to your therapist or to your support group to get some ideas. Better yet, find a quiet or inspiring place and just spend some time thinking by yourself. Imagine your future. Allow yourself to imagine it both positively and negatively, but steer your mind toward the positive. What kind of life do you want to lead? Think principles. As you continue to write, distill some of your thinking into a few simple, forward leaning positive sentences. Eventually you will start to formulate a mission statement. Here's what one looks like.

- It is my mission to appreciate simple stuff.
- It is my mission to cut right through the crap, mine or anybody else's.
- It is my mission to feel better.
- It is my mission to control my anger.
- It is my mission to regain my strength and confidence.
- It is my mission to return to active duty.

Or,

- I intend to do everything in my power to heal so that I can be the father to my son that my father never was for me.
- I will stop drinking and go back to school and learn a trade that can earn me a living.
- It is also my mission to help my fellow soldiers.

Or, simply,

- It is my mission to take and complete the fluid warrior basic training in order to heal.
- I vow to do it for my family, my country, my God, and myself.

For more on mission statements check out the book *7 Habits of Highly Effective People* by Steven Covey, he's the master. This mission to become a fluid warrior is just a stepping stone. This is your opportunity to decide where this stepping stone will lead you. You will work on and refer to your mission statement often during this basic training.

GEAR FOR THE TRAINING

Please obtain the following items before beginning this training:

- A blank notebook to be used as a journal.
- A simple quiet space with a chair, a surface to write on, a floor area large enough to stretch out on, some floor cushions, and a blanket or two.

- A timer with alarm (your watch may already have this).
- A water bottle. You are going to be drinking a heck of a lot of water, so you might as well make it special. Get a water bottle that you can write or tape inspiring words on, Semper Fi, Courage, or Forward, for example. Being reminded of your goal, or an attitude you want to promote every time you take a drink of water is greatly empowering.
- Pictures of people, places, or things that inspire you.
- Pictures of people with whom you feel connected—family, friends, service buddies.
- Artifacts that mean something to you—tokens from your deployment, military coins you've collected, mementos from your youth, gifts from family or friends, badges and medals you've earned.
- Loose, comfortable clothing.
- An MP3 player or CD player with music of different types (relaxing, inspiring, hard-driving).
- Some type of musical instrument: a drum, a harmonica, a guitar, or something you have played before.
- One of those big inflatable exercise balls.
- Light (5 to 10 lbs.) free weights, wrist and ankle weights, therabands or stretch cords.
- Therapeutic foam roller.
- An appointment book that includes your first (or a follow-up) appointment with a therapist (psychologist) and your physician appointments.

ELEMENTS OF TRAINING

The key elements and practices you will be involved with for this coming 12 weeks have been described throughout this book. These elements include:

- Water and nutrition
- Breathing and mindfulness practices
- Continuum movement practices
- Conscientious rest
- Journal writing and planning time
- Exercise
- Music
- Psychologist (therapist) and physician appointments
- Humor
- Bodywork
- Creation activity/hobby time
- Nature

- Community
- Teaching
- Service

Water and Nutrition

- We've talked about the importance of water. Getting in it, appreciating it, and drinking it. You've been hearing about this all your life. Now we are making it official, your doctor is ordering you to drink 8 to 10 glasses (8 ounces or more) of water daily. Drink your first glassful upon waking and last one an hour before bedtime. You'll find that water can help you to feel full when you thought you were hungry. It's the best way to start off any meal. You should be peeing like crazy and your pee should become almost clear looking. That's a good sign you're well hydrated. Coffee, beer, and sodas are not water. Real water, straight from the tap is what we're talking about. If you want to use it filtered or bottled, that's okay, too (but recycle the bottles). Your brain is 85% water and your body is 70%. Do you think that's a good reason alone to follow this advice?
- Eat real food. Read Michael Pollen's book *Food Rules*. Moderation is always the right answer when it comes to your nutrition. Eat whole foods, not processed. The less canned, frozen, prepared, processed, artificial, and exotic your food is, the better. Focus on fresh vegetables and fruits, complex, whole grains (whole wheat bread, pasta, or rice), healthy oils (olive or canola), low fat milk, and lean (not red) meats. Two thousand calories a day is plenty of calories, preferably divided over 4 to 5 small meals. Most importantly, eat slowly and enjoy the tastes of all of your food, don't rush one of life's simple pleasures.

Breathing

- Create periods of practice throughout the day. Use the breathing practices in Chapter 6 to get you started.

Mindfulness

- Any and all of the awareness practices listed in Chapter 6.

Continuum Movement

- Any and all of the practices listed in Chapter 7. As the training progresses, we'll add strengthening.

Conscientious Rest

- Time spent breathing, stretching out, unwinding, and moving and in any way that feels good to you. Then, just rest. Give yourself completely to gravity. You are completely shutting off. If you fall asleep that's fine, but there is no goal, except to rest.

Nature

- Time outside walking, sitting, or rolling in a wheelchair. Time spent with an animal. Just sit with a tree. Remember, it's a living thing, so think of it that way. Enjoy the sun. Enjoy the rain, the heat, the cold, and the wind. Become a weather connoisseur. The sky is never the same. Notice that. Take your journal if you like. If you live in a city, and can't make it to a park, think of the people around you and the city itself as a type of nature. Just observe.

Journal Writing

- Time spent free writing, telling your story, or working on your mission statement. Write about your response to this training.

Music

- Time spent listening and moving in some way to music. Anything you like, but preferably something slow and relaxing to start. Find a way to get your whole body to move to the music, particularly your spine. You may do this in a chair or on your feet.
- Time spent creating and exploring your own music: humming, sounding vowels, playing an instrument you're familiar with, playing an instrument that's new to you. Become fascinated with sound and patterns. Try to repeat some. Make something up by yourself, or, better still, and if possible, with a group. Move with the music you make.

Exercise

- Any traditional exercise: walking, hiking, swimming, running, biking, racket games, yoga, tai chi. Walking, running, exercising, or simply playing in water (a pool, a lake, an ocean) is the ultimate form of exercise. Feel the water flowing around you as you flow through it. See yourself becoming one with the water, one with the flow.

Friendship, Community

- Be with friends and family: Call someone you enjoy, a service buddy perhaps. Have an authentic conversation about what you and they are doing, what you are going through.

Humor

- Engage in some activity that makes you laugh. Get together with friends and watching a funny movie. Watch comedians on YouTube. Tune in to one of the many funniest home videos shows.

Bodywork

- As a way to help jumpstart your boot camp experience, treat your body to a new experience, and to help begin mobilization, get some bodywork by a professional, as described in Chapter 8.

Teaching

- The best way to learn something is share it with others. Part of your training is to teach others what you are learning and discovering. That makes it your own. As soon as you can, please share this information and these exercises with your family, friends, and fellow warriors. Go from being a passive sufferer who feels controlled by a symptom or a diagnosis, to an active teacher who can help others.

Service

- Being in service to others mobilizes all of your resources. Whether it's helping other Vets get through tough times, helping your brother-in-law build a deck, working as a volunteer in a community center, helping your kid with homework, or just walking some little old lady across the street, when you are helping others, you are helping yourself. You are the first person to receive the energy of helping, as it passes through you. You have to be in possession of something, before you can offer it to others. If you want to help yourself, you must help others as well. You'll be doing a lot of that. It's where your mission will ultimately take you. Keep your eyes and mind open to look for ways to be of service.

TWELVE-WEEK FLUID WARRIOR BASIC TRAINING

The ultimate goal of this 12-week training is to instill a lifelong habit of taking care of your own self. There are three tracks available for this basic training:

1. Full time: For those who are fully committed to becoming a fluid warrior and who have the time to dedicate themselves to an entire day of training, at least 5 days/week. This is your full time job.
2. Part time: For those who are committed to becoming a fluid warrior, but who are also balancing family and/or work, in or out of the military. You can either dedicate a few hours a day for the effort, or give more effort just a few times per week. To do this, just pick out a few of the missions or activities of the full-time training each day (say 3 or 4 hours) or simply do the schedule every other day. You may wish to progress more slowly than the full time schedule as well, give yourself 4 or 6 weeks before increasing the intensity. Go at the pace that suits your lifestyle or time available. Remember this is a lifelong journey. Just make sure you don't stagnate or be satisfied with completing only half the mission.
3. Samplers: For those who are exploring the ideas of the fluid warrior and who want to pick and choose some parts of the program or can commit only a few hours every now and then.

> *If a warrior is to succeed at anything, the success must come gently, with a great deal of effort but with no stress or obsession.*
>
> —Carlos Castaneda

Fluid Warrior: Basic Training

It will be helpful if you make a chart to keep track of the activities we are suggesting for this training, or you can use the ones included later on in this chapter. You can begin with a simple calendar or appointment book, but ultimately you'll want to put together some specific duty logs that break down your day into the segments of your mission that you can check off as you accomplish them. Regardless of how intensely you'll be pursuing this basic training, you should begin and end with the specific routines described here so that you prepare your body and mind for the healing activities of both the day and the night.

Step 1: Wake Up Routine

The following basic routine should quickly become a part of your life, regardless if you are diving in full-time or just dabbling. Although it may seem like a lot of time initially, giving yourself 20 minutes of time to prepare for the day, it really is not asking a lot if your goal is to become well and whole again. If you can, take a little more time for both of these on the weekends or whenever you can. It's like charging your batteries before starting the engine, cleaning and checking your gun, or stretching before and after playing a sport, there's no excuse not to do it right.

1. Water: Immediately upon rising each morning drink a full glass of water slowly with appreciation. Think of it as prescription medicine that you can't live without. Oh yeah—that's right—you really can't live without it. We suggest filling your water bottle the night before and having it on your bedside table.
2. Breath: Five minutes mindful breathing. Slow it to around six times a minute. That's about half your usual rate, or 10 seconds a breath; 5 seconds inhale, 5 seconds exhale. Thirty breaths, in and out, over 5 minutes. The timing is just a guide. Find your own slow natural rhythm. Your focus is on the quality of breathing, enjoying the long, slow process, feeling the air fill as much of your lungs and the nutrients reaching throughout your body. Nothing feels better than just focusing on this life giving process.
3. Movement: Either in bed, standing up, or on your mat on the floor, spend 5 minutes doing the *Unwinding the Animal Body* exercise (Chapter 7, Exercise #10).
4. Breath: Follow the exercise with another 5 minutes of mindful breathing.
5. You're ready to face the world and start your day. Eat a good breakfast to help power your body and brain.

Exercise #10: Unwinding the Animal Body

1. Sitting, standing, or laying on the floor, breathe, and stretch out in any position that feels good to you. Think about how a dog or cat stretches when they awake.
2. Twist and turn in such a way that it feels like you are wrapping your muscles around your own bones. Play at the edge of your range of motion. Don't try to push through. Use breathing to help you open and elongate. No forcing.

Step 2: Daily Schedule Routine (14 hours/day for 5 days/week)

Use the following daily schedule as a guide or suggestion. The schedule that follows outlines a full daily program of activity, but you can modify this depending on what your level of participation is, what your tolerance level is, and how you are doing. It's your choice how you specifically construct the schedule or build up your participation. You can try to do all elements of the program for shorter period of time at first and then build up, or you can just pick those elements that you want to start with and add other elements as you progress. As we've said before, it's not what you are actually doing that is as important as the fact that you are doing something and that you are doing them with passion and attention to how it makes you feel. If you decide to fully engage, begin with an hour of structured activity in the morning and afternoon, and an hour and a half in the evening for weeks 1 and 2. Increase this to 2 hours of activity morning, afternoon, and evening in weeks 3 and 4; 3 hours of activity in morning, afternoon, and evening in weeks 5 and 6; and 4 hours of activity morning, afternoon, and evening in weeks 7 and 8. By week 9, you will be able to participate in a full morning, afternoon, and evening of training. Continue this for the next 4 weeks. Although the weekends may be fully at leisure, see if you can actually find some time to do some of the structured activities and exercises then, too. As you progress along and increase your activity, you will see that more and more of your time is dedicated to recreation, hobby, volunteer, and service (teaching) activities. Incorporating breath and movement exercises into these activities is recommended. As tolerated, try and progress to work activities, as well. As noted, if you cannot either tolerate or afford to devote your full-time attention to this schedule, try and identify definitive times to take parts or pieces of the schedule and engage in them. The secret is to perform these activities to the level of your tolerance, to build up new strengths and abilities, and then to gradually increase your participation. Again, the goals are to use the specific tools outlined in this book (along with the other treatment and management techniques you have learned and are receiving) to help control or treat your symptoms, while targeting a return to full activity, participation and some type of work.

Step 3: Bedtime Routine (30 minutes)

Just as waking up in a way that will allow you to help to focus and energize your whole day is vital, so too is winding down and letting go of the events of the day. Restful sleep is one your body's strongest and surest tools, but as with everything else, you sometimes may need to consciously sharpen the blades on this tool to get it working well again. The goal is at least 7 hours per night of uninterrupted sleep, so be prepared to let go of some of the things that may have previously filled your day or night. Try and make time for pleasurable things, like sex, but don't force this. Realize that your physical urges will resurface as you better integrate your body and mind, as your body begins to feel whole and strong again. Although sex and sexuality can be restorative in and of itself, let it flow naturally and easily. The following simple nighttime routine is a guide to help bring out and sharpen the restorative sleep you so badly need.

1. Drink your last full glass of water of the day at least one hour before retiring.
2. Take a short walk outside for 10 minutes or so. Include your family if possible, including your dog. Think or talk about how the day went today.
3. Put on your sleep clothing. Make sure you use the bathroom no more than 30 minutes before getting into bed.
4. Read or write in your journal for 5 minutes. Avoid television, video, or computer screens, unless they are laughter inducing.
5. 5 minutes of *Unwinding the Animal Body* (Chapter 7, Exercise #10), repeated below.
6. 5 minutes of the *Luna Breath* (Chapter 7, Exercise #9) to quiet your nervous system.
7. 2 minutes of *Moving Cobra* (Chapter 7, Exercise #18)—even a minute or two of this can make a big difference. You can even do it in bed under the covers. Don't work at it so that your heart rate becomes elevated. Just think of it as a way to loosen and become aware of your upper back and neck. A little bit can go a long way.
8. Breathing into sleep: Heavenly sleep comes with a heavenly breath. One doorway to sleep is the fully experienced pleasure of breathing. We recommend always breathing through your nose and sleeping on your side. The left side is preferable because your heart doesn't press on your lungs and they can expand and relax more easily.

Exercise #10: Unwinding the Animal Body

1. Sitting, standing, or laying on the floor, breathe, and stretch out in any position that feels good to you. Think about how a dog or cat stretches when they awake.
2. Twist and turn in such a way that it feels like you are wrapping your muscles around your own bones. Play at the edge of your range of motion. Don't try to push through. Use breathing to help you open and elongate. No forcing.

Exercise #9: Luna Breath

1. Breathe easily through your nose and bring your attention to the back of the tongue and throat. Feel where your tongue is fastened at the back of the throat.
2. Gently pull the tongue back and up to the roof of the mouth and slightly close off the opening in the back of the throat.
3. Shape the back of your throat and mouth as if you are going to make a humming sound.
4. Breathe out of your nose.
5. Lengthen your exhale. The slight extra pressure generated by the smaller opening at the back of the nasal passages produces a quiet hissing sound. Listen and see if you can make it audible. Lengthen this breath and follow it with all of your attention until its completion. The image and sound of a space-suited astronaut walking on the moon might be helpful.

Exercise #18: Moving Cobra

1. Lay on your stomach with your legs together.
2. Place your arms close to your chest, elbows bent with your hands flat on the floor directly beneath your shoulders.
3. Start with your forehead flat on the bed. Press down with your hands, slowly tilt your head back and roll your neck back and then gradually up your spine until you are curving backward up from the waist. Do not strain. Do not hold. There is no effort here. Do not worry about "doing it right."
4. Play with pressing or releasing into the floor, curving, moving, and relaxing your spine. Enjoy your breathing.

Daily Guide to Fluid Warrior Boot Camp

What follows is a 12-week training regimen designed to fit with your life. Whether you are in a warrior transition unit, a day-to-day working person with family and kids either in or out of the service, being seen in the VA as an outpatient capacity, or in the hospital, this program can be tailored and shaped for you. There is a variation for you whether you are able or disable bodied. We've outlined a full style program that incorporates many of the ideas, activities, and exercises listed in this book, but you are invited to reshape all of the elements in a way that resemble the kind of life you have now and to take you in the direction you wish to go. You are encouraged to create a schedule for yourself from the ingredients listed that suit your particular life. All of this can be tailored to meet your needs.

Morning (4 hours and 30 minutes)

1. Wake up routine. Shower/hygiene. Get dressed in loose fitting clothing. Eat nourishing breakfast (full bowl of whole grain cereal or two pieces of toast, glass of low-fat milk, piece of fruit). Drink your second glass of water. (30 minutes)
2. Perform a breathing and mindfulness practice. (5 minutes)
3. Perform a Continuum movement practice. (40 minutes)
4. Repeat breathing and mindfulness practice. (10 minutes)
5. Spend time journal writing. (30 minutes)
6. Spend time enjoying or making music. Move or exercise to or with the music if you like. (30 minutes)
7. Take a conscientious rest. (30 minutes)
8. Drink a full glass of water. Drink water continuously throughout the morning.
9. Practice mindfulness. (10 minutes)
10. Exercise (walk, run, bike, swim, tai chi, use the gym). (60 minutes)
11. Spend time on a hobby or doing a chore. (45 minutes).

Afternoon (4 hours and 30 minutes)

1. Eat a light lunch (raw vegetables, low-fat cheese or yogurt, fresh fruit). Drink a full glass of water. Enjoy music, reading, or conversation. (70 minutes).
2. Take a walk, garden, or otherwise enjoy nature. (30 minutes)
3. Breathing and mindfulness practice. (10 minutes)
4. Perform a Continuum movement practice. Feel free to add some weights to your arms or legs during this session to help build strength. (30 minutes)
5. Spend time volunteering, teaching, or working. Drink a full glass of water. Drink water continuously throughout the afternoon. (110 minutes)
6. Spend time journal writing and reflecting on the day. (30 minutes)
7. Breathing and mindfulness practice. (10 minutes)

Evening (4 hours and 30 minutes)

1. Eat dinner with your family or friends (50% vegetables and fruits, 25% whole grains, 25% protein/meat). Drink another glass of water. (90 minutes)

2. Friendship and community time with family and friends. Call, Skype, or otherwise contact those people who you can't directly be with. Enjoy a light snack of whole grain chips, vegetable, or fruit dipped in hummus (chickpeas), tahini (sesame seeds), peanut or almond butter, or a low-fat spiced yogurt sauce. (100 minutes)
3. Humor and music time. (70 minutes)
4. Bedtime routine. (30 minutes)

Remember, you trained hard, to become hard, in order to go to war. Now you are training hard, to become fluid, in order to heal. In boot camp, the army, or the marines, or whoever, tore you down so that you could be built back up into something new: a warrior. Every day you worked hard to tear down muscles so that your body would build them back bigger and tougher. The body adapts. That's what's so incredible about it. You are going to be using the body's capacity to reinvent it. Where healing is concerned though, you are already torn down. This reinvention needs to be approached in a very different manner. This new training is about opening you up. It's about creating the space and the flow for something new to arise so that you can flow right through the effects of war and into your new life. That new life has already begun. It is right now.

Keep in mind that this approach to becoming a fluid warrior may be a 180-degree reversal from how you previously approached life or how you thought in the military. It's important to think about what are the principles, which guide the solid warrior in training, and what are the principles that guide the fluid warrior in training. Training to go to war is radically different from training for healing. If you thought that training to be a soldier or marine was hard, where you were being shaped and molded to meet the upcoming mission, becoming a fluid warrior and taking on your own specific mission is just as hard, because here, you're not just doing what some guy is yelling at you to do. It's all you. In the service if you disobey an order, you get demoted, go to the brig, or have disciplinary actions taken against you. Here, there are no such immediate consequences. You just don't participate with your own healing. It's highly likely that your health will just not improve or deteriorate. You don't have to do what *we* say; you only have to do what *you* say. Your enemy is not out there and there is no drill sergeant screaming at you. There is only you, and your own thoughts. Can you really bring the courage, self-discipline, and endurance of the solid warrior into this new boot camp to expand who you are and learn to become a fluid warrior? When we treat patients in clinics or hospitals, we're lucky if a third of our patients actually follow through with what we recommend or prescribe. When we set out to write this book, we hoped 25% of you would actually read this book and do this training. If you've gotten this far, we think the odds are much higher that you will. Could you really get up every morning and give this training your all for 12 weeks? That's 3 months. Do you have what it takes to go through one of these trainings that fit with your life? That's why this is so much harder for you than just following orders. Although we can provide the recommendations, the biggest part of this is really you making a plan from all this and having discipline to follow it. You may follow the one's we recommend or you may create your own.

Training for war is a particular training. Training for healing is a different kind of training. Training for life is a constant, but the environment around you may be always changing. Remember early on we said that things are always changing? That means your brain has to be open for anything. And, the responsibility for discovering your own way of thinking is yours and yours alone. We can set up this training for you, but unlike military training, there is no guy screaming at you, there is no physical or daily structure. There are no barracks and there's no being with a bunch of guys jumping out of bed in the morning at the sound of reveille to get your going. You're not part of a pack now. You're an individual. You are coming to stand alone. It is in that standing alone that you will learn to stand again with others. This entire book is about growth. Yours. It's about a lot more than just overcoming something. The title of this book is *Overcoming Post-Deployment Syndrome*, but it's much more than that. Just like in solid warrior basic training, it's not just about *overcoming* something; it's about *becoming* something. But you have to be open to it.

> A visitor came to learn fr.om a master. "Have some tea," said the Zen master. As the visitor put his cup forward the master poured the tea until it rose over the top and spilled all over the table. "Stop! The cup is filled, it will not hold anymore," said the visitor. "Just like your mind," said the Master "which you must empty if you are to learn new things."

This is a container for your healing. We know that that structure and discipline help create the rhythm of your healing path. This is a life process.

There is another response to horror besides self-destruction.
—Barry Lopez

12-Week Basic Training Schedule

The following training schedule offers a structured, weekday calendar for your basic training, with recommended activities; duration of overall morning, afternoon, and evening sessions; and other things to consider during the week. The schedule is set up to allow you to increase your participation by 30 to 60 minutes every 2 weeks, to get you to a full day of activity by the ninth week of activity. Don't forget to try and create a mission statement before beginning your basic training. Don't worry, you can change it on the way or even after you've finished this important next step. Also, make sure you have gotten together all of your gear for the mission before starting.

Weeks 1 and 2

	Duration in Minutes	Activities	Other
Wake-up	20	Standard Program	Breakfast is the key meal of the day.
Morning	60	Breathing Continuum Movement Conscientious Rest	Add some music or other creative activity. Drink your water.
Afternoon	60	Walking Breathing/ Mindfulness Continuum Movement	Add some music or other creative activity. Drink your water.
Evening	90	Community Time Music and Creative Time	Celebrate your hard work with family. Review your mission statement.
Sleep	30	Standard Program	Enjoy your restorative sleep.

Weeks 3 and 4

	Duration in Minutes	Activities	Other
Wake-up	20	Standard Program	Notice if you feel refreshed in the mornings.
Morning	120	Breathing/Mindfulness Continuum Movement Conscientious Rest Music and Creative Time	Try and add some hobby time. Think about the exercises you will be doing. Drink your water.
Afternoon	120	Walking Breathing/Mindfulness Continuum Movement Journal Writing	Try to plan what type of volunteer or teaching you will be doing. Drink your water.
Evening	120	Community Time Music and Creative Time Humor	Conscientious rest may be needed here.
Sleep	30	Standard Program	Review your journal.

Weeks 5 and 6

	Duration in Minutes	Activities	Other
Wake-up	20	Standard Program	Enjoy the effects of your morning shower.
Morning	180	Breathing Continuum Movement Conscientious Rest Hobby/Chore Time Aerobic Exercise	Add weights and strengthening to movement. Drink your water.
Afternoon	180	Walking Breathing/Mindfulness Continuum Movement Music/Creative Time Journal Writing	Try using the exercise all for Continuum movement. Drink your water.

Weeks 5 and 6 *(continued)*

	Duration in Minutes	Activities	Other
Evening	180	Community Time Music and Creative Time Humor	Think about how you can provide volunteer or service time.
Sleep	30	Standard Program	Notice how your body and mind feel.

Weeks 7 and 8

	Duration in Minutes	Activities	Other
Wake-up	20	Standard Program	
Morning	240	Breathing Continuum Movement Conscientious Rest Hobby/Chore Time Music/Creative Time Aerobic Exercise Journal Writing	Extend your sessions to as long as feels comfortable. Drink your water.

Afternoon	240	Walking
		Breathing/Mindfulness
		Continuum
		  Movement
		Music/Creative Time
		Journal Writing
		Volunteer and
		  Service
			Take time to notice how your body and mind feel before and after sessions.
			Drink your water.

Evening	240	Community Time Music and Creative Time Humor	Use this time to plan your weekend activities and next week's schedule.
Sleep	30	Standard Program	Review your mission statement at night.

Weeks 9 Through 12

	Duration in Minutes	Activities	Other
Wake-up	20	Standard Program	
Morning	270	Breathing Continuum Movement Conscientious Rest Hobby/Chore Time Music/Creative Time Aerobic Exercise Journal Writing	Vary the duration of individual sessions. Vary the types of creative activities you do. Drink your water.
Afternoon	270	Walking Breathing/Mindfulness Continuum Movement Music/Creative Time Journal Writing Volunteer and Service	Take time to notice how your body and mind feel before and after sessions. Consider sharing your journal with family or close friends. Drink your water.
Evening	270	Community Time Music and Creative Time Humor	Notice your energy level at the end of the day.
Sleep	30	Standard Program	

What Not To Do

You may have noticed that we haven't spent a great deal of time telling you what *not* to do. That's because we have wanted to focus on positive things that make you well. We are also convinced that if you slow down, cut out some of the outer and inner noise, do some or all of these practices, and listen to your deepest self, your natural intelligence will actually know what *to* do. We anticipate that *not doing* will not be a problem. That said, there are a few things we'd like to suggest that you should definitely consider *not doing*. If you smoke, drink, or do drugs, we think you should consider blowing all of them off for the duration of this basic training. If they are hard and fast friends of yours, we know putting them down can be extremely difficult. You may think of them as one of your only pleasures. But, you will find that the more you move toward your body's authentic pleasures, the easier it will be to throw off the false ones. As hard as it can be to do, waking up is life's greatest pleasure and the spring from which all other pleasures flow. Just do your best. Consider each moment a new one in which to decide. Even if you are halfway through a cigarette, or half way through a beer, you can flip that "do something else" switch. Good luck with it.

We don't have anything against alcohol. Very few self-respecting military men do. Having a few drinks with friends is one of life's greatest joys. A glass of red wine each evening with dinner or afterward with friends is not only pleasant, but it may also help you live longer and healthier. We encourage joy. A drink can be a pleasant way to relax. But, there are other reasons that people drink. Alcohol is a chemical that literally dissolves uncomfortable or painful feelings by intoxicating the cells of the brain. Temporarily, it acts as a de-inhibitor. But its effects as self-medication are extremely short lived. And the way it leaves you feeling . . . well we all know what too much alcohol feels like. The short of it is: it anesthetizes you. Eventually, it not only medicates the brain cells and nerves of the body, but it also kills them. Using alcohol to dissolve pain of any kind, physical or emotional, can be extremely dangerous. Despite how it may feel now, over the long haul if will actually work against your goal of recovery.

> *There ain't no way I'm not gettin' drunk every once in a while. It's the only time I feel good.*
>
> — PFC Lori Stefano

Even if you don't think you have trouble with alcohol, if the prospect of not drinking anything at all for the 12 weeks training seems even remotely daunting to you, you might think again. Alcohol is sneaky. You need to remember that evidence is mounting that the brain affected by PTSD, depression, anxiety disorder, and perhaps even concussion will actually deteriorate over time if the challenges it presents are not met head on. Alcohol will make it much more difficult, if not impossible, to meet these challenges, and there is no time to lose. If you suspect that you have a problem with alcohol or drug use, you should bring it up with your doctor or therapist and you should get help. Alcoholics or Narcotics Anonymous works as well as anything out there. Find a meeting with Veterans in it or even leading it. Go to one at your local VA. A community of understanding people is tremendously healing and the 12-step program that AA espouses has been a successful model of recovery and spiritual rejuvenation for countless people. Go and stick with it. It may be just the thing you need to get your mission on track.

WORKING WITH PAIN

Pain is a complicated thing. It can be physical, psychological, spiritual, or any combination thereof. It can be blinding or illuminating. It can be a signal to us that something has changed, or that something needs to change. It can tell us when there is too much chaos in the body or brain, and it can also tell us when there is too much rigidity. It is information. One way to look at it is as a signal to where there is the need for coherent flow. Acutely, pain is the way the body tells us that flow has been disrupted. It pulls our attention to where it is urgently needed. That part of it is a good thing. We certainly would not survive very long if these types of disruption were a pleasurable experience. But, pain can also sometimes take over our whole consciousness. Particularly when we chronically focus on pain as a thing only to be resisted and gotten rid of and there's no immediate danger or cause. When this happens, our body and mind sometimes amplifies the pain, compresses it, compounds it, and distorts it. The natural mechanisms that are present within our skin, muscles, soft tissues, and nerve endings are no longer working normally. Now it's not just physical sensation, but a whole attitude and a way of being. The training in this book is designed to teach you how to be with pain in a new way.

> *Our culture operates with the idea that healing means the absence of pain, but I've come to understand that healing doesn't mean that our pain and suffering go away. Healing is learning to live in a different relationship with our pain and suffering so it does not control us.*
>
> —Claude Anshin Thomas, Vietnam Veteran
> From *At Hell's Gate*

Although avoiding physical pain is a very smart thing to do, sometimes it is present, unavoidable, and will actually be the door through which you must walk. If you want to become a long distance runner for example, you come to recognize pain as the thing you must experience to become stronger. You have to learn to be uncomfortable. The old military adage "pain is weakness leaving the body" is an apt one. This is the realm of the solid warrior. Leaning into pain is a way of meeting it without resistance. Excellence in anything can be the result of "taking great pains." Being the last one shooting baskets, when you're exhausted and everyone else has gone home, is part of the road to mastery. Doing it so long that you develop a knee problem or some other such repetitive injury may mean you have not learned the language of pain, or that you are just flat out bullheaded. Our emphasis here is on nonresistance. We're trying to teach you how to breathe with the pain. It is in creating a larger space within you in which pain can occur, so it's not your main point of focus. Think of it this way; if your pain is all you're aware of, it's your whole life. If you are also aware of your breath, it has less than your whole life in its control. If you are aware of your breath, your relation to gravity, how you are sitting or standing, how the light is that strikes the dashboard of your car, the feel of air against your skin, the thoughts in your mind, and any of an infinite array of other things you can be aware of, then the pain is a much smaller portion of your consciousness, of your life. It shrinks in relation to everything else you are aware of.

One of the things our breathing practice does is allow us to step back a little from pain and identify ourselves not as the pain but as the space in which the pain occurs. The fluid warrior does not ignore pain. He or she is interested in learning its language. All of this is to say we seek partnership with the body, not dominion over it. What's your pain profile?

In a sense there is positive and there is negative pain. Pain can tell us when we are opening our boundaries, and it can tell us when we have crossed way over them. It is not possible to get through life without pain, and the attitude we have about it can determine the trajectory of our entire life.

- Do we avoid it at all cost?
- Do we seek it out?
- Do we identify with it?
- Can we listen deeper into the sensation of pain to perceive a deeper wisdom it is telling us?
- And, can we develop awareness spacious enough that we are not completely consumed by it?
- Can we see it as just one of a number of physical sensations and not the whole enchilada?
- What is it to live a life that contains some physical pain in it now, or even always? These are pertinent questions for those of us who are dealing with it.
- What does it have to teach us about living in a noble and humble way?

TEACHING AND SERVICE

One of the best ways to learn anything is to teach it to others. When you become a source of knowledge for those around you, you are taking things to the next level. If you can't pass it on, you don't know it. You are demonstrating the ability to not only integrate these actions and behaviors within yourself, but also you are beginning the process of integrating them with others. That's why we are encouraging you to share the stuff in this book. Particularly anything you have tried at enough to have an opinion about. In the military, your basic training taught you a lot about who you needed to be and what you needed to know to go to war. Until going through it, you really didn't understand the level of commitment needed to become a warrior. After you got there, you learned a whole lot more. You began to understand what it took and what it was all about. For most of you, you didn't know squat about healing after post-deployment syndrome. But, if you have read this book and gone through some or all of this training, now you've begun to better understand. Now, it's your turn to make this even more interesting and to become a teacher of others. To begin to be of service to them. As you go through this training, as you start to learn about these principles of healing and if start to take it with you we, we are encouraging you to become a teacher. Become the healing virus and spread this stuff around. It's not just to help others—it will also be of huge benefit to you.

11

The Return of the Warrior: A Lifetime of Success

*In oneself lies the whole world and if you know how to look and learn,
the door is there and the key is in your hand. Nobody on earth can
give you either the key or the door to open, except yourself.*

—Jiddu Krishnamurti

Your experiences in the military and civilian life may have been rougher than most peoples, but there isn't any easy way to just erase or even move past them. The life you've got now is what you've got to work with. We know that what you've gone through already qualifies you as having had a life that is anything but ordinary. There are a whole lot of special things you've seen and done that you wouldn't trade away for anything. But, there are also a bunch of things that you'd like to see changed in your life. How we respond to the challenges in our lives gives us the opportunity to grow, think, move, and even enjoy life in an entirely new way. In order to regain your health, you're going to have to set into motion a number of these changes. People around you who haven't experienced what you have may have little or no incentive to change, and that's fine. But for you, living just an ordinary life or going back to exactly what you had are no longer options for you. That's the good *and* the bad of it. Your experiences have changed you and for you to get your life back in gear, you'll have to make some changes. Your decision to make these changes will let you take advantage of all of the rich experiences and skills that you have and learn how to make those experiences a source of strength for your future.

*The greater the difficulty, the more glory in surmounting it. Skillful pilots
gain their reputation from storms and tempests.*

—Epictetus

THE SIX STEPS OF HEALING

In this book, we've covered a lot of things. What has started off as simple, six-step process actually contains many layers and elements that may seem complex. Although it's actually a good thing that there are so many ways to begin and grow the healing process and to tap into recovery, at times it can also feel kind of overwhelming. It's okay to feel that way and it's very understandable. No one said it would be easy. Most good things in life never are. To make our points, we've been fairly repetitious. In part that's because of the great deal of overlap in how the healing processes work. It's also because the road to recovery isn't a simple, straight line. It's more of a winding path that can back track on itself as it eventually leads you along. Actually, it's most like an ever widening spiral that can bring you to ever higher and higher levels. We wanted to make it clear to you just how many resources and tools you already possess and how many different ways you can use them. While reading the book, you may have tried some of the steps, tested out some of the exercises, or even given the boot camp schedule a try for a day or two. Everything you've done so far since your deployment from the battlefield has demonstrated that you want to return to normal, that you are willing to make whatever effort is needed to recover. Whatever parts of this book that you can take away and make part of your life will give you that much more to work with. If you've even read this far that shows that you're willing to try something new and to try whatever it takes to improve your health. Your efforts will not go unnoticed, your body and mind will see the results.

To take full advantage of the program introduced in this book, all the information, ideas, exercises, and strategies described here need to move from ideas and thoughts to actions. They need to become second nature to you. They can't be just words on a page or part of a book on your shelf. Just as your training as a warrior became second nature to you by going through basic training, drilling for hours, and literally living the skills every day of your life. Of course, it had to become a part of you—your entire life depended on it. Well, to put it in similar terms, now the entire *rest* of your life depends on you making wellness second nature to you. It's the only way you can be skilled enough to succeed in this new mission, the mission of healing. You were trained in the art of war and now you are training in the art of healing. In order to take this important next step in your life, you must get on and travel along the road to wellness. Let's take a look at this road again and see how some or all of the tools we've given you can be used to get on, stay on and finish this road.

- Step 1: Understanding Your Body's Symptoms. Developing a greater appreciation of what post-deployment syndrome (PDS) is accomplished by better knowing the nature of the common symptoms and medical diagnoses that are associated with it, and recognizing what type of clinicians may be able to help you with them.
- Step 2: Discovering Your Strengths. Understanding the role of breath, questioning, internal scanning, mindfulness training, and restoring flow to your body to start the process of both understanding and treating the symptoms and causes of PDS.
- Step 3: Applying Healing Principles. Using continuum movement therapy, rest and sleep, proper nutrition, aerobic conditioning, and strengthening exercises to manage the symptoms and causes of PDS.
- Step 4: Re-Establishing Normalcy. Appreciating how the brain works and how to optimize its functioning through effective psychotherapy techniques.
- Step 5: Integrating Health Into Your Life. Applying creative arts and activities to your life to improve PDS and to restore the fullness of your life.
- Step 6: Resuming The Productive Mission. Initiating both a short-term, structured program of activities to regain your health and reduce the effects of PDS on your life and then incorporating that program into your everyday life.

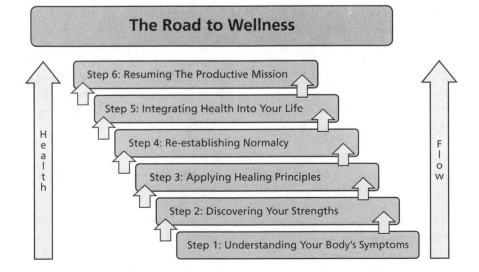

Seems pretty simple doesn't it. We can all follow simple steps. But, as we said previously, the journey to wellness that you are on is actually not a straight line or staircase. It's really an ever-enlarging spiral made up of these six steps and all of the tools to help get you up them. The steps themselves are more like ramps that you can progress up slowly (our recommendation) or race on up. The tools and resources help to provide the rails that you can use to pull you up the spiral and that can keep you on the right path. There are many ways to get onto the road and you can begin from wherever you are in your state of health. When you've made the commitment to get on this upward spiral, the key to success is to realize that the further you get on this road, the better you'll feel and the easier it will be to keep going. Using the range of tools we've reviewed in this book will help you to stay on the road, but don't worry it's a wide road and it's hard to veer off too far to one side or the other. Just keep moving. You can set whatever pace you like. How fast or far you get on the road is up to you, but you can hitch a ride or turbo charge your travels by using many of the techniques contained within these pages.

Each of the six steps has been built around easily accessible tools and techniques, and each of these steps builds on the one before it. Breathing exercises calm us down and help to open our mindfulness. Mindfulness practice increases awareness of sensation to what's on the screen of the mind, building your illume. Continuum movement practices increase the ability to feel, create healing in the physical body, and mobilize flow in the stuck emotional body. This allows for innovation in the body and mind. Tracking allows us to observe and name what is happening in our bodies, in sensation and emotions. Because this observation can often overwhelm us with all that we are experiencing, we learned how to pace ourselves in the process. We stressed the importance of finding a good therapist you are comfortable with, to help you to examine all of this in a beneficial way. We have talked about the importance of making creativity and time with nature an integral part of your life, and of how re-incorporating community and service back into your life can bring you back to your warrior's mission. That's a whole lot of things to work on. So, what are we still writing about now? Before you put the book down, we'd like to invite you to read on a little bit more so we can introduce you to another step (or two) that are near the top of the spiral. A further exploration of just what you can do to further your mission.

The same immense energies that create the symptoms of trauma, when properly engaged and mobilized, can transform the trauma and propel us into new heights of healing, mastery, and even wisdom. Trauma resolved is a great gift, returning us to the natural world of ebb and flow, harmony, love, and compassion.

—Peter Levine

Heartfulness: Thinking with Your Heart

As you take these steps and do the work of becoming a more fluid warrior you will discover that you feel more alive. The question that has been running through this book—*What is alive in me right now and what can I do to increase this aliveness?*—will become more vital and easier to answer. You will know exactly what you need in the moment. It may be mindful breathing, movement, rest, water, friendship, nature, work, play, medication, a talk with a therapist, or none of the above, but you will know and act accordingly. This aliveness means that you are summoning your inner strength, finding your mental clarity returning, and seeing your physical body is healing. It also means that you will experience more connections within your self, with people, and with the whole world around you. Although the logistics of these connections may occur in the prefrontal cortex of the brain, the heart is the organ that senses connection. In the final analysis it is not only your body, or even your mind that you are helping to heal or bring into flow—it's your heart. We think of the brain as the instrument of intelligence, but the heart has its own kind of intelligence, it's own kind of knowing. You may remember that the heart is even directly linked to the brain through the vagus nerve. So, when you can get your heart into the game, it's not thinking alone. It's actually working in unison with the brain. If you want to increase your brainpower and expand your mind, then let the fluid warrior training increase the intelligence of the heart.

A key to your healing entails learning to be okay with what has happened to you, whether it makes sense or not. There is freedom in this acceptance. To tap into this freedom, the only thing with the power to do that is your heart—*your* heart—no one else's. You must come to see that you are not salvaging your life, but instead that you are growing into a new one, a life that couldn't exist any other way. As you move into this new life, you will bring all that has happened along with you. It will make you who you are. In spite of the title of this book, you are not just *overcoming* something, you are also *becoming* something. Your heart will awaken to the fact that at some essential level, you are already whole. There may be many areas for improvement and much room for growth, but where you are starting from is the perfect starting point. With that recognition, the heart unclenches and does not resist. This means two things: (1) everything is alright just as it is, and (2) in coming to this attitude, you have opened the flood gates to allow the maximum flow of healing energy. It's a paradox isn't it? The more you accept where you are, the more you will see where you can go. So, it becomes your task to look into your heart and see what you find. Again, this is quite literal and involves focusing your attention on the physical sensations of your heart and understanding how you are influenced by them.

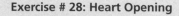

Exercise # 28: Heart Opening

- Enjoy a little breathing practice, scan the sensations in your inner landscape, and come into open awareness for a few minutes.
- Enjoy some of the awakening dragon exercise to free your spine.
- Bring your awareness into the large spiral shaped muscle that is located in center of the upper left part of your chest. It's the one that pumps all the blood through your body. Find some awareness of your heart.
- Use your imagination and breathe directly into your heart, as if it were a lung. Do your best to feel completely into your whole heart, front, back, sides, top, and bottom. Remember? It's the thing that hurts if your boyfriend or girlfriend dumps you.
- Contract and release all the muscles surrounding your heart to increase sensation.
- Place one or both hands palms flat and directly on the chest over your heart. Feel it beating. If think you are too cool or tough to do this, buck up. Make the connection.
- You are allowing the sensation of your heart to saturate your whole mind. You are bringing your brain into alignment.
- Now, imagine these following situations and feel the accompanying sensations in your heart.
  - Relaxed, full or open heart: Try and remember or think about your girlfriend or boyfriend, being with your buddies, or a day at the beach or park. Think of any time when you felt peaceful and connected.
  - Neutral heart: Remember a time when your heart was neutral; maybe going to the store, doing your laundry, or chatting with someone you didn't know in a line. Imagine chatting with an acquaintance about the weather.
  - Contracted or closed heart: Remember, and then use your imagination to come to images that conjure the feeling of a closed or contracted heart. What you've seen in war is probably what comes most readily to mind, but it can also be a time with a difficult person, someone with whom you've had angry words. Or, think of times when you were frustrated and fit to be tied, or how much you may have hated the enemy or even people who just looked like him.

How do each of these situations make your heart feel? Really become curious. You are getting to know more and more intimately the condition of your own heart. That knowing means you can be informed by your heart but not always so jerked around by it. Over time you will feel more compassion for your own self. That, in and of itself, opens the heart and allows for more flow. Compassion for self leads to compassion for others and vice versa. This helps you relax and create flow in your emotional body. You are coming to the heart's intelligence. When the brain and the heart work together true intelligence is activated.

Thinking with the heart is what we do when we work with guilt, shame, pride, grief, or gratitude. We could call this a seventh step or ramp for your recovery, but it's an ongoing step that every person on earth, whether they know it or not, is continually taking.

> *The wages of trauma, as I have written it out in my life, is anger. The resolution of that anger, say the therapists, breaks the grip of the traumatic event. But to resolve anger – and this I got on my own – it's necessary to love. It's not enough just to arrive at the place where no one, not even yourself, is to blame. You have to go further.*
> —Harvey Fleming, Bravo Company
> Second Battalion, 27th Infantry
> Military Historian, from *Resistance* by
> Barry Lopez

Guilt, Shame

> *The platoon was the faith, a greater cause that, if you focused on it entirely, made your fears go away. It was an anesthetic that made you aware of what was happening, but strangely fatalistic about the outcome. As a soldier, the thing you were most scared of was failing your brothers when they needed you, and compared to that dying was easy. Dying was over with. Cowardice lasted forever.*
> —Sebastian Junger, from *War*

In war, there are wounds deeper than flesh or effects more devastating than the fear-frozen brain of stress disorders. There are wounds of the soul. Although we are urging you to move forward up the spiral, there are some things that are beyond the symptoms and diagnoses of PDS. These things aren't just real, they can stop you cold. Guilt and shame are two of those things. They can freeze you in your tracks. They take you out of life's parade. Although warriors are trained to buck up and drive on, you cannot drive on from guilt or shame, they ride with you. You must understand them and sometimes take action to alleviate them. Guilt and shame are painful. They may be the most painful things a human being can know. They can stab directly into the heart of a person's self worth. Although this knife may be delivered from outside of you, the knife-edge is wielded from within you.

Shame and guilt will eat at you and drag you down, but it is your own hand that won't allow the wounds to heal. Overcoming them is not simply a matter of time. People carry guilt to their graves. To have any chance of working with and through them, you must come to see and understand them. There is much to learn. Guilt and shame are both major obstacles to improving and a source of your greatest healing.

> *But clinicians are often challenged by patient deficits not found in most texts on psychotherapy. The fear response may lie in the hardware of the limbic brain and may be successfully deconditioned. But guilt and shame reside in the brain's software or soul and require more creative, psycho-spiritual approaches.*
>
> —Wilfred Busse, PhD

Guilt is a problem with something you did whereas shame is a deeper problem, involving who you think you are. Although guilt and shame have different definitions and may live in different regions of our heart and mind, they tend to affect us in similar ways. They are difficult subjects for all of us, but they tend to be particularly difficult for a warrior. Warriors ascribe to a certain mental toughness and aspire to a certain code of honor. Just having guilt or shame of any type can mean that that code has been broken. Shame and guilt are in and of themselves, shameful. Here are some of the common causes of a warrior's shame and guilt:

- Feeling responsible for the death of others.
- Letting people down.
- Surviving when others did not.
- Killing in the line of duty.
- Enjoying killing.
- Killing innocents.
- Being weak and not being able to suck it up.
- Looking disfigured or different.
- Having lost your skills.
- Feeling incompetent, when athletic prowess is so valued.
- Not having enough money.
- Not being able to control your own emotions.
- Not being able to control your rage.
- Yelling at your spouse or children.
- Drinking, using your medications to excess, or taking illicit drugs.

- Not being able to work.
- Feeling so different.
- Not able to provide for your family.

Any or all of these reasons or feeling can be drivers of shame and guilt. Accompanying these reasons are five basic responses to the internal pain of guilt or shame:

1. Avoiding the feeling, often by using drugs, alcohol, or other forms of addiction. Alcohol literally "dissolves" and drugs block or alter the internal chemicals of guilt and shame, at least temporarily.
2. Withdrawing from any circumstance where shame might arise. Not seeking work, not attending social events, and not having an apartment or home that requires paying rent are examples of this. Shame may be a major cause of Veteran homelessness.
3. Attacking yourself. Self-sabotage or the debilitating inner talk of self-worthlessness. *It's my fault. I should have done something.* Addiction to self-obliteration can also serve this response.
4. Attacking others. Shame is so painful that it can lead to anger and the need to seek release in rage at others. This is especially true when others are thought to be the source of that shame, if someone else has been the perceived source of dishonor. Sadly, most school shootings are the result of this.

Some or all of these are common responses to shame and guilt that do nothing to alleviate it. Indeed, they perpetuate it or make it worse. They drive it deeper into the psyche and your biological system. But, the fifth response is different:

5. If you can withstand the painful experience of shame long enough to use your inner illume on it, what it's trying to tell you will become clear. You will learn from it and move on.

Thinking of guilt or shame as a spotlight that tells you where attention should be given and where learning must take place, can turn the nature of your pain completely around. Bringing mindful attention to the sensation of guilt is what will eventually allow that sensation to subside. Sharing your thoughts and feelings with others who understand and can help you to better understand it is crucial. You may learn your entire response or how you have interpreted it is in error. You may come to realize that no one could have saved your buddy or the children that got in the line of fire. You may learn that the difficulties you're having aren't your fault or can be improved. You may learn to forgive yourself.

On the other hand, if you come to see that you've done something that you think is morally wrong, you might come to see how acts of restitution might be made. You might come to the realization that becoming dedicated to healing, both to your own, and to the world around you, is the only antidote to your shame. You may come to understand that learning and serving, living a life of kindness, is the only thing you can do to make up for something you did or participated in. Remember, nothing about us is permanent. We are not actually defined by who we are, but rather by who we are becoming. It's what you become *in this moment* that is relevant. It is how you handle guilt and shame *in this moment* that imprisons or liberates you.

Grief

> *I'll miss Will forever. I would switch places with him right now if I could. When it comes right down to it it's by far the most painful thing for me. It was so painful; I couldn't even feel anything any more. The only thing I could feel was being pissed off.*
>
> —PFC Lori Stefano

Grief is a natural response to loss and the inevitable residue of war. In war grief usually comes suddenly and horrifically. Every warrior knows this. When you lose a buddy, a mentor, see innocents killed, lose a limb or abilities, or lose your sense of the way you think life was supposed to be, grief arises. Individual responses to loss can be all over the map—anger, depression, shock, confusion, disbelief, despair, or numbness. Grief is a part of war and it must be honored. You do not honor the dead or the life that you had if you only try to leave them behind. Grief must flow within you or it ceases to be natural. When it just sits inside of you, it becomes toxic. It must flow through you in order to become a part of you. The practices in this book will help you feel again and help you create flow. The heart opening practice earlier in this chapter is extremely helpful in this regard. It is also imperative that you create a time and place where grieving is something you consciously do. You can do this alone or with others. When possible, it is particularly helpful to be with others who understand best, those who were there. That is what has made the Vietnam War Memorial such a powerful place. Sharing your grief with others who understand is a primary means of facilitating its process. You are learning to deal with grief intentionally, so that it doesn't have to take over your whole life.

But there is something more to understanding and dealing with grief. Grief is only possible because of love. You cannot grieve what you do not love. Grief is the way that the things you love leave their mark on you.

It's a cliché, but sometimes we do not even know how much we love until grief instructs us. When the things we love leave us, grief is the energy they leave behind. With a little illume and a little time, you can see grief differently. You can think of grief as a way you are still touched by someone or something you love or loved. It can actually be a source of strength. It can give your life meaning. It's extremely healthy to stay in touch with what you love.

Gratitude

If healing were bread, then gratitude and appreciation would be the yeast and leavening, there to help provide the needed lift. In the midst of all that has happened to you, the horror you may have seen, the pain you have experienced, what are the things you are still grateful for? Name them. Write them down. Use your journal. Focus on them. Take a few of these questions and elaborate your experience of them. Remembering what you're grateful for liberates an energy that flows directly from your heart. The more this energy flows, the more you will be lifted. As you work to lift yourself, you will lift all around you.

Gratitude Exercise

Ask yourself:

- What areas of my life am I grateful for?
- Do I have friends for whom I would do anything, or who would do anything for me?
- Do I have family that has been by my side through this?
- Do I have children?
- Do I have an amazing dog?
- Can I see?
- Can I see the sky?
- Can I hear?
- Can I hear music?
- Can I walk?
- Can I roll?
- Can I breathe?
- Do I have both arms?
- Or even one?
- Do I you have a sense of humor?
- Do I have enough to eat?
- Do I have some shelter?
- Do I have work?
- Can I still laugh?

THE FLUID WARRIOR COUNCIL

> *People think that soldiers are addicted to adrenalin. What they are really addicted to is brotherhood.*
>
> —Sebastian Junger

As you climb to the top of your wellness spiral, we want you to consider creating and being a part of a fluid warrior council to practice all of the healing steps in community—breathing, mindfulness, continuum, music, writing, exercising, hiking, laughing, and service. Practicing all of this with fellow warriors is like taking your journey beyond turbo charging, right to nuclear power. Call your buddies, ping them, text them, Facebook them, Skype them, Tweet them, or whatever you need to do to create your community. Arrange a weekend or weeklong retreat. Even if you start with just one other person, you will feel your strength grow. This is an important step that you need to do, but do so only because it feels right to you, not because we said so. You know that being with your fellow soldiers is the best. But what would it be like to be with them in a fully conscious and intentional way? What would it be like to be with them where you know up front that you are all there to help each other create your new lives? What would it be like to have a group process that you went through? What would it be like to bring the camaraderie you experienced in battle to this new battle to overcome PDS? Imagine that in this fluid warrior council you come to know each other so well that you can tell each *others'* stories, not just your own.

 Weekend Fluid Warrior Council Retreat

Here are some possible activities for a weekend fluid warrior council.

- Breathing and mindfulness practices.
- Group continuum movement exercise.
- Time set aside for sharing writings or stories.
- A discussion of the six steps from this book.
- A discussion of how to be of service to others.
- A drum circle.
- Sharing meals and stories together.
- Watching a funny movie.

You can love the sword and you can love the battle. You can love the skills, the power, the mastery, the passion, and the exhilaration of war. But, you cannot love those things more than the men and woman you serve with. We do not see how any book about healing cannot speak about the power of love. That love will heal you, if can open to it. Being part of a fluid warrior council is one way to do that. It is a way for you and your fellow soldiers to be of service to each other.

Wisdom: Becoming an Elder

As you practice these steps, learn the art of healing, feel the heart awaken with connection, and reach out to help each other and the world, you will do more than just *overcome* PDS. You will *become* someone with a new mission. Do you remember the Native American warrior culture we described where warriors are trained to use ritual to become ready for war? Well, these same warriors used other rituals when returning from war—sweat lodges, trials, time spent in solitude, vision quests, and warrior councils—to reintegrate themselves back into their culture. We are advocating a modern version of that for you, with the same results in mind as a goal. You will slowly come to wisdom and you will have the opportunity to grow into an authentic elder. Becoming a wise elder is not just the result of how long you had been alive, but how deeply you have looked into the face of death. Our culture needs the wisdom of those who have looked into the face of death or fear. What did you learn? What does your soul know now that it did not know before? Is there something deep down that wants to be born in you? What can you teach the rest of us? We cannot go where you have gone and can now go. We are clinicians and teachers. We have not seen what you have. Think about it: you've studied war, you've been to war, and now you're studying healing, and you're healing. How expansive does that make you? Wisdom is so hard to come by that at some point, you may even come to see what has happened to you as a kind of gift.

Weird and Magical Times

We live in weird times. There is a lot of fear. There is fear of terrorism, environmental degradation, and economic collapse. There is the fear of not having enough. There is fear of people who seem different. The left side of the political spectrum is afraid of the right side and the right side is afraid of the left. The news is filled with the latest school shootings, natural disasters, and man-made catastrophes. People wonder where their money will come from. People are afraid. They are afraid of being in pain. They are even afraid of just being uncomfortable. They don't know what's going to happen to them. They are afraid of death. The lists of fears are endless. But, you have already experienced the worst that people can imagine. You have experienced their worst fears and have lived to tell about it. Your brain may still be acting like it's under fire, but when you get through all this, the debilitating effects of fear will be a thing of the past for you. Not because there will not be any more fear in you, but because you have learned to deal with it. You'll be able to see fear for what it is and act anyway. As you well know, that's what *courage* is.

How does a guy like Max Cleland, a triple amputee from the Vietnam War, go on to become a congressman and national leader? Or, how does John McCain get through years as a tortured prisoner of war torture and then go on to be senator and presidential candidate? Or, explain the strength within Tammy Duckworth that has allowed her, after losing both legs and part of her right arm in the Iraq War, to go on to become an assistant secretary for the Veterans Administration? The human spirit is pure magic that matches the magical times we live in. Technology is constantly evolving. There are new astonishing gadgets created every 5 minutes. The human genome has been mapped. Even space travel is old news and cloning is a done deal. Diseases are being cured and vaccines developed. There are breakthroughs in medicine every day. Modern military medicine has made the battlefield yet another frontier to conquer. Many of you would not be here at all if it weren't for those breakthroughs. You are a product of this magical world.

This is where you come in. You have seen and experienced the worst of what this world has to offer and you're still here. It's one of the reasons that when you came home and you saw how much abundance there was and heard people complaining about how hard everything was that you might have felt like this country you lived in was filled with a bunch of babies. You came home alright, but your home and your world are not the same. You're not the same. We don't know about divine plans for the universe, it's beyond our pay grade. But, something makes sense about the idea that your coming through this is a way that will help to contribute to a sense of sanity coming to this world. As you get better, you will teach people what's really important just by the way you are.

This is a weird time on the earth for all of us. We know it's also weird time in your life. It seems like everything is chaotic or rigid. Everything seems overheated and inflamed. It seems like almost everything needs to be healed in some way. For most of this book we have been talking about what *you* need and how *you* are going to heal. You've been listening to us. But we need to be listening to you. The truth is: *we need you to heal us.* All of us, your families, your friends, your fellow soldiers, your doctors, therapists, nurses, and this whole world need you. We need men and woman like you. Men and woman with warrior hearts. Those of us who have not been to war, who don't have a clue—who have not known the fear, the courage, the exhilaration, the pain, the intensity, the boredom, the heat, the dust, the bonds, the pride, the guilt, the confusion, the clarity, the anger, the sadness, the heartbreak, and what it's like at the edge of life and death—need *you* to help *us* heal. It is not only your actions that heal this world, but who you are, who you become.

THE NOBLE WARRIOR

We realize that going from seeing yourself and your body as a weapon of mass destruction to seeing your body as a garden in which you grow healing is a tremendous leap. But if you've come this far, we think this cutting edge life of yours and its closeness to death, makes you a particularly fine candidate for this work. When it comes to doing this kind of work, all the power and intensity you've experienced in your life gives you an advantage. Digging deeply into the questions of what it means to be alive and what it means to face misfortune, and then rising from the destruction to live a life that really means something is a real warrior's life.

But we, like you, also know that having a full and authentic life doesn't mean there is no suffering. Suffering is not equally distributed, but no life is without it. This is where warriors become so important. Because facing suffering without complaint is what warriors do every day. And turning suffering into blessing is what the wisest, most noble warriors do. In the midst of this battle there can be a shift. You can be that shift.

Resources

We think continuing education is extremely important. Fluid warriors are curious about and open to new ideas and perspectives. We think the act of reading or listening, like the act of writing, trains and improves the mind, and we strongly recommend doing some every day. Below is a list of books for further reading. Many people enjoy listening to books on tape. Check to see if any of the titles below are available in that format.

BOOKS ON WAR, WARRIORS, PHILOSOPHY AND RECOVERY

Epictetus, *The Enchiridion (The Handbook)*—The work of the great Greek stoic philosopher; the strength and foundation to many a fine military man's philosophy.

Charles Hoge, M.D. (Col., U.S. Army, ret.), *Once a Warrior always a Warrior: Navigating the Transition from Combat to Home–Including Combat stress, PTSD, and mTBI*—Written by one of the nations preeminent military psychiatrists, this book is primarily concerned with the Cognitive Behavioral Therapeutic aspects of treating the returning warrior.

Keith Armstrong, L.C.S.W, Suzanne Best, Ph.D. and Paula Domenici, Ph.D., *Courage After Fire: Coping strategies for Troops Returning from Iraq and Afghanistan and Their Families*—An excellent and extremely accessible general guidebook for the returning warrior.

Ed Tick, Ph.D., *War and the Soul: Healing Our Nations Veterans from Post–traumatic Stress Disorder*—A clinical psychotherapist's view of the deepest issues involved in warrior healing throughout history.

Nancy Sherman, *The Untold War: Inside the Hearts, Minds, and Souls of our Soldiers*—A military philosopher and psychoanalyst's insights about the aftermath of war.

Sebastian Junger, *War*—A war correspondent's account of his time embedded with marines in the mountains of Afghanistan: an accurate and compassionate view of young marines in action. He gets it. A must read for young modern warriors seeking some perspective on themselves.

Claude Anshin Thomas, *At Hell's Gate: A Soldier's Journey from War to Peace*—The title says it all. Highly recommended.

BOOKS ON MEDITATION, CONTINUUM, THERAPY, AND NUTRITION

Eckhart Tolle, *The Power of Now: The New Earth*—the best selling author's modern guides to the present moment and the liberation of suffering.

Jon Kabat Zinn, *Wherever you go, There you are*—An introduction to meditation by the Doctor and Harvard professor most responsible for bringing mindfulness practice into mainstream medicine.

Venerable Henepola Gunaratana, *Mindfulness in Plain English*—The definitive introduction to meditation practice.

Bonnie Gintis, DO, *Engaging the Movement of Life: Exploring Health and Embodiment Through Osteopathy and Continuum*—An essential book on Continuum and its principles.

Emilie Conrad, *Life on Land: The Story of Continuum*—A fascinating autobiography of the founder of Continuum.

Byron Katie, *Loving What Is*—A simple, direct and powerful method for dissolving dysfunctional thinking and the suffering that accompanies it.

Peter Levine, PhD, *In an Unspoken Voice: How the Body Releases Trauma and Restores Goodness*—The originator of Somatic Experiencing outlines his philosophy and method of trauma resolution.

Darlene Cohen, *Turning Suffering Inside Out: A Zen Approach to living with Physical and Emotional Pain*—A wonderful book about meditation, opening awareness, and the art of acceptance to take the primary focus off of pain; extremely helpful.

Daniel Siegel, MD, *Mindsight: New Science of Personal Transformation*—The state-of-the-art book on meditation, neurobiology, and personal growth.

Wendy Palmer, *The Intuitive Body: Akido as a Clairsentient Practice*—An Akido masters take on awakening our, and our body's natural intelligence.

Stephen Covey, *The Seven Habits of Highly Effective People*—The classic book on enlightened executive function; essential reading for those who want to order and improve their lives.

Michael Pollen, *Food Rules*—The simplest and most modern handbook for what to put into your body.

INFORMATION ON THE INTERNET

As anyone with access to the Internet knows: information is not only easy to come by; it's easy to drown in. The amount of information on even the most obscure topic staggers the mind. We think you know, for example, that just by searching PTSD you will have access to a lifetime of reading. Like all things Internet, some of it will be enlightening, some of it will be entertaining, some of it useless, and much of it downright junk. So be careful. It's also important to recognize that screens can be another form of addiction. Recent research suggests that too much time spent with the Internet encourages attention deficit. It is our opinion that mindlessly surfing the net for more information is a counterproductive substitute for the work of everyday healing practice that this book recommends. It will not move your mission forward. Despite having said all that here are a few reputable and comprehensive sites that may prove helpful to the returning warrior.

www.militaryonesource.com—One stop web surfing for veterans and their families.

www.ptsd.va.gov—The Veterans Administrations The National Center for PTSD The Center aims to help U.S. Veterans and others through research, education, and training on trauma and PTSD.

http://yogawarriors.com—Yoga for warriors, by warriors.

http://ravendrumfoundation.org—Raven Drum Foundation— An organization dedicated to healing warriors through drumming.

MUSIC

Most of us have a pretty defined taste in music. It's a part of our identity; part of who we are. Whether you like country, rap, hip hop, rock and roll, jazz or classical, or all of the above, we encourage you to make time to listen, move, and exercise to the music you love. Life loves, and is, rhythm. We also encourage you to listen to flowing and soothing ambient music. It slows you down and provides a space to relax within. It offers a counterpoint to the intensity of war as well as to the speed of our culture and is complimentary to the Continuum movement practices in Chapter 7. If this kind of music is new to you, give it a chance. Listening alone can be a mini-vacation, with measurable effects on heart rate, blood pressure, and the nervous system.

Index